v10-03

DATE DUE			5/01
JUN 27 '01			
JUL 14 '01			
AUG 04 '01			
AUG 30 '01			
SEP 22 '01			
NOV 16 '01			
MAR 05 '02			
GAYLORD			PRINTED IN U.S.A.

A BOOK OF
REASONS

A Book of
Reasons
John Vernon

HOUGHTON MIFFLIN COMPANY

BOSTON   NEW YORK

1999

For information about permission to reproduce selections from
this book, write to Permissions, Houghton Mifflin Company,
215 Park Avenue South, New York, New York 10003.

Library of Congress Cataloging-in-Publication Data

Vernon, John, date.
A book of reasons / John Vernon.
p. cm.
Includes bibliographical references (pp. 259–72).
ISBN 0-395-94477-5
1. Vernon, John, 1943–   — Family. 2. Novelists,
American — 20th century — Family relationships.
3. Collectors and collecting — Psychological aspects.
4. Eccentrics and eccentricities — United States.
5. Brothers — Death — Psychological aspects.
6. Recluses — United States. I. Title.
PS3572 E76Z465   1999
813'.54 — dc21
[B] 99-15173   CIP

Book design by Anne Chalmers
Typefaces: Adobe Minion, News Gothic

Printed in the United States of America

QUM 10 9 8 7 6 5 4 3 2 1

Lines from "The Four Wishes of Saint Martin" are from *Gallic Salt:*
Eighteen Fabliaux, translated from the Old French by Robert Harrison.
Copyright © 1974 by the University of California Press.
Reprinted by permission of the author.

AUTHOR'S NOTE
To protect the privacy of friends and family,
I've changed some names of people
and places in this book.

For Pat and Jack Wilcox,
for Holly and Frank Bergon,
for Bob Mooney and family

Special thanks to Lenny Davis
for suggesting the idea for this book

Finally, for my sons, Charles and Patrick
The secret to life? *Clean your room.*

Grateful acknowledgment is made to the
National Endowment for the Arts for a fellowship
that gave me the time to write this book, and to the
State University of New York at Binghamton
for its additional support.

These times are the ancient times,
when the world is ancient.

— Francis Bacon

If one knew the facts, would one have to feel pity even for
the planets? If one reached the heart of the matter?

— Graham Greene

\

CONTENTS

PREFACE

THE PREMISE of this book may be simply stated: I've chosen a three-month period of my life — late February to early May of 1996 — and attempted to trace the historical roots of the everyday occurrences and objects in it, from something as commonplace as buying a thermometer to something as singular, yet clearly familiar, as attending my late brother's wake. The roots of such events in history, science, and mythology are legion. And, I'm convinced, they can be communicated only from the vantage point of a positioned mind, in a specific place and time, harnessed to a limited point of view. The narrative of this three-month period is the vantage point I've chosen.

But my choice was not arbitrary. These months contained a chain of events that followed my brother's death, and impelled me to reflect on and examine both his life and my own. In a sense, then, this is two books: one a memoir concerning the things I learned about a lonely and troubled man I barely knew — a brother fifteen years older than me — the other an account of everyday life and its sources. That the life of a recluse may launch speculations about everyday existence only demonstrates my thesis: history in its minute particulars touches us all, and in the least expected ways.

So: a book of reasons. Reasons for my brother's way of life and death, reasons for my response to his death. I am aware that any search for reasons in our time has a lot to contend with. For one thing, the gratifications of consumer technology have infantilized us all. Our interests are mostly passing, and we satisfy them with distracted attention, as unconscious of reasons and their historical roots as of the farthest galaxy. For another, our most characteristic science, the one that appears to best express the spirit of the age—chaos theory—implies a universe so random and complex that we can never know who or what is responsible for anything. Chaos theory purées causes, dissolving such notions as responsibility. Reasons, by contrast, assign responsibility. This book walks the broken ridge between the two. Reasons, like chaos, can be multiple and diffuse, scattered to the corners of space and time, unless a search threads the mess and snags for it a shape. Then, as I've learned, the act of searching itself also becomes an act of taking responsibility.

Reasons, finally, are one means of learning to bear painful news. For me, this meant bearing the sad and strange things I learned about my brother after his death. Referring them to history doesn't mitigate a wasted life. But referring them to history is my way of trying to understand that waste. As a novelist and teacher preoccupied with the past, I've spent much of my career digesting research into story. I've written about French and American explorers, about the Ute Indians, about women miners in Colorado. This book reverses that process: it takes a true story, recent and personal, and refers it to the past, to the surprising and irregular upheavals of history. And though the story is my brother's, it is also mine. It is the story of a voyage, of my search for a way to comprehend a life that left behind not splendid monuments but ordinary wreckage.

I
HEAT

1

PAUL

I was driving to a Wal-Mart in southern New Hampshire to buy a thermometer the day the world grew unfamiliar. My mind unclogged, it seemed — as though whatever I'd previously known turned out to be some sort of a blockage in a drain. It started slowly, even coyly, with vague irritations: heavy traffic on Route 28, the bum air conditioning in the van my brother'd left me, the resulting open windows, the heat and humidity, the fumes from idling cars. I passed May's, where we'd ordered the flowers for his funeral, passed the mini-malls, Granite State Potato Chips, the rows of yellow construction equipment lined up like Tonka toys behind a chain-link fence.

The worst was over, I'd been thinking. I could indulge in a little complacency for a change. I'd be driving home soon, back to upstate New York. And I was heading toward a Wal-Mart, the ultimate sanctuary of choice in Emporium America.

A car behind me honked, but it barely registered. Stupid chatter began running through my head about the value of my brother Paul's house and his adopted state's 18 percent inheritance tax, which applied horizontally to siblings but not vertically to parents or children. How strange, I thought. A child has only half your genes, after all. This tax clearly favored hierarchies dimly remembered from English common law. I was explaining this to someone in my head, and explaining the fact that Paul had never married, when, of its own weight, a picture slid from a brain cell — jogged by these thoughts — of Paul as a boy

holding in his hand the branch of an apple tree, half hung with apples. The rest, miraculously, had broken into blossom.

Memory works in the brain like brachiated lightning unloading its contents in faded afterimages. The picture weakened but still, in a sense, I remembered the memory, then something else happened. A line shooting up through walls of tissue guttered and caught, bisecting me vertically. It pulled on my heart like a cord on a tent: the first ache of sadness for my poor brother. And just an hour ago I'd been stupid with joy!

He held out the branch with fading reluctance like a boy who'd been bad. Was he returning it to someone? Other images drifted in, visual analogs of overlapping whispers—the double and triple exposures of memory. It felt like spilling water on a newspaper and reading tomorrow's weather through yesterday's scandal. Through Paul and his branch I saw my grandmother's house, smelled wet ashes in her driveway, felt the warmth of the rose quartz sitting in the recesses, tall and narrow, beside her front door. Ghosts more solid than the honking world around me. Where had that picture of my brother come from? He'd lived with my grandmother in central Massachusetts when I was growing up, and my parents and I had visited every weekend. By the time I was a child Paul was past his teens, and I thought of him more as an uncle than a brother. An uncle with a hobby—through the walls of Grandma's house I saw Paul's room hung with model airplanes, each suspended on a wire from the ceiling, each pieced together from balsa wood and cardboard with X-Acto knives and small, precise fingers.

Then I remembered. The picture of my brother was literally that— a newspaper clipping I'd found in his house three months ago, after his death. For twenty years he'd lived alone in New Hampshire, and his sudden death left me in charge of his affairs, including the obligatory sorting of remains. Most of it was junk, overwhelming trash, but I thought my mother would want this clipping, and she did in fact gaze at it wistfully before putting it in a drawer to be forgotten. Now it came back with urgent clarity: nine-year-old Paul offering to the viewer his amazing branch, half blossoms, half apples. So he'd been a child too, though beyond my witness — this was six years before my birth. And he hadn't been bad, hadn't stolen or broken anything, he was just camera shy: head tilted forward, dark gash of hair slung across his brow, black reluctant eyes not unlike a cautious dog's. He held the branch up like Liberty's torch, though faced with a camera Liberty looked slumped, and the torch was no higher than Paul's sunken chest.

The car honked again. I must have been Sunday driving. Past all the malls, I was still creeping along at 20 miles per hour on the two-lane highway. The car pulled out to pass me on a curve — a lipstick-red Grand Am — and a teenage male on the passenger side *flipped me the bird*, in our zoological slang.

Fuck you too, I mumbled — my atavistic twinge. I couldn't really get angry, though. I felt dazed, numb, saddened by the loss of an older brother whose life had barely left an imprint on the world. He'd been a recluse and a loner in a throwaway society, and here I was bent on the same course, driving to a store to buy something I didn't need, a cheap thermometer. I maintained my granny pace. Like a needle reading normal, I sat with one hand on the wheel, poised between distractedly complacent and obscurely annoyed. The Grand Am had thumped past like a war machine, with those booming woofers heard first in the bowels, and even now the sound lingered. I felt miles and months behind everyone else. Spring had arrived — summer was imminent — but me, I was still adjusting to winter, still wondering whether I needed a jacket. Once again, the revolutions were outpacing me, the wheels forever spinning, the days and weeks scrolling, but flapping like shades glued to the slower roll of the seasons — the earth itself cartwheeling on its axis at a speed of 22,000 miles a day, and revolving around the sun at 18.46 miles a second . . . statistical Drano for sluggish minds. I smiled to myself. The cosmos is a giant flywheel, said

H. L. Mencken—but at least we flies are permitted to think that the wheel was constructed to give us a ride.

What happened to that boy with the branch? Where do youth and potential go when a life unravels?

I tried conjuring more memories of Grandma's house. Wasn't there a Victrola in, of all places, the bathroom, and hadn't my brother taken it after her death? Possibly, but I hadn't seen it in his house, though it could have been buried under piles of debris. His remains were of the sort one might find in a cave. He must have had that Victrola — Paul, I knew, was especially attached to my father's mother. My parents were living with Grandma when he was born, having moved in with her after their marriage. But when Dad found a new job and he and my mother moved to South Boston, where I grew up, they left their seven-year-old fifty miles away in Wire Valley with Grandma. I'd heard various reasons. The prospect of moving frightened young Paul. Besides, he was cute, and Grandma loved him so much that she might as well keep him to relieve her solitude. Also, the new apartment was small, and my parents would visit every weekend, a practice that continued after my birth and throughout my childhood. Finally, this was 1937 — the Great Depression — and many families split up to go where the work was. Or so I'd been told when I asked about those years. I realize now that no greater mystery exists than the time before our birth, always darkened by the shadow that we ourselves cast.

Later, when I was a zit-faced adolescent, Grandma died and Paul joined the army, then lived with us in Boston, sharing my room. He stayed there after I left home, never dating or marrying, until he purchased the house in New Hampshire for which I was now buying a thermometer.

In the Wal-Mart parking lot I found a slot, rolled up the windows, locked the doors. Outside, the knots of people drifting toward the entrance possessed the glow of families converging on a church. We searched each other's faces for signs of recognition, exchanging looks that said, I'm just buying an apron (or a thermometer), but isn't it in-deed just, right, and meet? This Wal-Mart had been dropped beside an empty highway like a modern country Assembly of God; there was nothing else here, no other stores. Around it were pine trees and still naked birches, some returning to earth as though swung on by one of the boys in Robert Frost's poem, those too far from town to learn about baseball.

From Route 28 came the sound of screeching tires, but no crunch of metal. Robert Frost's farm, now a museum, was six miles up the road.

On the store's pale blue pediment, a sort of packaged, shrink-wrapped extract of sky, were the red words *Wal*Mart,* and at the apex, where the cross should have been, a yellow happy face. Jefferson was wrong, I thought: happiness is not a state to be pursued but an em-balmed yellow decal to slap on buildings and T-shirts. In the twenty-first century we'll hold up happy faces to ward off vampires. I looked around for the Grand Am, mildly worried that the teenagers were here too, to stock up on guns, but not one car in the parking lot was red.

Inside, the store smelled of motor oil and popcorn. A kindly Saint Peter in a silly blue apron welcomed me to Wal-Mart. Behind him, the department known as Kids' Clothes resembled a landscape of dead bunnies. I was floating, not walking, still in a fugue state, past picture cubes, portable ab rollers, cylinders of cheese puffs, and bread-slicing "systems"—past curling irons, Jockey shorts, *101 Dalmatians* tooth-brushes, CD storage towers, and electric massage mats, looking for the thermometers. And I marveled at our long and complex human his-tory, at our evolution of an upright posture and grapefruit-sized brains, at our discovery of fire and burial rites, our development of language and ritual and dance, our paintings in caves, our invention of tools and farming and jewelry, our beautiful material cultures, our an-cient cities, our aqueducts and looms and solar calendars, our models of the universe, our invention of the telescope, our discovery of the calculus, our balloon flights and steam engines and space stations and computers, and at the maze of mental and psychological organizations that trailed behind or pioneered these mounting stages of the past, all leading to this, to *101 Dalmatians* toothbrushes and slipper socks and *Cats in the Sun* calendars and boxes of talking Michael Jordan dolls.

Amid designer thermometers with the circumference of basketballs and nice paintings of ducks and reeds on their faces, I found a plain outdoor thermometer for $2.59 and headed for the checkout.

Then I remembered I didn't have a hammer.

"Hickory," I said to the clerk in Hardware. It was stamped on the handle. "I wonder where they make these things." I was hefting it as hammer buyers do, to feel its forward weight. The heavy iron knot on the tip of the shaft makes one's blow more powerful.

"Right there." He pecked the handle. He possessed the sort of broadax face that barely turns and boom, it's a profile. Sunken eyes and teeth. He was anywhere between forty and sixty, and had a hard time mustering the Wal-Mart smile.

"Taiwan?"

"You want to buy American, try the Stanley, but it's more."

"I like the idea of hickory."

"They're all hickory."

The hammer was only $8.39. We were just chatting. "I was reading in the paper. You know Richard Reeves?"

He shrugged.

"Writes a column? He talked about buying hardwood furniture, early American, and it all turned out to be made in Malaysia. So he did some research and found out that Indonesia has thirteen thousand islands covered with hardwood, and they're all being clear-cut. I bet that's where they got the hickory."

"They got it from the moon for all I know. Sir."

I was tempted to tell him about the great cutover in Michigan and Wisconsin a hundred years ago — twenty-three million board-feet of lumber worth four billion dollars, clear-cut from the upper Midwest.

They floated it down to Chicago and milled it for balloon frames to build the new America.

In Japan they mill the iron that makes the heads for hammers used to build the iron mills.

But he'd turned to tidy up the duct tape across the aisle. The large, small, and medium rolls each had their own horizontal skewer, and some rolls had been misplaced. "Look at that." He turned back and held out a box of allergy pills.

"Pharmacy," I said, then felt odd for saying it. "What's it doing here?"

He showed me it was empty. "They take out the pills and leave the box behind."

"Steal them, you mean?"

He looked at me with no expression at all.

Back at my brother's house, I cleared away some thorn shoots beneath the kitchen window with a dull saw I'd found in the basement that morning. It was a crosscut saw made for carpentry, not brush, and didn't cut so much as mangle. My father, I'm sure, would not have approved of this misuse of tools.

The house was an older-style ranch, on one acre in Kingston. A dirt road forked behind the pie-shaped lot. The front door faced Twist Run Road.

Behind a field across the road were dozens of chicken sheds, all with smashed windows.

My brother's place was half boarded up where its windows were broken. Paul had lived in Boston with my mother the last two years, having abandoned his house to vandals and rats. It needed a new roof. The front-entry stairs were gone. The brown aluminum siding was in pretty good shape, though, despite some pits, perhaps made by hail. The trim everywhere—around windows, eaves, and doors— was peeling and rotten. And the landscaping surrounding the house consisted of weeds, shrubs, and thorn bushes. But the white pines towering over the place, also one spruce, were impressive. They might help to sell the property. And this southern New Hampshire town was rapidly becoming a bedroom community. A twenty-minute drive down Route 111 led to I-93, thence to Boston, a mere hour away.

Thorn shoots kept getting caught in my pants—why on earth was I doing this? At last I was able to stand on a chair I'd salvaged from the house to nail up the thermometer. Entering the house made me uneasy, because of the smell, so the prospect of returning the chair was not something I looked forward to, but it had to be done. The real estate agent was coming today, and I'd have to show him through.

A cement truck drove past, heading for the new subdivision up the road, Kingston Estates. Bees flew in and out of the letterbox on the back porch, beside the lilac bush. I tore the cardboard backing off the plastic bubble and pulled out the nails and bracket for the thermometer. The nails had spiral grooves up and down their shafts.

Freeze the frame there. Why was I doing this?

I was doing it because my brother had died and left me his house, and I had to sell it. I was doing it because of the laws governing alienable property and inheritance in families in the United States and the state of New Hampshire, laws modeled on English common law and rooted in the end of feudalism and the rise of capitalism and the concept of property. I was doing it for money. What is money? A system of exchange. One pays $2.59 for a thermometer, $8.39 for a hammer, prices in America always end in nines. Money is a delicately balanced mechanism of credit and faith, a shared fiction made of paper and pixels of light on computer screens in banks.

But why was I doing this?

I hadn't been that close to Paul. It wasn't just the fifteen years between us. He was odd; some would say he wasn't normal, though he'd held down a job all his life and managed to function in a presumably normal world. By the time he retired, however, he'd withdrawn from that world's pervasive engine of arrangements and become a recluse. At his death, lacking his own family, he left me everything he possessed, and in sifting through this legacy I'd come face to face with the mystery of his life, and what I'd seen had frightened me. I'd thought about it a great deal since his funeral, and my thoughts had spread to include not only the way he'd arranged his solitude, but the way we all do—the strangeness of marriage or of living alone, of work and money, of the sorrow of possessions—the oddity of cars and streets and interstates, of owning houses, of central heating, of buying fast foods and paying bills and using hammers and selling property and nailing up thermometers outside kitchen windows.

I was doing it because we live in houses, having tried the alternative—living in caves—which didn't work. From caves and rock shelters we moved to pits, skin tents, brush shelters, cliff dwellings, thence to houses, villas, castles, and palaces. I was doing it because even beavers build houses, and snails carry them around. Because a house is a sign of our dominion over the earth. Be fruitful and multiply and subdue the earth. Moderate extremes. Manage nature, don't let it manage you. Live in warmth where it is cold and in coolness where it is hot, and don't live like my brother, who wound up fouling his own nest.

Inside a warm kitchen, boiling up some Kraft macaroni and cheese for dinner, one reads the temperature outside and shivers not with cold but with a sort of *frisson*. "Let it freeze without, we are comfortable within," said Sir Walter Scott. This, I knew, was important in New England. In a word, it was homey. Who knows, it might even encourage a prospective buyer to become an actual owner. Although there was a hitch. One could not be cozy in Paul's house once winter came, nor boil macaroni in his kitchen, since neither the furnace nor the plumbing was functioning. No problem, I thought, some American do-it-yourselfer would fix them, someone who likes a bargain.

He might need a strong stomach, though. After the plumbing and heating stopped working, and the toilet became inoperative, someone began using the cold-air return in the living room as a urinal. The results of this practice were evident in the basement: the large rectangular duct of sheet metal leading to the furnace had been torn open by rust. And worse had been done. Since the floor grate covering the cold-air return was removable, this convenient repository in the living room contained human excrement as well. It must have been vandals, I told myself.

Yet everything I'd found in the house before having it cleaned—the enormous piles of trash, the scarred and splintered walls, the garbage, the twenty-plus years of utility bills and junk mail, the mildewed photos, the damp stacks of lurid magazines, the charnel house rot of a life in pieces—suggested it wasn't vandals, it was Paul.

And none of these things, not even the grate, was the source of the smell.

I held the bracket to one side of the window and nailed the first nail in.

Why was I doing this?

2

REASONS

REASONS ARE NOT answers. Reasons are recipes for making sense of the world's arrangements and accidents. They are explanations of why things are, how they work, what they mean, where they came from, how they began. We need reasons when we feel dislocated, when ordinary things seem unfamiliar and contingent, when there are no easy answers. Why is that tree there, who invented the nail, how large is the universe, what happens after death?

As a pundit observed on *The NewsHour with Jim Lehrer,* "Americans think everything can be explained." In one respect this is true, but in others, not. We are a practical people, we love information, but living as we do in a cornucopia of commodities, we tend to feel that things are their own explanation, and so take them for granted. In a world of Wal-Marts, a world of juxtaposed goods arranged on shelves by category — "Appliances," "Hardware," "Stationery" — reasons seem neither possible nor necessary. Wal-Mart is not a narrative or sequence, not a system of cause and effect, but a self-replenishing material utopia of the useful and useless, cunningly integrated so that the useless seems useful and the useful an array of indulgent treats. We are not intended to reflect on the merchandise, which is why our stores have the feel of anthills, assemblages of parts whose origins are irrelevant. In a world of Wal-Marts, we attend to the local, as unaware of reasons as of the oxygen we breathe.

In other words, we disconnect. We are the revenge of Descartes's pineal gland, his bottleneck connection between mind and body. A friend of mine once sat on her Exercycle, then discovered that an hour had passed and she couldn't remember whether she'd exercised or not. That has happened to me while driving to work. We occupy a world in which the things we do or use are taken for granted, and so are done or used mechanically — but then again, so do pigs.

Yet tools did not show up full-blown at Wal-Mart like fruit picked off trees; they have a long history. Nor was the thermometer of recent invention, like the cellular phone. And to understand that every step we take, every act we perform, is woven into networks connected to both the past and the stars can be positively breathtaking. I'd liken it to the time my father first thumbed the back off his pocket watch and I stared at the spinning wheels and ticking levers. Reasons may vary from culture to culture and century to century, sometimes even from decade to decade — still, they are the lifeblood of cultures. They enable us to cross the street, read a newspaper, conduct a ceremony, name a newborn, and perhaps even comprehend our suffering or happiness. When we brush our teeth, when we sit down to eat, when we stare into a fire, we live, one could say, among leftover reasons. Like our furniture and homes, they probably preceded us, and will undoubtedly survive us.

Sitting down to eat, for example. In the Middle Ages, Europeans ate with knives and sometimes spoons, though both implements merely supplemented fingers. The individual fork—as opposed to a large meat fork with two prongs—wasn't introduced until the sixteenth century, and, slow to catch on, was considered by some to be "a diabolical luxury," in Fernand Braudel's words. A German divine quoted by Braudel pointed out that God would not have given us fingers if he wished us to use such an instrument as a fork. Even Louis XIV was praised by Saint-Simon for his skill at eating chicken stew with his fingers without spilling a drop. It took a long time for fingers to be replaced by forks, and during that time they were often used together. Fashionable Greeks in the eighteenth century helped themselves to olives with their fingers, and with their fingers impaled them on forks, in order to eat them as the French did. As for the blunt-tipped knife of today's table settings, it was introduced by Cardinal Richelieu in the seventeenth century when he noticed a guest picking his teeth with a knife. Richelieu flew into a rage and ordered the tips of all knives in his household filed down to rounded ends.

I first became interested in reasons and their arcana when I was given by my father-in-law a deteriorating leatherbound 1911 edition of the *Encyclopaedia Britannica,* twenty-eight volumes of tissue-thin paper still perfectly white inside covers that pebbled and smeared in one's hands. A dubious gift, I thought at first—then I started using it. The 1911 *Britannica* is said to be especially reliable in its literary and historical entries but outdated in its science and technology. I found both assessments to be off the mark. The literary and historical entries often turned out to be Western imperial ethnocentrism at its worst—

the white man's burden—whereas the science and technology were a cabinet of wonders, a window into the ingenuity of the human mind when its information is insufficient and it must therefore chew more than it can bite off.

Our information is also insufficient, of course. There are things we don't know that others will know in the future, and one hundred years from now our encyclopedias will also be quaint. "We can easily imagine," says Vladimir Nabokov, "people in 3000 A.D. sneering at our naïve nonsense and replacing it by some nonsense of their own." Consequently, reasons have to be ingenious. They are machines tacked together with the resources at hand, like the box kite and bicycle that became the first airplane. I like to think of our legacy of reasons as eloquence rooted in the human vernacular.

In my decaying *Britannica,* I read about Ludwig's stromuhr for measuring blood flow; about hatters who separated the finer fibers of furs by striking with a pin the string on a huge bow suspended above a worktable; about the alternatives to oral administration of mercury for syphilis patients—fumigation of the naked unfortunate huddled beneath a blanket while seated on a cane-bottomed chair, or injection of the mercury directly into his buttock; and about abiogenesis, the belief that animals and insects can be spontaneously generated from dew, piles of old clothes, the slime in wells, and mud. I read about the English "Jury of Annoyance," appointed by an act of 1754 to report on highway obstructions; about the Chorizontes, those ancients who believed that two different people wrote *The Odyssey* and *The Iliad;* and about heart burial, defined with impeccable deadpan as "the burial of the heart apart from the body," an honor accorded to, among others, Louis XIV, Robert the Bruce, and Shelley.

Often the entries revealed a past quite different from that in history books, with their organized landscapes of dates, political alliances, and anonymous armies. The difference was like that between seeing the world from an airplane and walking around in a hallucination of close-ups, hideous and fascinating. It was the past through a microscope rather than a telescope. Occasionally, too, an entry revealed unexpected links between myself and the past. One of my earliest childhood memories had been of watching my father in his print shop pecking away on a Linotype machine, an apparatus whose ability to raise and lower itself with enormous thuds and clunks seemed at odds with the ordinary flitter of typing. What I didn't know was what I later learned in the *Britannica* article on "Typography": when my father finished a line and pulled the lever, inside the machine a jet of molten metal shot from a melting pot into a mold against the matrices of type, thus casting the slug, which he gave me to take home and store in my dresser drawer, my own cabinet of wonders.

From Linotype machines to sponges and other tunicates, to sections of the brains of turtles and sharks, from wombats and conveyors ("mechanical devices designed for the purpose of moving material in a horizontal or slightly inclined direction") to roofs and crustaceans, all illustrated in exquisite detail, the appeal of the *Britannica* gradually unfolded: it displayed the secret insides of things, their penetralia. It x-rayed and dissected, it cut things in half, it showed the inside and outside of life side by side. Its project was the same as the Viscount's in Italo Calvino's novella about a man cut in half, *The Cloven Viscount*. "If only I could halve every whole thing like this," the Viscount says while contemplating a divided octopus, "so that everyone could escape from his obtuse and ignorant wholeness. I was whole and all things were natural and confused to me, stupid as the air; I thought I was seeing all and it was only the outside rind."

In other words, most of the machinery of our daily lives operates beyond our senses, either buried in the ordinary or lost in the monstrosities of space and time. Take organic life itself. Life may be, as Samuel Beckett's uncle liked to say, a disease of matter — and we may enter matter from we know not where, go round in a circle several thousand revolutions, then depart whence we came — but the ride touches worlds far beyond the personal, worlds that have no experience of being us. The origins of life required the presence of carbon, with its bonding properties that enabled strands of DNA and RNA to exist. And carbon was born in the stars—in their nuclear reactions—then blown off as dust. Add to this the possibility that clay was a likely medium for the polymerization reactions that were necessary for life, and we have the prospect of life's origins spanning biblical clay and the outer reaches of space. Our human slime, smeared upon clay, is wired to the stars.

Webs and nets are much in the news these days—the Internet, the World Wide Web, our figures for illusory global villages. I see those particular webs as labyrinths of warehoused information not unlike Wal-Marts in their hash of the useful and useless. The web of reasons that enmeshes us, though, is not a digital toy but a medium as pervasive and invisible as air. It has countless strands that tie us to a world inconceivably large, and at the same time connect us to the other pinpricks of subjectivity in that world, our fellow human beings. *Middle-aged man nails up a thermometer and feels the ripples spread through the universe.* To see the ripples, I freeze the frame and step out of the picture. To illustrate the myriad connections, I trace a few of them.

And to unravel the question of why I was doing this, I develop the negative, inspect the shadows, search for hidden clues. Why nail a thermometer outside my brother's window? It undoubtedly began as happenstance, a whim. In my worked-up state, I believed that a thermometer would dignify the sorry house I inherited, would endow it, however superficially, with a civilized bearing. Perhaps I thought the thermometer, like a mark on the door, would spare my brother's house from destruction. It might even warm it, the way a burglar alarm makes possessions more valuable. Still, there's more. Even now, cut in half between the one writing this and the one standing on that chair, I can see the thermometer as my little pry-bar, my pick for unlocking Paul's place in the world.

Or his lack of place. What most of us do is what Paul did not do. He had few friends, did not marry, cared little for appearances, seldom bathed or washed his clothes. His domestic arrangements were the daily adjustments of someone caught in a slow landslide. By the time he paid someone to board up his windows and moved in with my mother, his unheated house had become a calamity. So my cheap thermometer was a sad joke too, a comment on both the customary behavior we all take for granted and the latent arrangements of everyday life. We think of a thermometer as a sign of domesticity, of our victory over nature. Yet some, like Paul, lost. What was it he lost? What was at stake? I see my thermometer as an archive, a scroll sealed inside a jar. It contains its own chapter in the chronicle of the struggle humans have waged ever since the first tools, its branch of the story of how we tamed fire and turned cold into heat. In it I can see, like homunculi in a tube, the faces of those who still haunt us today, whether or not we think about history—floating faces, bulbous and thin, of those kitchen scientists who, tinkering in their pantries, whipped together our world: Galileo, Fludd, Pascal, Descartes. They haunted Paul too, even if he never knew it.

3

A BRIEF HISTORY OF
THE THERMOMETER

IN 1647, on one of his rare visits to Paris, René Descartes, the father of modern philosophy, looked up Blaise Pascal to inquire about his claim that he'd created a vacuum. Descartes was fifty-one, Pascal twenty-four. Descartes, by all accounts, was a mousy little man with a large head, projecting brow, long bony nose, eyes wide apart, and hair growing down his forehead nearly to his eyebrows. Pascal, on the other hand—the young upstart mathematician–cum–natural philosopher—was said to be handsome, with a prominent and manly nose, full mouth, and large eyes. As a child, he'd constructed from scratch Euclid's first thirty-two propositions. He'd written a treatise on conic sections at the age of sixteen and, the same year, invented the first calculator, to relieve his father of the burden of doing sums. His father was a tax collector.

Descartes brought with him three friends and three boys; Pascal had by his side Gilles Personne de Roberval, "the greatest geometrician in Paris and the world's most disagreeable man," according to a friend of the Pascals'. Pascal demonstrated his creation of a vacuum, a simple replication of the famous experiment of Evangelista Torricelli, performed three years earlier: he poured mercury into a basin and filled a narrow glass tube, closed at one end, with the same substance. Then, with his middle finger plugging the open end, he turned the tube upside down, plunged it into the basin, and removed his finger. The liquid in the tube dropped, leaving a space that had to be a vacuum.

No, said Descartes. Didn't Monsieur Pascal know that air was a substance finer than wool, and its fibers had penetrated the glass of the tube? Roberval ridiculed this idea. Later, when Pascal gave his friends an example of a fantasy for which obstinacy alone could win approval, he cited Descartes's opinions on matter and space—something like the story of Don Quixote, he said.

Descartes suggested an experiment. Pascal should climb a mountain with his basin and tube to see whether the mercury in the tube would be lower at the top than at the foot of the mountain. It should be lower at the top because, Pascal claimed, the weight of the atmosphere determined the level of the mercury, and on a mountain, the atmosphere would weigh less. Parenthetically, Pascal's creation of a vacuum was also evidence for the existence of an atmosphere.

But Pascal was too weak to climb a mountain. He suffered from intestinal tuberculosis and tuberculous pseudo-rheumatism, and could hardly walk. So Descartes advised him to stay in bed every day until he was tired of being there, and to drink a lot of bouillon.

Three years later Descartes died, before fulfilling his promise to the world to prolong a human life by several centuries.

Pascal did take Descartes's suggestion, however, by proxy. He instructed his brother-in-law to climb a mountain in central France, the Puy de Dôme, with his basin, tube, and mercury—an embryonic barometer, in fact—and register the mercury's level at the base and at the summit. At the foot of the mountain it was 26¼ inches; at the top, 23⅙ inches. Pascal had won.

After Descartes's death, in the 1650s, Pascal wrote in his *Pensées,* "the great Pan is dead." I like to think he was referring to Descartes. In the spirit of impish dismissal, it doesn't take much to see Descartes as Pan. Pascal called Cartesianism the "Romance of Nature," and Pan in mythology was nature, earth, body, intoxication, bestiality, sexuality, and worse, perhaps—obscurantism. The hairy goat-god with horns and hooves and a prominent chin, who lived in woods and caves and raced across mountains, whose sexual appetite was inexhaustible, may have looked like Descartes too, or a parody of him. Didn't Descartes inspire his adversaries with terror, just as Pan had done to mortals?— hence our word "panic."

Pascal, on the other hand, is best thought of as Mercury. One wonders whether he or his brother-in-law knew what the ruins were on the summit of the Puy de Dôme: a Roman temple dedicated to Mercury. He probably drained the mercury market in France when he was performing his experiments. Mercury was swiftness, flight, cleverness, air, commerce, mind, culture, and clarity of message. Descartes as Pan, the Calibanistic grotesque, and Pascal as Mercury. They could have been brothers.

All at once, on that chair, nailing up my thermometer, I saw my brother Paul hunched over an oscilloscope, as he'd once hovered over his balsa-wood airplanes. I'm not sure what he was doing—running tests, checking data. I'd found it in his attic after his death, the same oscilloscope he'd built when I was a teenager. Heavy and cylindrical, the size of a vacuum cleaner.

The chair was so shaky I couldn't absorb the recoil of the hammer without bringing it to the verge of collapse. I had to tap the nails lightly. This didn't seem to matter. I could have pushed them in with my thumb, it seemed, the window frame was that rotten. The bracket was flimsy, the thermometer plastic, and neither of them would last the first windstorm, I suspected.

Chaney Instruments in Wisconsin. White thermometer, red liquid. Markings for both Fahrenheit and centigrade. Sixty-nine in the shade.

Around the front of the house, a school bus drove past. I just caught the yellow blur.

What *was* that red liquid that indicated the temperature? Not mercury, surely. Perhaps colored alcohol, or maybe ethylene glycol, something that can't freeze up. It resembled a thin line of blood, I thought. My *Britannica* tells me that in their early incarnations every conceivable liquid was tried in thermometers: water, spirit of wine, linseed oil, mercury, *l'eau second*—an acid solution of copper nitrate produced in refining gold—turpentine, alcohol, petroleum, *l'eau de vie* (brandy), saturated salt, olive oil, oil of chamomile, and oil of thyme. Food appears to be a theme in the history of thermometers; no wonder we mount them outside kitchen windows.

The liquid in the tube had been sealed inside a vacuum, or so I assumed. Light and heat pass through vacuums, air and sound do not. We take vacuums for granted today, or, to be more accurate, partial vacuums; the perfect vacuum is still somewhat elusive. Light bulbs and picture tubes operate in vacuums, we vacuum pack coffee, we've even coined a verb: to vacuum means to clean. But vacuums were once hotly debated, for religious as well as scientific reasons, and the history of the thermometer is hopelessly entangled with that bitter debate.

DEATH OF THE GODS

As it turns out, Pascal was not the one who formulated the epithet "the great Pan is dead." It had wide currency in European history. Milton used it, as had Rabelais earlier, and Eusebius before him, and other Christian apologists. Of modern thinkers, Nietzsche mentioned it in *The Birth of Tragedy.* It can be traced back to Plutarch's *De defectu oraculorum,* "The Decline of Oracles," an essay written about claims that the years are getting shorter, the ancient oracles and religions are withering away, and the gods are really demons. As Plutarch tells the story, a ship was passing the island of Paxi when someone shouted that the great Pan was dead, and those onboard should announce it to the mainland.

Christian apologists fastened on this story as a passing of the torch: the death of the old gods, the birth of Christianity. Pan was paganism incarnate, the god of nature, the universal god of the pre-Christian era. Furthermore, it's clear in Plutarch's essay that his point is a shocking one: the gods in fact can die, since the gods are really demons.

And what happens when they die? "The eternal silence of these infinite spaces terrifies me," said Pascal in the *Pensées.* He answered himself in the same work by declaring that the Nothing depended on the All, and one leads to the other. Just as Pan's death coincided with Christ's birth, so Pascal's vacuum — his Nothing — was really a proof of Christ's existence, since Christ is our All. But this was dangerous territory. The Church disapproved of vacuums. The notion of a vacuum had been championed by such atheists as Epicurus and Lucretius, both enemies of religion. And a vacuum, most philosophers thought, was simply illogical. It posited nothing where something — space — existed. And if a vacuum did exist, neither light nor sound could pass through it, and we could never detect it.

They were right about sound, at least. Experiments conducted in the early seventeenth century, with bells inside vacuums rung by a magnet outside, confirmed that a sound couldn't pass through airless space.

HERO

Pascal's interest in vacuums was encouraged by his father, Étienne, who'd given him a copy of Hero's *Pneumatics*. Hero (or Heron) of Alexandria, a first-century A.D. contemporary of Plutarch, was famous for constructing machines that provided miracles for temples. In the *Pneumatics* he describes pipes and vessels from which wine and water alternately flow, or from which wine flows when water is withdrawn, or from which wine flows when water is poured into a neighboring vessel. He describes a machine for producing the sound of a trumpet when a temple door is opened, figures made to dance by fire on an altar, and statues that pour libations on a fire lit between them, thus extinguishing it. His best-known device was a machine for opening the doors of a temple when a fire is lit on an altar outside them. All these contrivances work by means of gears, secret tunnels, heated air, and siphons created by vacuums. And all of them were hidden behind false walls or underneath floors — *vide* the Wizard of Oz.

Some accounts say that Hero worked in Ptolemy's museum at Alexandria, whose library became the most famous in the world. If so, we can guess how far the gods had fallen by Hero's and Plutarch's time. They'd become museum pieces, relics and statues and toys and automata. Chants of their priests had been exchanged for blueprints for building mechanical birds that pipe and flap their wings and lay wooden eggs. And mortals were left to buy dream books, and leave offerings at a rock whose significance escaped them, and dance around a pole without remembering what it meant.

GALILEO AND FLUDD

Hero firmly believed in a vacuum, and predicated his inventions on it. Vacuums created siphons that extracted liquids from containers, reducing their weight, thus activating counterweights—and opening temple doors. His work with heated air and airtight compartments and the creation of siphons became known to Pascal and other Europeans through a series of translations, first into Italian (1547), then Latin (1575), then Italian again (1589 and 1592). Galileo knew of Hero, as did Robert Fludd, two of the four or five or six men, depending on your historian, credited with independently inventing the thermometer. Galileo's instrument was probably the first, though Fludd's had a scale, making it a true thermometer.

Fifty years before Pascal's experiment on the Puy de Dôme, Galileo was puttering around in his kitchen. Here's how an eyewitness describes it:

> He took a small glass flask, about as large as a small hen's egg, with a neck about two spans long and as fine as a wheat straw, and warmed the flask well in his hands, then turned its mouth upside down into a vessel placed underneath, in which there was a little water. When he took away the heat of the hands from the flask, the water at once began to rise in the neck, and mounted to more than a span above the level of the water in the vessel. The same Sig. Galileo had then made use of this effect in order to construct an instrument for examining the degrees of heat and cold.

Italy's Hero, Galileo went on to invent the geometrical and military compass, pendulum regulators for clocks, and vibration counters derived from the pendulum; to build telescopes and microscopes and binoculars; to discover the phases of Venus and spots on the sun and Jupiter's moons; and to be "vehemently suspected of heresy" by the Inquisition for his advocacy of the Copernican system. After his death, his finger was cut off and preserved in a confection of crystal and silver similar to those medieval reliquaries used for the body parts of saints. It may be seen today in the Science Museum in Florence. Mounted on a stem, the crystal bubble with its finger inside bears an odd resemblance to some of Hero's designs, and to Galileo's early thermometer.

Reliquaries for the pious, thermometers for the practical. Perhaps the thermometer is Pan's reliquary. Of the other claimants for the invention of the thermometer, Robert Fludd is the strangest. Not only did he know Hero well, but in one of his many scientific/theological treatises the great Pan appears and narrates the text, as Fludd's Principle of Universal Nature.

Fludd, also known as Robertus de Fluctibus, lived and worked with one foot in the Middle Ages, one in the Scientific Revolution. A graduate of Oxford, a fellow of the London College of Physicians, he was also, in the words of a contemporary, a "Trismegistian-Platonick-Rosycrucian Doctor," and a "cacomagus" (a black magician) who believed in geomancy (divination from the pattern of thrown pebbles) and in the weapon-salve, a medicine he defended in *Doctor Fludd's Answer unto M. Foster, Or, The Squeesing of Parson Fosters Sponge*. The weapon-salve was an ointment concocted of human tissue, blood, and fat. It was said to heal wounds by being applied not to the wound itself but to the weapon that caused it. Smear the salve on the weapon and keep the wound clean with a linen cloth dipped in the patient's urine, and a cure would be effected . . . by magnetism.

Unlike Galileo's, Fludd's embryonic thermometer, or "weather-glass," had a scale, though the scale by our convention was upside down: cold was up and hot was down. In *Mosaicall Philosophy*, Fludd's last book, he claims that Moses invented the weather-glass and received it "figured or framed out by the finger of God" (not of Galileo). God operates in the world by attraction and repulsion, or contraction and expansion—or cold and heat. God's divine spirit is light—another form of heat—and we humans assimilate it into our bodies in the process of breathing. Our lungs then carry it to our hearts, where it separates into our vital spirit and the gross parts that mix with blood to nourish flesh.

And how do we know this? We look at the thermometer. "I would . . . have each discreet Reader to understand, that, when he beholdeth this Instrument's nature, he contemplateth the action (as it were) of a little world," Fludd said. Like the human body, the thermometer is a microcosm of the universe, and God's vital spirit circulates inside it—expands and contracts—as it does in our bodies. "This formall Champion of Light, namely Heat, warreth perpetually against the cold gardian of Darknesse . . . and all this is effected by the Act spagerick or separative Act of God's Spirit or Word." And: "It must needs follow, that [God] is the agent, as well in the contraction and dilation generally, without the Glasse, as particularly within the Glasse."

That should give some of the flavor of Fludd. His thermometer is not just "an experimentall Instrument" but a "spirituall weapon." And in his later work it comes to replace the universal monochord as a symbol of the living (expanding and contracting) universe with its calibrated harmonies scored and tuned by God, a universe permeated by His divine spirit, or "aerial quintessence." It was relatively easy for Fludd to adapt the weather-glass to baser functions too, for example to uroscopy—diagnosis by means of gradations of color in the patient's urine—and to the illustration of pulse rates, with musical notes punningly arranged on a "scale" to demonstrate the tempo. Pictures of both instruments, identical to the thermometer, appear in his books.

WIND CHILL

If Fludd was correct that God impressed nature with secret characters at the time of Creation, and that our job is to read them and understand the maker's majesty, then all this history was written in the thermometer I was mounting outside my brother's kitchen window. And God was in the liquid inside the glass tube, that thin thread of blood. No wonder nailing it up warmed the house.

I tapped in the other nail and could tell it hadn't bitten. When I pulled on the bracket both nails came out. I'd have to find another spot. I climbed down and checked the time: 12:45. Then I moved the chair over to try the window's other side, and, climbing up, grasped the chairback and stood there testing out the wobble, shifting my weight and going lighter where I could, first one leg, then the other, to countermand the chair's collapse.

Chaney Instruments of Wisconsin now told me it was warmer. The thin red line had climbed above 70. But I realized I'd been holding the thermometer in my left hand while nailing with the right. Holding it, that is, with three fingers clamped against my palm, my thumb and forefinger gripping the nail. Such dexterous monkey tricks.

We take temperatures in our social life too. A guy is hot, a nose ring cool, a woman frigid, an interest lukewarm.

Do thermometers lie? They're often inaccurate. "Wind chill," for example, means that heat loss due to the wind's convective cooling can make any warm body considerably colder than the indicated temperature. But aren't all measurements a fiction, regardless? The melting point of butter once was proposed as an absolute extreme for the thermometric scale. Seven times in the twentieth century, the Consultative Committee on Thermometry, a subcommittee of the International Committee on Weights and Measures, revised the International Practical Temperature Scale, established in Paris in 1927. Thermometers *lose* their accuracy, being little machines — exchanging energy for matter — and thus subject to entropy.

The early thermometer had more serious problems. In a handbill printed in 1631, a London firm offered a thermometer for sale:

Note that this water ascendeth with could [cold] and descendeth with heate. If in 6 or 8 howers the water fale a degre or more it wil

sureli rain within 12 hower after. . . . You may bye the glasses . . . att
the signe of the Princes arms in Hale Street.

This is a thermometer yet sounds like a barometer. But the barometer
hadn't yet been invented. And that's my point. It took Pascal's experiment on the Puy de Dôme, and the subsequent evolution of the
barometer, to complete and seal the invention of the thermometer by
Galileo and Fludd.

PASCAL REDUX

The device described in the 1631 handbill was evidently based on
Fludd's weather-glass; the language is the same as that in his *Medicina
Catholica,* published two years earlier. Why this instrument could
forecast the weather as well as measure temperature, no one quite
knew. Nor did anyone care, at least not for several decades. Thermometers were becoming popular in Europe—people really did hang
them outside windows—and so what if they happened to serve a dual
purpose? Actually, their purpose wasn't thought of as dual except in
retrospect. It takes a keen mind to recognize a problem where no
problem exists. Enter Pascal. In a letter describing the results of the experiment on the Puy de Dôme, he wrote: "From [this experiment]
there follow many consequences, such as . . . the lack of certainty that
is in the thermometer for indicating the degrees of heat (contrary
to common sentiment). Its water sometimes rises when the heat increases, and sometimes falls when the heat diminishes, even though
the thermometer has remained in the same place." (Keep in mind that
the scales of the first thermometers were upside down relative to ours.)

Pascal's point is that there are times when, according to our senses,
the temperature is hot but the thermometer doesn't show it, and vice
versa. Having created a vacuum, and having discovered why vacuums
are difficult to create—not because nature abhors a vacuum but

because we live beneath an ocean of air—Pascal realized what was wrong with those early thermometers: they were open to air. This is exactly what Fludd admired about them, since in his universe air was akin to vital spirit. But being open to air also meant that thermometers responded to the pressure of the atmosphere as well as to temperature—and the pressure of the atmosphere was what Pascal measured when he created a vacuum on the Puy de Dôme.

Pascal offered no solution to this problem, not once he abandoned science for religion. Maybe he thought the answer was obvious: to seal the glass tube. Besides, science for Pascal was not a spiritual weapon, as it was for Fludd, and the two realms of science and faith were separated by an unbreachable wall. As a scientist, Pascal scoffed at his contemporaries who parroted the ancient axiom "Nature abhors a vacuum." "I can hardly believe," he said, "that nature, which is not animate nor emotive, is susceptible of horror, since the passions presuppose a soul capable of feeling them." As a believer, he titled one section of the *Pensées*, "Nature Is Corrupt," but an editor's note beneath the title explains that "though Pascal allowed for this heading he allotted no fragments to it." In other words, in his new dispensation, nature hardly merited a mention.

The mystical Fludd and the dry, pious, skeptical Pascal were early-seventeenth-century contemporaries. The antagonism between scientific and mytho-theological thinking is such a given in Western history that we tend to forget those, like Fludd, for whom the two were inseparable. For Pascal, they were opposites. Pascal's view won. Today nature doesn't breathe or possess vital spirits or bear God's signature or prove the Bible.

It took one of the last of the Medicis, Ferdinand II, the grand duke of Tuscany, to surgically disjoin the thermometer and barometer. He couldn't have known he was also dividing science and religion. Actually, it took his glassblower to do it. Ferdinand suggested that in making a thermometer, sealing the glass tube would eliminate the effects of atmospheric pressure. So the thermometer as we know it was born. Ferdinand also published instructions for marking the scale of degrees on the tube. But the impulse to codify the thermometer's measurements — to create a scale — opened up a final Pandora's box.

SCALES

The thermometer measures heat, but what is heat? Fludd's idea of contraction and expansion was closest to the truth. His contemporary Francis Bacon, though, is the one usually credited with our definition: "When I say of motion that it is the genus of which heat is a species I would be understood to mean, not that heat generates motion or that motion generates heat (although both are true in certain cases) but that itself, its essence and quiddity, is motion and nothing else. . . . Heat is a motion of expansion, not uniformly of the whole body together, but in the smaller parts of it."

Bacon wrote this after thermometers were invented. So the quiddity called heat wasn't defined until the instrument for measuring it had been created. That seems sensible — or does it? The makers of the first thermometers didn't understand heat the way we do today; most of them assumed that heat and cold were opposites, not aspects of the same thing. In other words, the pioneer scientists — or, as they called themselves, natural philosophers — didn't first discover the nature of heat then deduce a way to gauge it. The gauge came first. First one conceives of measuring something, then the object becomes endowed with quantity, which is the same as saying it becomes an object.

Therefore thermometers created heat, and it is true in more than just a fanciful sense that nailing up a thermometer outside my brother's window warmed his house. And in the same spirit of reasons thrown up like flying buttresses before the church is built, the thermometer's scale predated even the invention of thermometers. The scale came first, then the instrument, then last, the corpus delicti, heat.

Our experience often shows this. We know the effect before the cause. This is the way history unfolds when history isn't yet history but something being experienced. When history becomes an object of study, it's usually the opposite: we know the cause first, thus robbing both cause and effect of human interest.

Galen conceived of the notion of degrees of heat and cold in the second century. In the fourteenth, the Schoolman Nicole Oresme of Paris said that for measuring things of continuous quantity such as motion or heat, "it is necessary that points, lines, and surfaces, or their properties be imagined. . . . Although indivisible points, or lines, are non-existent, still it is necessary to feign them."

To feign them. Then all scales are fictional, and an upside-down thermometer is just as meaningless, or meaningful, as a right-side-up one. It depends on what we agree upon, on our social contract. The notion that there could be a "natural" or "true" scale was a chimera pursued by early thermometrists who, in pursuing it, multiplied existing scales until they had to be mounted on boards ridiculously wide, to accommodate all the competing systems. One thermometer built in 1841 had eighteen scales, not just the Fahrenheit and Réaumur, but the Old Florentine, the New Florentine, the Hales, Fowler, Paris, H. M. Poleni, Deslisle, Bellani, Christin, Michaelly, Amontons, Newton, Société Royale, De la Hire, Edenburg, and Cruquiu, making it the Babel of European science.

Why so many scales? Before a scale could be standardized, it needed at least one fixed point, preferably two. For the cold end, the temperatures of snow, of ice, of a mixture of ice and salt, of a very deep cellar, and of the freezing point of water were all proposed. For the warm end, the temperature of the human body, of melting butter, and of boiling water. A consensus eventually developed around the freezing and boiling points of water, but not on how many degrees should divide the space between the two. Even those points weren't absolute, however, since water boils at different temperatures according to atmospheric pressure. The Catch-22 of scales was this: the constancy of freezing and boiling points of water had to be assumed, because there was no scale with which to measure them and determine their constancy. Those points would in fact create such a scale—but how could they do so if they weren't fixed?

The solution was to pretend they were fixed. Today we say that the temperature of steam over pure water boiling at normal atmospheric pressure, along with the temperature of melting ice—not affected by atmosphere—determines our thermometric scale. And what is normal atmospheric pressure? That which exists at sea level. And why is it normal? Because most people live there. In science as in the rest of human history, "normal" and "natural" mean what most people do.

In a recent book, Lennard Davis has shown that our meanings of the words "normal" and "norm" are relatively young; before the mid-nineteenth century, normal meant perpendicular, and norm referred to a carpenter's square. As the century progressed, normal evolved into average, and came to be associated with the normal distribution curve, a.k.a. the bell curve. Once the normal was so defined, it established a range that produced the abnormal at the curve's extremities. It's no coincidence, then, as Davis points out, that the nineteenth-century statisticians who borrowed the bell curve from astronomy (where it was known as the "error law") were also eugenicists who thought the race could be improved by lopping off its extremities and abnormalities.

So with temperature scales. One reason the freezing and boiling points of water were proposed to frame a scale may well have been our shared experience of extremes. Between those two points lies our body's temperature—a natural and moderate compromise. So the scale becomes a line displaying natural states, and helps define a range of normal distribution, and weathermen compare each night on the news the actual temperature with the norm for that date.

Moderating extremes is a recent innovation in human history, relatively speaking. Aristotle could define virtue as a mean between extremes—as with courage, a mean between cowardice and foolhardiness; or thrift, a mean between prodigality and parsimony—because by the fourth century B.C. some human beings around the Mediterranean Sea had learned how to live in moderate comfort, inside houses lit by oil lamps, with slaves to do their work and braziers to keep them warm. To put this in perspective, as Carl Sagan tells us, human beings lived outdoors for 99.9 percent of human history, following game and crops. Some still do. But most don't; and what most people do or don't do, by definition, is the norm.

What most people do is nail up thermometers outside their kitchen windows, or install weathervanes or bird feeders, or plop lawn jockeys down beside their front steps. In other words, they find ways to announce a domesticated environment. The thermometer as a sign of civilized behavior and nature brought to heel suggests fire captured and tamed, cooked food, private life, central heating, and comfort. The thermometer is also a fiction that measures something real—heat and cold—and to call it a fiction is simply to acknowledge its role as a cog in the immense machinery of human culture. Take away the thermometer—or the nail, the word "bread," the magnetic coil, paper money—and the whole interlocking edifice collapses. No one has that power, of course—to remove the gears and wheels that keep our lives turning. But some, like my brother, do remove themselves.

Had Paul ever nailed up his own thermometer? The evidence suggests that he hadn't, although they don't last forever, those cheap thermometers like the one in my hand. I'd found some solid trim on the window's other side. Several relics of nails, minus heads, stuck out of it, left from the plywood shutters that had boarded up the house. Perhaps, when the heat was still functioning, when he'd first bought this house, a thermometer had been here. Paul could have consulted the temperature one day and decided not to go to work, not to brave the subzero cold outside. How much more inviting to brew up a pot of tea, to watch *The Price Is Right* in pajamas, robe, and slippers.

But gradually, one by one, his domestic servomechanisms failed. He replaced them at first; the boiler was only ten years old, installed by Sears in the late eighties—I'd found the receipts. The water pump, however, looked to be ancient, constructed mostly of rust. I'll never know the exact sequence of events, or the manner in which Paul's vigilance eroded. Perhaps it felt akin to that vaudeville routine in which a man runs back and forth behind a long table to keep a row of plates spinning while an impish assistant continually hands him new plates to add.

He retired. He grew old. Things got to be too much for him. The water heater sprung a leak. The front steps collapsed, and in a spasm of industry he cleared away the rotten wood. Then the toilet would not flush, the plumbing ceased to function, the phone line went dead. The ride-around mower, left out all winter, wouldn't start, and its four tires went flat. Eventually the central heating broke down, and what good would a thermometer be then? Especially in a cold climate, the thermometer marks the boundary between a managed environment and the larger world that exceeds one's supervision. For Paul, that boundary no longer existed.

Male menopause, I've heard, occurs at the age when one can't even muster up the will to change a light bulb. Most of the bulbs in Paul's house had burned out. He did manage to do something, though. Among his voluminous papers, I'd found a receipt for nursing home insurance, bought a year before he died.

HEAT ENGINES

Once a common and acceptable temperature scale was agreed upon, it was possible to measure the thermal expansion of metals. Engineers could then compensate for thermal effects, enabling them to build more precisely calibrated machines and instruments. This helped make the Industrial Revolution possible.

As Fludd's Principle of Universal Nature, the great Pan isn't so much dead as irrelevant. He's been replaced by heat. Sadi Carnot, fascinated by the first steam machines, devised the theory of heat engines that fueled the enormous industrial expansion still heating up the globe. In 1824 he said this about heat; as you read it, try substituting "Pan" for "heat":

> It is to heat that we must attribute the great and striking movements on the earth. It causes atmospheric turbulence, the rise of clouds, rain and other forms of precipitation, the great oceanic currents that traverse the surface of the globe and of which man has been able to harness only a tiny fraction for his own use; lastly, it causes earthquakes and volcanic eruptions.
>
> From an immense natural reservoir we can draw the motive power we need; nature in offering us all sorts of combustibles has given us the means of generating at any time and anywhere the latent motive power. To develop that power, to appropriate it to our own use is the purpose of heat-engines.

Parenthetically, the internal combustion engine, made possible by Carnot's theory, relies on a piston to be returned to its position — after being fired to the top of a cylinder — by air pressure. So Pascal and, through him, Hero of Alexandria still haunt the modern world.

Pascal talked about a hidden God. Our hidden God is heat. Thermometers with their fictional scales transform heat, a thing of nature, into heat, a thing of culture. Nature, of course, was the object of science, or emerged as such in the seventeenth century. But to talk about a nature that "emerged" is a figure of speech. What emerged was a new way of framing the world on the part of human beings. We saw things differently and had a new meme, "nature." A meme is Richard Dawkins's term for a unit of culture — wearing baseball caps backwards, for example — that evolves out of other units, just as morphological and biological characteristics of organisms (via genes) change through evolution. That nature could be thought of as a unit of culture is not, by the way, a recent notion. Pascal said as much in his *Pensées*. Number 126: "Nature is itself only a first custom, as custom is a second nature."

As for my brother Paul, perhaps the reason he never nailed up a thermometer outside his kitchen window is that he wasn't normal. "Normal" is our way of regulating nature. One way to achieve it is to manage deer herds; another is to nail up a thermometer, as I was doing now. This proves that I myself am normal, does it not?

II
TOOLS

1

OSCILLOSCOPE

HAMMER IN HAND, still perched on that chair, I stood and admired my all-white thermometer, now properly mounted beside the kitchen window. It was sticky, as everyone says in New England — pre-summer muggy, before the trees break out and turn on their fountains. The insides of my elbows felt damp. On Twist Run Road, around the front of the house, a car pulled up. I listened for its engine to cut.

The thermometer — an instrument of benign domestication — looked official yet cozy against the dull brown siding. My feelings of pride were severely out of whack with the magnitude of the task, of course. I stepped off the chair. My hand still held the hammer, so I slid it in my belt; its claw helped to keep it there.

Claw. I pictured the word in my mind; it felt dangerous and evil. It sounded and looked exactly like its meaning, and seemed forged in those flattened spikes on the hammer, made for bloody digging. I thought of two-toed sloths and saber-toothed tigers emerging from the swirling primeval butter, of young mindless power stretching its limbs, hard and amoral. It doesn't take much to become a Neanderthal. *Soft-spoken novelist goes cowboy apeshit with skull-crunching claw-headed hammer in his belt.*

The car door slammed. What to do with the chair? I wanted the house to look halfway presentable, so I flung it in some bushes below — it was on its last legs anyway — and rounded the corner to meet Jerry, the agent.

The appraiser appointed by the probate court after Paul's death had recommended Jerry and given me his card. His father owned the local Coldwell Banker agency. Small towns, I thought—go with the network. Big smile on his face, arm extended, he crossed the wilderness of front yard to greet me. "Doing some work?" He'd spotted the hammer.

"Nothing much."

Jerry was the sort who looked as if he'd never wilt. He carried a leather portfolio in one hand. White shirt, floral tie, no coat. Short and bull-necked, he was fresh out of college and had the jaw of a nutcracker, but only a noselet. I trusted his smile; it seemed genuine enough.

We went in through the basement, as I still couldn't get the back door to work. "This could be a problem," he said. We were climbing the open basement stairs past blackened cobwebs, heating ducts, and wires. The place smelled of rust and wet, sandy soil. Behind me, Jerry asked, "What about the front door?"

"No steps."

Upstairs, the door into the kitchen hung open at an angle, one hinge ripped off. The smell inside the house was overwhelming. The humidity made it worse, I realized. I had to breathe through my mouth. "Looks like you got it cleaned up pretty good," said Jerry.

"It was a hell of a job."

"Who'd you finally get to do it?"

"Some guys up the road. The kid who runs the Mobil station got a crew together. I called something like six cleaning companies. Three showed up and two walked away. The one who actually gave me an estimate, for six thousand dollars, called back and said he'd changed his mind, he didn't want the job. So I asked around town. The gas station guy knew someone, he said, then he thought for a minute and said maybe he and his buddies could do it. I told him he better take a look at it first." We were trolling the house, breathing through our mouths. I hoped he wouldn't ask about the scratch marks on the walls, made by desperate claws. The doorjambs too were splintered and ripped. None of this had been noticeable before.

"Floors look tight."

"That was a surprise. We got the rugs up and found hardwood floors."

"They're in pretty good shape."

I'd made sure that each room had at least one working light, if only a bare bulb. The rooms still looked filthy, despite the shop vac I'd used to finish the cleaning. Two bedrooms, a small formal dining room with a fake pewter light fixture, a kitchen, and a living room. What they call snug. The rooms echoed our footsteps.

"What happened to all that ham radio equipment?"

"I sold it." I'm not sure why I lied.

"Probably worth a lot, all that stuff."

"Actually, Jud, the guy from the gas station, he sold a lot of it. He sold quite a few things. I told him they could have whatever they found. He knew everyone, that guy — every scavenger in town, every salvage and scrap man, every ham, you name it. Appliances, junk. They came out of the woodwork. He made a killing off this place. We had words about it."

"Wadeedo?"

"Pardon me?"

"What did he do?"

"Who?"

"Your brother."

I looked at him. We were standing in the living room. I walked across the room, to lead him away from the cold-air return; its grate was back on. Around the perimeter of the room, scummy bits of rug and backing still clung to small nails in rows on the floor. Most of the windows on this end of the house weren't boarded up. "What do you mean, what did he do?"

"For a living."

"Oh. Retired."

"I mean before that."

"Electronics. Raytheon."

"Engineer?"

"No. Assembly. Amateur engineer, though, I guess. I found lots of notes and drawings for inventions. They looked like inventions." Jerry's eyes widened and he faced me smiling, feigning interest in my brother. I found myself clamming up and drifted off the subject. I didn't really understand Paul's inventions, not being familiar with electronics and microwaves. He'd told me a few years before his death that he was on to something that would make a lot of money, and intended to give the profits to our parents, to ease their old age.

I thought of his airplanes hung on wires in Grandma's house. As a teenager, he'd built a replica P-47N Thunderbolt that really flew—I'd seen photographs of him grinning like a proud father, this specimen in his arms. My mother enjoyed mentioning in company his ability to use a slide rule. When he moved in with us after Grandma's death, he built CB radios, two- and ten-meter-band transmitters and receivers, the oscilloscope. Yet he'd barely finished high school and never learned how to spell. His handwriting consisted of carefully constructed block letters. In my box of his effects in the van were his notes on "Reinventing the Notch Filter"—his "possible new marketing item," as he'd written across the top of the page—his moneymaking device that would buy Mom and Dad a lifetime supply of vacations in Hawaii. I'd found the notes packed in a Tupperware container after his death:

A FEW MONTHS AGO, DUE TO CURCOMSTANCES AT WORK, I WAS ABLE TO TRY OUT SOME OF <u>MY</u> IDEAS ON NOTCH FILTERS, AND THE RESULTS SO FAR, SEEM TO HAVE BEEN WORTH THE EFFERT! TO SIMPLIFY THINGS, ALL I HAVE DON IS TAKEN A GIVEN PASS BAND CAVITY, WITH A

GIVEN LOOP DISIGN, AND MODIFIED THE LOOP TO GIVE A
NOTCH. THIS WAS DON BY OPENING UP THE GROUND SIDE
OF THE LOOP, AND ADDING GOOD QUALITY VARIABEL
CAP'S. BY THE SIMPLE ADDITION OF TWO JOHANSON VARI-
ABAL CAP'S, (AT A COST OF APPROXIMATLY $12) AND TWO
TYPE "N" CONNECTOR'S, (AT THE COST OF $15, ONE OF
OUR HIGH Q CAVITYS CAN BE MADE INTO A PASS/NOTCH
CONFIGURATION THAT WILL GIVE THE USOR A PASS BAND
BETWEEN 400 TO 500 MHZ WITH AN INSERTION LOSS OF
.5 TO 1.0 DB, AND A NOTCH OF UP TO 70 DB THAT IS
TUNABEL PLUS OR MINUS 50 MHZ FROM THE PASS BAND
FREQUENCY.

This had something to do with filtering interference from radio transmissions, I knew, but mostly it sounded like gibberish. It frightened
me a little, as runes in a cave might. It went on for several pages, and
had been rewritten and painfully recopied a dozen or more times, then
typed with the spelling cleaned up and the exclamation points taken
out—by someone else, I assumed—and apparently circulated as an
interoffice memo, dated a few years before his retirement. Also in the
plastic box were test reports on these "reentrant notch cavities," and
blueprints and pictures of what appeared to be the standard bandpass
cavity filters—steel cylinders with knobs and a sprinkling of other
gadgets on top, about the size of beer kegs.

It occurred to me to wonder how much of what I'd written in my life
would be gibberish to Paul, from poetry to literary criticism to novels
about failed visionaries. In his house, I'd found a copy of my first novel
with a bookmark on page 8. I'd also found five or six homemade cavity
filters in one of the junk cars he'd left behind the house. I piled them
outside when I was emptying the car, only to discover the following
day that Jud from the Mobil station had sold them when his crew
cleaned out the place. So I'll never know if they were worth anything.

I did find a letter from Paul's employers, commending him in vague terms; it didn't mention notch filters.

Suddenly I was full of questions for Jerry. "The agency takes what, six percent?"

"That's standard," he said.

"How long's our contract for? You brought it with you?"

He patted the portfolio. "That's something —" he started. "Standard is nine months. I'm okay with — whatever —"

"You think fifty-six thousand is a fair price?"

"That's the appraisal. I think you need wiggle room."

"I don't see how we can sell it with this smell. Does it seem worse to you?"

"I think when it's warm —"

"Can we do anything about it?"

"It's not that bad, really. What this place is, is a handyman's special. The market's hot now, this location is good, and the price, you could set a price in the sixties. That's rock bottom. Someone comes in and rips out the walls and puts up new Sheetrock, there goes the smell."

"I was thinking about some industrial-strength cleanser or deodorant. I don't know. The guys who cleaned it out said a smell like that gets into the studs and joists, even. You can never get it out."

"It's not that bad, really."

"A friend of mine got skunked one time and used vinegar and tomato juice."

"The hell you say! It's not as bad as a skunk."

"It's inconceivably worse."

"Horseradish. Can I try the front door?"

We were standing in the little entryway between the living and dining room. Jerry opened the door and looked out. Instinctively, we both inhaled deeply.

"Door works fine," he said. "Lock works fine."

What's your point? I thought. To exit the house, he had to get down on his hands and knees then back out with his weight on his forearms. It was three or four feet to the ground. I followed.

"He must have had stairs here once," he said.

"You think we need some now?"

"It's up to you. I can't see taking people in through the cellar. And the back door won't open, and even if it did, the back porch is caving in and it constitutes a safety hazard. The floor boards are rotten."

"I was hoping to start home after we signed the papers."

"Go ahead. It's not all that bad. We'll go through the cellar."

"You just said you couldn't."

"It really doesn't matter. It's psychological. If you go in the front door, that makes a better statement. But with this being a handyman's special, it probably don't make any difference anyway."

By now we'd begun to walk around the house. I'd gotten rid of three junk cars outside, but Paul's rusting ride-around mower, on four flat tires, still sat in the back. The man I'd sold it to, for fifty dollars cash, hadn't picked it up yet. "You know someone who could do it?" I asked.

"Build some steps?"

"Don't worry about it. I shouldn't have mentioned it. Completely up to you. Heck, it's your house. What's that?" We were walking down the slope behind the house, past a tangle of bushes.

"Chair. They must have missed it."

Jerry turned to face me. We'd reached the dirt road that ran behind the house whose named I'd never learned; there was no street sign. Across this road were remnants of a stone wall, and arthritic apple trees in the thorny field behind it. They looked ready to burst into blossom right now. "You could call a pre-cast," he said.

"You mean pre-cast concrete?"

"I know a place in Haverhill that delivers."

Half an hour later I was driving to the Home Depot in Salem, having signed on with Jerry and Coldwell Banker, having phoned his pre-cast people from the Mobil station. Steps for Paul's house would cost $530, not including delivery.

Too much. I felt chained to my duties, and didn't like someone younger than me rattling the chain, and didn't care about the house, but knew it needed front steps. At red lights I tapped my fingers on the steering wheel, feeling cheap, then feeling proud I felt cheap. I found myself honking slow starters when the light changed; why not flip them the bird too? Also, I was cultivating a minor irritation regarding Jerry's failure to notice the thermometer, and every few minutes poked it a little to see if it was there, like a loose tooth.

I'd have to phone the Red Roof Inn if I stayed another night, since I'd checked out that morning. I mentally ran down a list of have-tos. Call home. Get money. Enough irritants existed to supply me for days. Then, walking through the Home Depot, I felt some sort of grit on my soles, and longed for a rug to wipe my feet. Whenever I shopped at this store, it seemed, I found myself wiping my hands on my pants.

Home Depot, the Wal-Mart of do-it-yourselfers. Sheetrock, lumber, glass, furring strips, trim, doors, cinder blocks, shop vacs, hoses . . . electric trucks and forklifts beeping madly through the aisles. Wal-Mart equals blue, Home Depot orange. The shelves on which all these goods sit—items for sale at ground level, inventory above—fit nicely under warehouse-metal roofs a good thirty feet high and are made of a distinctive construction-strength steel, painted orange and bolted to uprights. Adult Erector sets. In the lumber department, large enough to house a drive-in movie, T beams and girders, instead of shelves, hold stacks of wallboard or plywood or doors. Here the help seemed especially busy. I found someone to ask if they sold pre-made steps, though I suspected the answer.

"Pre-made? No. We got pre-cut stringers."

"What's that?"

He looked at me and smiled. His face seemed to soften and harden simultaneously, as though wanting to help me but lacking the time.

Yet he took the time. His beard and cloudy eyes appeared flaked with ashes, but he looked somewhat distinguished, save for some raw red patches of skin. He could have been a doctor—thin lips, gray hair—but one arm, I noticed, was bulkier than the other, a sure sign of a carpenter of the old school, one who uses a handsaw. "I take it you never built no steps. It's pretty simple. What's the total rise?" Voice soft and flaky.

"I'm not sure."

"What's this for, anyway?"

"Front steps to my brother's house, which I'm selling. I just want to get people in and get them out. I mean prospective buyers. It's a handyman's special. Whoever buys it, of course, will put in something permanent."

"Like pre-cast?"

"Sure . . ."

Back at the house, I laid out my supplies and equipment. I already had a hammer and saw, I'd assured the clerk. To go with them, I'd purchased a norm, but no one calls them norms anymore, they're carpenter's squares. And nails, plus stringers and one-by-fives for treads, but nothing for risers—the steps would be open. We'd taken the time to talk about the project, and the Home Depot clerk had suggested that I buy some posts too. Since the stairs had rotted off, the sill was probably also rotten, hence I couldn't attach the stringers to the house. Instead, I'd have to box out the steps.

The stringers cost only $7.49, and the rest of the wood plus the norm and nails brought the total to just under $50. So I should have been happy. But the saw was dull from misuse, and making just one cut through a four-by-four post took a good ten minutes. Also, I didn't have a level; I had to eyeball everything. If I worked fast enough, I told myself, I still might be able to drive home today. Home to Hannah and our children. It was already mid-afternoon, though. I was hungry too, having skipped lunch. And it was hot; on this side of the house I had to work in the sun.

Every second of every day, the sun loses four million tons of its mass in the process of sustaining its huge production of energy. Of that mass, 4.3 pounds of light hits the earth each second. And the light is hot, especially if you're working. Am I my brother's keeper?

I cleared out some weeds and brush first. Then scraped at the dirt with the hammer's claws to level the paving stones I'd found in the basement, on which to set the stairs. The clerk was right: below the closed door, the exposed sill was rotten. In fact, a gap had opened up between the bottom of the door and the interior floor, large enough to vent the house's smell as I worked.

I took out my frustration by banging nails hard. I'd bought nails, not screws—the obvious choice, the clerk had assured me. And I did not just stare at the hammer-Thing, as Martin Heidegger calls it. I'm sure the English is more charming than the German: "The less we just stare at the hammer-Thing, and the more we seize hold of it and use it, the more primordial does our relationship to it become." Cool.

The all-purpose nail—our universal hyphen—is also primordial, nails being stark and simple. The nail is blue-collar, the screw white-collar, even though "screw" comes from the Latin *scrobs*, meaning the hole a pig makes with its snout. "A nail is heroic and exciting," says the Mexican essayist Fabio Morábito. "In a screw the brusque commands of the nail have been transmuted into dialogue and negotiation."

Nails and screws both go back to Roman times. The ancient Chinese also made nails. The Romans had claw hammers, also folding carpenter's rules, as did the Egyptians. A first-century A.D. Roman nail-heading anvil was discovered in Bavaria in the nineteenth century, and the author of a book that reports it—*Ancient Carpenters' Tools*—assures us that a junk dealer named Faust, in Pennsylvania, had witnessed a blacksmith named Emory, in Philadelphia, around 1877, making nails and rivets on a similar anvil. Before the Industrial Revolution, England's center for making nails by hand was the country near Birmingham; there, nail masters kept women and children, who worked in filthy sheds attached to their houses, in effective slavery by paying them for piecework on the truck system, or so my *Britannica* reports.

America pioneered the machine-made nail, in 1790. Forty years later, Stendhal's famous description of a nail factory opened his novel *The Red and the Black:* "No sooner has one entered the town than one is startled by the din of a noisy machine of terrifying aspect. A score of weighty hammers, falling with a clang which makes the pavement tremble, are raised aloft by a wheel which the water of the torrent sets in motion. Each of these hammers turns out, daily, I cannot say how many thousands of nails. A bevy of fresh, pretty girls subjects to the blows of these enormous hammers, the little scraps of iron which are rapidly transformed into nails." In the nineteenth century, nail factories set the standard for noise; even Lewis and Clark, complaining of the noise at an Indian village, compared it to that of a nail factory.

Hammer and nails. Bedrock. Manhood. I'd practiced as a boy on scraps of two-by-fours, but choked up on the hammer too much, my father said. He told me nails should be driven in two or three blows, and joints should be square. As I built my brother's steps, I remembered Dad building similar steps for my uncle's house in Worcester, when I was young. Uncle John's emphysema was so bad by then he could barely walk to the bathroom; he hadn't been to the second floor of his house in two or three years. My father has it now, emphysema. Paul had it too, though he died of an aneurysm.

Dad's work seemed effortless—his stairs built themselves. This was not the case with mine. I resented every cut, every blow of the hammer. What good did it do to check each joint repeatedly with my norm if I couldn't correct it? I'd seen a carpenter once, after framing a closet, wallop the uprights with a sledgehammer to force it into square. Me, I can never get anything square—I lack patience and skill—and this feels like a shameful flaw in my character. All my life I've misused tools. I used a crosscut saw to trim brush, a hammer's claws to clear away debris and level the ground. At home, my few tools sit in judgment on a shelf in a corner of my basement. Tools are profoundly conservative. They dictate a right way. Building Paul's steps, I realized too late I should have bought a tape measure. Why hadn't I thought of it?

At least the rhythmic motion of sawing calmed me down. It was just as primordial as swinging a hammer. I sawed and sawed. My shoulder grew sore, but I sawed through the soreness. Both Dad and Paul had been good with tools; maybe I was the odd one, not my brother. In the army during World War II, Dad worked as an auto mechanic at Fort Devens in Massachusetts, being too old for the fighting overseas. Later, when I was growing up, he tinkered with our car on the street in South Boston, often after supper while I held a flashlight. Leaning into the engine, he never bothered to explain all the fabricated viscera — those wheels, cylinders, hoses, belts, and bars, those hooks, teeth, needles, wires, rotors, and blades — that smell of gasoline, burning oil, and rubber, that sound of the motor clicking and bubbling — not that I demonstrated any urgent curiosity. Instead he whistled, to convince others of his happiness, occasionally breaking off to recall me to my duties. *Shine it right there!* My attention always wandered.

Paul was a more meticulous tool user and worked at a bench. After Grandma's death, and after his own stint in the army, he moved in with us and arranged with our landlord to set up a workshop in the basement. We lived on the top floor of an old duplex, and the owner lived down. At a bench in our half of the basement, Paul gradually progressed from making airplanes and miniature balsa-wood houses (for model train sets) to piecing together — beginning with the circuit boards — radios, transmitters, and finally the oscilloscope, an instrument whose purpose seemed quasi-religious to me. It was profoundly mysterious yet strangely dumb and repetitive, stuck on one operation: the manufacture of glowing lines that looped across the screen. Yet its grids and its sine and sawtooth waves, its flickering green porthole, possessed a power to hypnotize, and most evenings I found myself wandering down to the basement to watch the oscilloscope over Paul's shoulder.

The floor of our basement was solid concrete. Above the oscilloscope on my brother's bench—above the pegboard attached to the wall behind it—a half window revealed the feet and calves of neighbors walking past on the sidewalk outside. I often visited this spot after school as well, when Paul was off at work, having discovered his magazines cached in the chassis of a radio on the bench. Even now, the smell of a soldering iron suggests white teeth, full breasts, and dangled G-strings.

Like my father, Paul was short on explanations regarding his machinery. Oscilloscopes operate through a sweep circuit, he said. They're just tools, he pointed out, but I thought of the instrument he'd built more as a shrine. He did explain that the line on the screen was an electric signal, and electric signals were everywhere—and this screen was how you saw them.

Later, my brother learned Morse code and obtained his ham license. He built a rotating antenna and installed it in the attic, with controls in our bathroom, then set up his transmitters and receivers on a thick plywood board across the bathroom tub. The bathroom was where I'd been doing my homework on a folding tray; once my family had a television set, it was our apartment's only quiet room. Now I was banished to the kitchen with earplugs, while the TV blared the *Texaco Star Theater* and Paul, in the bathroom, held cheerfully redundant conversations with strangers on the two- and ten-meter bands. For the convenience of my father and me, he took to leaving a coffee can outside the bathroom door, so that only my mother had the power to evict him when she had "an emergency."

Saturday mornings, he dismantled the machinery and removed the board for those who wished to bathe. To save hot water, after his bath

Paul left the plug in so I could use his water. The habits of thrift taught us by our parents had been learned in the Depression. This was how I cleaned myself: by lowering my body into Paul's gray opacity rimmed with a sort of soapy pond scum—and by staying there forever. By launching blankets of water down my legs with my palms, then waiting for them to crash and roll back, choked with Paul's dirt, while at the same time ignoring my family's repeated knocks and shouts to be allowed into the bathroom.

At last my posts were cut to size. I propped them on the house and leaned the stringers against them, distractedly calculating how to stabilize the framework. I could cut more four-by-fours as crosspieces, I thought. But I might have to notch them to nail it all together.

It suddenly occurred to me that Paul was never odd. At least he wasn't then. When had I learned to see him as different? I realized I'd spent my life fleeing his example—first to college, then graduate school, then academia, by means of which I slipped into the middle class, as though into a room one could only enter sideways. The middle class, I thought, where tools were meant for other people's hands. I was wrong, of course.

2

HAMMER STONE

WE ARE TOOL-MAKING animals, said Benjamin Franklin. But the way we make tools often looks either ingenious or harebrained, depending on your point of view.

In 1527, the Spanish explorer Cabeza de Vaca and the 242 men he was stranded with on the coast of northern Florida stripped the stirrups and bridles off the horses they'd ridden there and heated and hammered them into nails and axes for constructing boats that would take them to Mexico.

In 1804, while wintering with the Mandan Indians in what is now North Dakota, Lewis and Clark gave their hosts a corn grinder. The Mandans already knew how to grind corn, with a metate, or saddle-stone—the way all tribes did it, the way the ancient Egyptians had done it too. But the corn grinder proved useful anyway. They deconstructed it, using the metal for arrowheads and hide scrapers, and the crank (with part of the casing still attached) for a pounder to crack open buffalo bones, to get at the marrow.

Skip ahead to 1935. In Africa, Louis and Mary Leakey, about to discover the world's oldest tools, drive their car into a ditch and have to dig it out with table knives and two enamel dinner plates. Sixteen years later, now famous, they find themselves near the Tanzania-Kenya border when the springs of Mary's car break. Louis replaces them with goatskins and wooden splints.

Now 1969. Archaeologists and paleontologists at Koobi Fora in northern Kenya find tools even older than those the Leakeys found—two and a half million years old, in fact. Each afternoon, the research team wash their clothes by hand in nearby Lake Turkana and fish with nets for tilapias, to make their evening meal. And each morning, searching for fossils, they dig and sift down through hardened sediment, one painstaking inch at a time, with dental picks.

Like Cabeza de Vaca, the Mandan Indians, and the Leakeys, the archaeologists at Koobi Fora misused tools—that is, they used them for purposes other than the ones for which they were intended. Misuse in this sense is hardly a crime; call it shrewd appropriation, or cunning adaptation via improvisation and found materials.

Maybe we are the tool misusing animal.

CHOPPERS, FLAKES, AND HAMMER STONES

The researchers at Koobi Fora, attempting to learn how ancient tools were made, developed a discipline they called experimental archaeology. That is, they made stone tools themselves, to see if they looked like the tools they were discovering.

Early tools don't display especially distinctive marks; to a layman's eyes, they just look like old rocks. Experimental archaeologists prove the rocks are tools. With a hammer stone, these members of the species *Homo sapiens*, in these ancient times—the late twentieth century—strike chunks of volcanic lava, knocking flakes off the core, and find themselves producing the same telltale conchoidal fractures, the same bulbs of percussion, and the same ripple marks that appear on ancient stone tools. When they do this several times on the same chunk, turning it as they go, they have themselves a chopper, which some consider the earliest manufactured tool. It was used, guessers guess, for hacking, mashing, cutting, grubbing roots, also scraping hides and pounding bones for marrow.

The process of making choppers, though, also makes flakes, which other archaeologists consider the truly earliest tools. That is, they assert that the pieces whacked off the original chunk were more valuable to early tool users than the chunk itself, because they were thinner and sharper—call them primordial knives. Experimental archaeologists have succeeded in butchering an elephant with such flakes.

But wouldn't the hammer stones used to knock the flakes off the core have to be considered the earliest tools? Before a tool can be used, or misused, one has first to make it with a hammer stone. Furthermore, the hammer stones employed to make tools could have been the same with which early humans cracked open nuts. Perhaps we're the animal who misuses one tool to make another. It would be interesting to know what tools the Mandans used to take apart Lewis and Clark's corn grinder.

The hammer stones that made tools became modified through use. In fact, repeated knapping with a hammer stone results in its taking a spherical shape. In the early 1900s prehistorians guessed that the spheroid stones they were finding at fossil sites were used as bolas, hunting devices they were already familiar with from Argentinean Indians in the Pampas. Bolas consist of two or three spheroid stones tied to either end of a thong. Thrown at the legs of game, they trip them up and bring them down. But experimental archaeologists, in making stone tools, discovered that using a hammer stone to flake cores for about four hours results in just such stone spheres—a more plausible reason for their existence.

Of course, once they'd finished using them as hammer stones, and discarded them, prehistoric people could have found the stones again and misused them as bolas.

Stone tools are the ones that last through time. We have no way of knowing whether bones cracked in half, exposing sharp edges, were also used for tools, or whether branches of trees were used in this manner, or large bone clubs, as in Stanley Kubrick's movie 2001. In 1953, the anatomist Raymond Dart claimed that early hominids used the sharp bones he'd found at a fossil site in South Africa for weapons, and the skulls for scoops and bowls—and therefore concluded that our ancestors were predators who killed and dismembered their prey, "slaking their ravenous thirst with the hot blood of victims and greedily devouring livid writhing flesh." Later experimental archaeologists are not so sanguine in their prose, and have determined that the bone fractures found by Dart were more likely produced by animal predators.

Maybe Dart had been reading his Bible—who knows? Bones as weapons have a long pedigree in our culture, beginning with Samson's using the jawbone of an ass to slay the Philistines. Was this a case of misuse of a jawbone? Did the hominid in 2001 misuse the bone with which he whacked his enemy? Do chimps misuse hammer stones (used for cracking nuts) when they throw them at each other? We are the animals who misuse tools to discover what they're good for.

PAN AGAIN

In making their ersatz ancient tools, experimental archaeologists use several techniques. They hold the hammer stone in one hand — invariably the right — and the core in the other, and strike the core. Or they use a boulder to brace the core while they strike it, or swing the core against the boulder, or even throw it at the boulder, all to produce choppers and flakes with the same scars displayed on early tools. To understand the range of injuries early hominids may have incurred from this industry, the archaeologists also shun protective clothing. They are acting, in a sense, from the most ancient scripts, playing musical scores two million years old. Just as we fall asleep by counterfeiting the posture of a sleeping person, they counterfeit ancient postures and gestures in order to counterfeit tools, which become authentic counterfeits.

Maybe we are the animal who counterfeits tools.

All manufacture is counterfeit to a Platonist, and all tools are imitations. We who misuse tools, we who counterfeit tools, even we who think about tools, are really closet Platonists. We build steps that fall short of the steps in our souls. We see ideal shapes in the tool before us, see dental picks as diggers. And we counterfeit tools with a template in our heads, setting in motion a kind of feedback loop between the ideal shape and the material object, perhaps the same feedback loop evolutionists contend fueled human development: toolmaking resulted in bigger brains, and bigger brains in turn made better tools.

The Ape of Nature was a seventeenth-century figure often pictured on the frontispiece of books, representing imitation as the motive power of learning. On the title page of Fludd's *History of the Macrocosm*, for example, the ape squats in the middle of a circle, pointing with his stick at segments fanning out from the circle, in each of which tools of industry or of the arts are represented. It may have been this tradition of the Ape of Nature that led taxonomists to name one of the six major types of ape *Pan* (*Pan troglodytes schweinfurthi*). In other words, like the god Pan, apes stand for nature. But they also stand for the process by which our work in the world imitates nature. This process is sometimes described as follows: early stone tools, taken from nature, are thought of as improvements on nature, and become synthetic teeth, jaws, horns, claws, et cetera. Even now, our names for tools often conjure up animals: monkey wrenches, rams, cranes, rat-tail files, crowbars, bullnose planes. Tools are also thought of as improvements of the human body, so that, as Freud said, with our tools we humans become prosthetic gods. Maybe the god we become is Pan.

So: we are the animal who counterfeits tools, and we are the animal who misuses tools. And one person's misuse is another person's ingenious appropriation, which his fellows will counterfeit, and so on and so forth. As much as shoddy carpentry, this makes Platonists of us all.

MAY I BORROW YOUR HAMMER?

In the 1960s, Jane Goodall observed her favorite chimp, a *Pan* she named David Greybeard, fishing for termites with a stem of grass. He plunged the stiff stalk of grass inside a termite nest, then removed it and ate the insects off the stem. When he left, Goodall aped the ape's behavior: "I picked up one of his discarded tools and carefully pushed it into a hole myself. Immediately I felt the pull of several termites as they seized the grass, and when I pulled it out there were a number of worker termites and a few soldiers, with big red heads, clinging on with their mandibles. There they remained, sticking out at right angles to the stem with their legs waving in the air."

We trust she didn't eat them. Later, she observed David Greybeard stripping leaves off a twig to use in fishing for termites, the well-known first recorded instance of chimps modifying an object to make a tool. When she notified Louis Leakey about this, he replied, "Ah, now we must redefine *tool*, redefine *man*—or accept chimpanzees as humans!"

Since then, the reports of chimps using tools has steadily grown: they fish for termites, ants, and honey; they use sticks to clean their teeth and leaves to clean wounds or scoop brains from baboon skulls; they threaten each other with brandished clubs, use stones to pound nuts and sticks to dig the nutmeat out of the shell, and sticks to extract the marrow from bones. All this has led anthropologists on a wild scramble to update Ben Franklin's definition of "man" as the tool-maker. Instead, we've become the *skillful* maker of tools, the *habitual* maker of tools, the tool *standardizers*, and the *social* user of tools. In my view, none of these succeeds in distinguishing *Homo sapiens* from *Pan*, except by degree; but the intent is to distinguish us by kind. Maybe Jay Leno came closest when he said that if chimps were really human, they'd just borrow each other's tools and not return them. Kathy Schick and Nicholas Toth, two experimental archaeologists who counterfeit early tools, have found this joke to be "remarkably prophetic." Chimps in the Ivory Coast, they say, have been observed to beg, borrow, and even steal each other's hammer stones, which they use for cracking nuts.

How *do* we distinguish humans from chimps? Are we who misuse and counterfeit tools, and construct a culture of them, part of nature —are we animals, like *Pan*—or, with our technology, are we utterly opposed to it? At what point in our evolution did we stop becoming animals and start becoming human? And why do we backslide? Or is it really backsliding?

THE HAMMER AND THE AX

Evolution does not proceed by design or move toward a perfect state; it improvises its path through random mutation and natural selection. (The title of one of Richard Dawkins's books expresses this view succinctly: *The Blind Watchmaker*.) Yet, as even evolutionists acknowledge, humans have developed the means to control their evolution and have done so through technology—in other words, by making tools.

This making of tools takes two divergent paths: we misuse one tool to make a new one, thus increasing the diversity of tools; and we counterfeit existing tools according to a template in our minds, thus conserving the inherited culture of tools. Toolmaking may have started through happy accident, but it proceeded in the direction of strategy and intention.

Just as grunts became words, and so stopped being grunts, tools also became less "natural" in their history, less modeled on bodily functions, whether human or animal. A hammer stone may have been the first tool because it does certain things better than a fist. But does a flake, or any sharp instrument, do things better than teeth or fingernails, or does it do things entirely different? Can teeth and nails butcher an elephant carcass? Tools are tools because they do what we can't do. That's why we misuse them, to find out what else we can't do—and thus to do it.

My own speculative history of tools would go something like this: Begin with a hammer stone. Find another one. Knock them together and you've got yourself a flake. Do this enough times, rotating one stone, and a chopper results. It somewhat resembles a half-eaten pear. Hammer stone and flake: hammer and knife. Chopper: hammer plus ax. The tools seem to be implicit in the stone every bit as much as David was implicit in the marble for Michelangelo. The Dani of New Guinea, who still make stone tools, believe that the ax exists in the rock and they simply free it.

It took more than two million years to fix handles and shafts on stone tools, and though the history of tools during this period may appear to be stagnant, it was accompanied by a doubling of brain size in the genus *Homo,* from 600 to 1,200 cubic centimeters. Think of early tools as cells that divide. This, in my view, is one of history's great branchings. I see the chopper as the ur-cell, the egg that came first, fertilized by the hammer stone. Since it's made for both pounding and cutting, the chopper mothered the two most fundamental tools, things that strike and things that cut—the hammer and the ax. The ax includes, in this schematized history, all cutting instruments: adzes, knives, swords, saws, even spades, which are basically dull adzes. Hammers include all things that pound and crush: war clubs, battering rams, pestles, punches, manos.

The hammer is crude, the ax sharp. Goliath and David. The hammer is might, power, rage. It flattens and pulps, it doesn't slice apart. It leads to weapons of percussion, such as guns, which have hammers. Clocks also have hammers, to strike the hour, and some roofs of large buildings in the Middle Ages were built with hammer beams, whose very name expresses the violence of forcing open the crown of a closed space against the pull of gravity. But I'm racing ahead.

The ax, on the other hand, is cunning and made for division. It splits things apart. It relies on force too, like the hammer, but its force is precise. Still, the hammer has precedence—in the form of a hammer stone, it came before the chopper, which later gave birth to the hammer as we know it (thus solving the problem of chicken and egg). So the hammer's more primordial. The sheer application of force is about as fundamental as it gets, and one usually does it rhythmically, since pounding makes a connection to the heart. Therefore hammers lead to drums, and perhaps ultimately to men's groups emitting grunts around a fire—making the hammer our first figure for the primitive, and the ax our first for civilization.

The hammer is improved by addition—with more weight it

pounds harder—and the ax by subtraction, that is, by being sharpened. The hammer's blunt, the ax crafty. Thor and King Arthur. Arthur removed his sword from a rock, as though to acknowledge that steel began as stone. And Thor's hammer was forged by two dwarves, as though to concede that violence and force could be improved by industry.

Did Arthur ever hack his own foot with Excalibur, or Thor bang his thumb with Mjollnir? While demonstrating axmanship to Cub Scouts as a teen, I swung the ax right into my toe.

The ax clears the way, the hammer throws up walls. Together they make the mazes we thread, the boxes we rest in. The ax is the future, movement and discovery, the opening of forests. Prehistorians agree that the ax is associated with the rise of farming communities, because it cleared the forests. But then we had wood where before there were trees. And the wood became used to make buildings and cities—requiring hammers. The hammer is protection and retention, storage, enclosures, order, stasis. In other words, walls—and front steps of houses. The ax opens, the hammer closes. Cross hammer and ax, you get the grid of time and space. Parallel, the two tools would just slide through history, hardly changing much, but cross them and right away they snag time and space and honeycomb their crevices. Thus forests were cleared, roads and cities chartered, palaces and towers and ramparts built.

METAL

Around eight thousand years ago, metal was first used to make tools. They'd been fitted with handles and shafts long before; their uses had multiplied and, with them, their shapes, and in addition to tools we had musical instruments, beads and bracelets, sacred objects, temples, coins, dwellings. We needed the last on this list—dwellings—to live in, of course, but for storage as well, since tools are also possessions, after all. And the more tools we had, from sickles and harpoons to awls and spears, the larger the place we needed to put them.

Henry David Thoreau: "Men have become the tools of their tools." Martin Heidegger: We are "chained to technology."

Tools increased our mobility by clearing the way, then wound up impeding it by weighing us down. We were cunning, however; we got animals to help us, as beasts of burden. In this way, we distinguished them from us. We had to catch and train them first, and in the process they themselves became tools and possessions.

Was there a time when we *didn't* have tools? The question is meaningless. We've always had tools because they define us as "we." The Shoshone Indians tell a story about the origin of sewing which slyly undercuts toolless innocence. Wolf and Coyote are making the world. Let's not have sewing, says Wolf. If we want to make anything like shoes or clothes, let's have it so we can just press the skins together and the things are made. No, says Coyote. Let's have needles and threads, that's a lot better. Then the girls will prick their thighs and we can lick off the blood.

Wolf and Coyote are animals, of course, but with the power of speech. Animals used to be people, like us; we all walked around, humans and animals, and talked and lived together in the same world. If this belief sounds quaint, it shows the distance we've come. The single thing that split the seamless world apart between animals and humans was the use of tools. It initiated culture. To say the same thing: most animals reverted to being animals, while those animals with opposable thumbs found ways to divide their nature from themselves and call it being human.

The benefits were immense. So were the costs. The Kutenais, most of whom today live in northern Idaho, have a story, "Why the Indians Had No Metal Tools." Two boys who visit the spirit of the Sun Dance return with gifts in two boxes, which they've been cautioned not to open until they've walked for three whole days and the sun is at its zenith.

At first the boxes feel light as feathers. But as the third day approaches, they get heavier and heavier. When the boys can hardly carry them, they rip them open and find, to their dismay, strangely shaped pieces of metal—embryos of tools. They've been seen before having fully gestated—aborted, in a sense. There is, however, one metal knife, the only tool fully ripened in this miscarried gift. Now every time they use it, they'll remember. They wanted the gift of tools, and they wanted their mobility and innocence, but they couldn't have both.

3

RAISING CAIN

I FINALLY HAD the stringers boxed out and up against the house. Not bad, I thought. The treads would strengthen the structure. They might even pull it into plumb, who knows? The main thing was to make the stairs look normal. I wondered, should I paint them? The question wasn't serious. I had no intention of painting this folly, and raw treated lumber looks better anyway—it has that feeling of newness.

Bent nails stuck out from the thing at odd angles. With enough overlap, the treads might hide them. I could pile some brush around it. From the road you couldn't see them.

My body ran through wooden grooves of memory as it crouched to saw, as the hammer raised up. I seemed to remember my father not measuring the treads before he cut them when he built my uncle's steps—instead, he laid them over stringers already nailed into place, and cut them there.

This must have been one of those funhouse-mirror memories. I could see right away that the moving saw would hit the house.

All *I* had to do was to move my steps away from the house—they weren't attached. I could cut the top treads on the stringers easily—two for each step—but as I went lower, my saw would strike the ground. The solution was to cut and nail the highest step, then use that as a template to cut the others, then nail the rest and drag the whole thing back against the house.

I felt competent and professional.

It was half past five already—I would not be going home. I would finish the steps and eat in Salem, at the Thai-Mexican restaurant, Pepe's Lucky Dragon, something like that, and check back into the Red Roof Inn. I would take a shower and feel good about having done my duty. Buy a quart of beer. Watch TV. I was thinking all these things when the hammer struck my thumb.

I did what we all do, yelled "Shit!" and dropped the hammer, shook my hand briskly, blew on the thumb, stamped one foot. This was not a glancing blow but a perfect bull's-eye, the kind that wastes the target. I stuck the thumb in my mouth, as though to extinguish it, and tried to relax. It felt like a blowtorch. Something odd occurred to me: when I was a toddler, had I sucked my thumb? Most human beings can't recall such things. If we could, the memory itself would be suspect, since sucking one's thumb is a way to tune out and erect a shield against future memories. In other words, to remember such a thing would be a sign one hadn't done it.

My thumb throbbed and glowed. I kept shaking my hand. Whom should I sue? Wal-Mart? The tool company? Suppose I called up Wal-Mart to find out how their hammers were made, just to sound them out. I could explain that I'm writing a book about the reasons that connect us with the past and with the universe. You throw the light switch and make a link with distant stars. Where did the fuel in our gas tank come from? That sort of thing.

Sounds like you've got your work cut out for you.

That's just it.

Wait a minute. This isn't something like, the head flew off, they make these things cheap.

I'm not an investigative reporter, no. I'm a novelist and poet.

Really? Me too . . .

I felt as if I'd been hung by my thumb, and stood there now with it in my mouth, three hundred miles from home. At least it tasted sweet. I didn't realize it was bleeding until I picked up the hammer and spotted the blood, a perfect thumbprint on the shaft. I must have done something wrong. I'd been booked into solitary confinement, it seemed, since pain is a mental prison. I felt sorry for myself. Yet when the pain slowly lessened, as though in little doses, I discovered that I missed it. So I clung to it, I licked it—a dog with a wounded paw. We all live in one river of flesh, after all. Whether or not we wade against the current, we're still one with the animals when we feel pain. The skin was split beneath the nail, the thumb had swollen up, and the nail was turning black.

In a poem, Alan Dugan points out that anyone can nail his own hand on a cross, but only the first hand. To nail up the second you need a friend, a wife, or a brother.

FATHER TIME

Paul, I realize now, seemed to thrive in small places. He worked with his tools at that basement bench, or in our bathroom, or later in his microbus. His Volkswagen van—we called them microbuses then— was the first of those vehicles seen in our neighborhood, long before they became flower-child icons. He proved obsessively ingenious about squeezing ham equipment into this bus while leaving room for sleeping quarters. Fitted out by Paul with shelves and curtains, with a thick, wide board on which he'd thrown a mattress, underneath which his radio gear was arranged, the bus became the wonder of our block. I was proud of it too, and showed it to my friends. He'd taken to driving it to hills around Boston to see whom he could contact on two or ten meters. Once or twice a month he paid me to wash it. He was very meticulous. When the body was clean I had to scrub the wheels and tires, while Paul, wearing socks dipped in solvent on both hands, rid the engine of grease. When he was done, it looked freshly born.

More than a decade later he gave me that bus, after Hannah and I had married during my last year of graduate school. An oblong can on wheels, pocked and rusty, it was still reliable but seemed considerably smaller than it had been in Boston, even though he'd emptied it. Paul hadn't come to our wedding; instead, six months later, he showed up unannounced at our doorstep in California, one wedding gift in the driveway—the VW bus—the other on our porch: my grandmother's old Morris chair. Hannah'd never met him. We biked home from campus that day and found him seated on the Morris chair, chuckling when we spotted him. He planned to visit for a week, and I recall an inability—stemming from hippie tolerance, no doubt—to account for my discomfort. Only when he offered to take us and our friends out to dinner did it occur to me to wonder whether others would find him strange.

At the restaurant, we moved two tables together and placed my brother at the head. A close friend named Sarah marveled at the fact that, well into his thirties, Paul lived with my parents. Her reaction was to humor him, to treat him as a pet—to tease him, as nurses tease the elderly in nursing homes. I tried to hold back from this subtle mockery, but couldn't decide whom to be more ashamed of, my friends or my brother. Paul lapped it up. Sarah was beautiful, I should add; he was still asking me, twenty years later, whatever became of her. She had a habit of glancing down at her arm, half attentive, of looking absently at her forearm, turned to reveal its white fillet of flesh underneath. But when her head lifted, her face engaged yours with a wide Lauren Hutton gap-toothed smile. She seemed to be watching both Paul and me for signs of brotherhood or imposture, one or the other. She called him Father Time and he beamed; she was trying, at least. The others ignored him. She could draw him out, it seemed. It was just friendly teasing, and I laughed with the others until, when Paul left to use the men's room, another friend announced his intention to order the menu's most expensive dish, since my brother had insisted. This friend was cunning and cool and could recognize Paul's generosity for what it must have been, a bribe to curry friendship. So why not take advantage?

These memories are painful. That evening in our little toy house, a rental cottage behind a professor's shingled ranch house two blocks from campus, Hannah and I lay in bed and talked. We lived in California, that Garden of Eden, in the pastoral innocence of graduate school. Outside our windows were cherry and avocado trees, and we rode bikes to campus and never knew want. Now here was my brother on a couch in the living room, in the midst of our idyll, not exactly a snake, too harmless for that — more like a pocket gopher. "What's *wrong* with him?" Hannah asked.

"Nothing. I don't know."

"Has he ever had a girlfriend?"

"Not that I know of."

"How come he still lives with your parents?"

"Look at the Irish. Irish men and women live with their parents until their thirties or forties. It's a Boston thing."

"You're not Irish."

"Three quarters."

Behind a composition-board wall, in the next room, Paul lay on the couch and listened. I'm convinced of that now. As my despair mounted, so did our voices. I defended my family, my home, my background — this was class warfare, I thought — then bewailed Paul, then excused him. The following morning he seemed to have retreated into the smallest space he'd ever occupied. At breakfast, he sat sadly bent and withdrawn, legs crossed, one hand tucked between his knees. I must have mirrored him. Full of guilt for my betrayal, for talking about him when he could hear, I'd already begun to think it was deliberate, though I still can't be sure.

As we ate, as we talked in monosyllables, I *saw* him, it seemed, for the first time in my life. Baggy pants, belt like a noose, shirtsleeves too long, mouse-colored crewcut. A vaguely unpleasant smell. Mule-faced and hung with a head that didn't fit, like an ancient leather mask of resignation, he pursed his lips and smiled bravely to himself, only thirty-eight. This was his two-week vacation. He worked at Raytheon by then, his lifetime employer, sitting, I imagined, at a bench against a wall, as he had in our basement.

He announced with strained bonhomie that he'd changed his plans. He was leaving today. Could I drive him to the Greyhound station? He wanted to catch a bus for Bakersfield that afternoon, to visit an old army buddy, he explained. From there, he would make his way to Los Angeles, then fly home.

A year later, the microbus was stolen—and I hadn't bought insurance, as Paul had told me to do. Why would someone steal an old car like that? I asked the cop. They use the engines for dune buggies, he told me, and junk the rest.

MONSTERS

My thumb had swollen up and still broadcast pain. I sat before Paul's house and held it in the sun. Imagine the first man who used a hammer—hardworking, eager, semi-conscious of his purpose. If he'd banged his thumb with it, another thousand years may have passed before someone else dared try it. But in this history a thousand years is nothing.

Then the ax. He learns how to chop down a tree. One tree leads to another, the ax grows dull, he cuts the earth with it instead. He's already graduated from being an animal, but any slip could send him back. He's learned how to farm. He's a dedicated and nervous husbandman, and tries his best to please.

His brother, meanwhile, is still herding sheep, and seems to have it easy. He lives with the animals, content with simple things. He's guileless, it appears.

The first one, the farmer, is the one with the tools. He makes a house for his brother, but it isn't square. He botched the job, again. He resents his shepherd brother's hermit existence, his skin clothes, wild hair, and dour look—his smell. All he does is herd sheep and eat berries and nuts. His life is unreal. Look at him, thinks the farmer, what a mousy little man, with bad posture and little cat feet and uncalloused hands. His pastoral existence is farcical, is it not? He won't even live in a house like the rest of us. He fouls his own nest.

Meanwhile, farming, for the first brother, shackles him to an uncertain future and to his tools. And it's backbreaking work. It is a fact that when humans first turned to farming, their body size decreased. Rickets and arthritis increased as bones grew thinner. The official view of farming is that it enabled people to store food for the first time, thus creating leisure. Tell that to a farmer.

God speaks to the brothers: *Make me a sacrifice.* The farmer, of course, brings offerings of crops. His brother brings a fat sheep. God smells the sheep. *This is pleasing to me, but not this, the turnip.* The farmer's demolished. All that hard work . . .

Why did God reject Cain's offering? The usual answer is that he gave a grudging portion—he was cheap. Another is that, because he was a farmer, his offerings were made from an earth that was cursed because of Adam's sin. Abel, on the other hand, had recaptured Eden. His rustic shepherd's life meant he didn't have to work and subdue the earth with tools and the sweat of his brow, only live with it on its own terms. As Elaine Pagels says, Abel was united with the earth, Cain opposed to it. In other words, if Cain had tools and Abel didn't, and if Cain envied Abel, it was the envy of someone chained to his tools directed at someone who lived in blissful innocence, before the use of tools. No wonder Cain resented his brother for getting away with regaining Paradise — Cain, after all, was paying dues for losing it. This had to be the first class division.

But whether such differences explain God's capricious preference is another question. Maybe nothing can explain it. Maybe it reflects any distracted father's behavior toward his children. In the opening scene of Proust's *Du côté de chez Swann,* the child who fears his father's punishment (for being weak and jumping out of bed and intercepting his mother to ask for a kiss) instead receives an amazing reprieve: his mother will sleep in his room that night. Maybe justice is not so much fair or unfair as it is whimsical. But how else can one attain a sense of irony?

The biblical story is memorable because it doesn't explain things. We are left with a God who can afford not to fool around with reasons. And Cain is left to cultivate irony, or nurse his resentment, take your choice. He chooses resentment, and it grows into the sin crouching at his door. *Come out with me to the fields, brother Abel.*

Cain was later thought of as the father of all monsters. The giants in Genesis 6 are the progeny of the sons of God and the daughters of man, and early commentators took this to mean the sons of Seth and the daughters of Cain. Later, through Ham, Nimrod and Goliath were born, and still later, in the Dark Ages, countless dragons and trolls, including the monster Grendel and his mother, said in *Beowulf* to be descended from Cain. Monsters are often outward signs of inner aberrations. *Monstrum* means an evil omen, and *monstro* means to show or display. Monsters are spectacles. They are also unnatural. Nature tampered with becomes monstrous and abnormal, as in Mary Shelley's *Frankenstein.* Beneath the shades of meaning of the word "unnatural" lie the specters of cannibalism and bestiality: humans eating humans instead of animals, humans coupling with animals instead of humans. In other contexts, it should be mentioned, both cannibalism and bestiality are natural—for example, in a world where animals are people. Montaigne: "Every man calls barbarous anything he is not accustomed to."

But the world in which animals are people is not the biblical world; Adam was given dominion over animals from the beginning. Yet the story of Cain and Abel may allude to that dividing line that haunts the human race: Abel still lives with the animals, whereas Cain, as a farmer and user of tools, has crossed over into what we call the human. From the point of view of each, the other looks unnatural. The shepherd looks at the man who tills the earth and sees his activity as a foolish effort to tame and conquer nature. The farmer looks at the man who lives with sheep and suspects him of what shepherds throughout history have always been charged with. And the word "unnatural" becomes not so much a moral standard as an acid showering disfigurement on others, while leaving oneself indelibly normal.

RIP

In subsequent years, when Paul visited my family, he often slept in his car. He began to smell of unwashed clothes, a sour and musty odor, like something stored in a trunk. Yet, I told myself, we'd done him a service. If in fact he overheard our conversation that night, it must have woken him up, because a year or so later he'd bought his own place in southern New Hampshire and no longer lived with my parents. I visited a few months after he moved in. Until his death, this was the only time I'd ever seen Paul's house. The story was that a carpet dealer had owned it, and had covered the walls of one bedroom with remnants, cleverly hiding the closet doors. He'd also cut an opening in one side of a bathtub, then lined it with shag to create a love seat. The house looked new then, and fresh, and somewhat charming. I felt happy for Paul. He seemed reborn. Maybe he'd get married, I thought. At least find a girlfriend — even a boyfriend. In one room, I remember, ham equipment was stacked to the ceiling, piled on a sideboard and on a pool table. It seemed that Paul accumulated objects easily.

It was Christmas. I'd just begun the second year of my first teaching job. As a present, my parents had printed up business cards for me, with my name, department, university, and phone number. My sweet mother didn't seem to know any better — professors do not use business cards — but I acted enthusiastic, or tried to. When the holidays were over, I drove up to see Paul in his new house. It surprised me to learn that he owned several dogs, also five or six cats, since we'd never had pets growing up, and neither to my knowledge had Grandma. One of the dogs, a German shepherd, had given birth just a few days before, and I made the mistake of going down to the cellar with Paul to see the pups. Curled up around her babies in a box, the mother lunged for my leg and bit me on the calf. When I jumped back, I knocked my head against a beam and grew instantly confused. Paul was shouting commands, it seemed — *"Rip Rip Rip!"* — to either me or the dog. Was I supposed to do something?

Later on, I realized that was the mother's name.

The sudden pain had shocked me, a hot explosion of light. Then slowly the pain numbed and spread through me like a wave of cold needles, and I looked at the dog, still baring her teeth. Terrified and angry, I backed away toward the stairs while Paul scolded Rip. I'd never been bitten by a dog before. The wound was deep and hardly bleeding; the flesh had puffed white around four puncture holes, each slobbered with saliva. I began to feel faint, but anger kept me conscious. I was yelling at Paul, asking why he hadn't warned me. He retreated into silence. He drove me to the ER at Parkland Hospital, and I don't think we said two words to each other. Silently I blamed him, silently he shriveled up. He looked more and more hangdog and tight-lipped as he drove, but whether this meant regret or resentment I never did learn.

The next year, Paul loaned Hannah and me one thousand dollars to help with our first house. A year after that, he wrote us a letter in painful block letters forgiving the loan. He said he didn't need the money.

PLOWSHARES INTO SWORDS

Trying not to use my thumb, I drove down to the Mobil station, and by some miracle, it seemed, the convenience store there had one box of Band-Aids left, of the Day-Glo variety. Now that we'd settled and I'd paid his overcharges for cleaning the house — the extra weight on the dumpster, the cost of the backhoe — Jud was cool toward me. I couldn't hold it against him. Nobody else had wanted that job, certainly not me. I'd sooner burn the house down. He probably thought he'd discover a treasure in the place, a cache of gold coins perhaps, but I knew my brother — that wasn't his compulsion. He was not the type to hide money and forget it. His money was in banks.

Tall and skinny, full of blinks, a stutterer, Jud nodded at me when I paid his clerk for the Band-Aids. He was back making coffee at the counter near the rest rooms. "Any offers?" he said, meaning on the house.

"Not yet."

When he'd won the job of cleaning the house, he'd called me twice a week with new verbal offers from people dropping by the gas station. I told him I didn't want anyone seeing it until he cleaned it out, because I knew how they'd react. But he took people up there, I'm sure of it. What could I do? I was two states away, and anyone could pull off a shutter and climb in. His potential buyers all evaporated, scared off by the smell. I didn't want to do it, but I had to walk past Jud, to clean off my injured thumb in the bathroom.

"Whadja do to yourself there?"

"Banged my thumb."

"Take care of that. Looks—looks nasty."

"I intend to."

I'd asked him once if he knew my brother, to which he replied he knew who Paul was—he'd come in now and then to gas up or buy cigarettes, until the last few years. People talked about him, said Jud. They wondered who lived in that place. Didn't the town get on his case too? Kids breaking in, that sort of thing?

"That's when he had it boarded up," I said.

"Didn't stop—stop the kids."

"What did people think of him?"

He burst into shrugs. "Wondered who he was. Didn't say much. Live and let live. There's plenty others like him."

I washed my still-throbbing thumb in the sink. A Band-Aid wouldn't do much good, I realized. I needed something like a large rubber crutch tip. I still had to nail treads on two more steps.

Back at the house, I tried using the crook of the carpenter's square to hold nails in place for the first several whacks. In this manner, I struck the carpenter's square once, twice, thrice. I'm sure I threw it out of square.

Cain had tools but Abel didn't—we presume he didn't need them. So Abel was powerless to defend himself when Cain lured him into the fields and took his life. What a horrible story. Horrible and fascinating.

With what did Cain kill him? The Bible doesn't specify. This has invited widespread speculation in commentary, legend, art, and literature. The Bible does say that Abel's blood cried out to God, and blood-spilling violence requires more than hands, so it must have been a tool, something hard and portable. The *Zohar*'s version, that Cain used his teeth, is memorable but hardly mainstream. He could have used a weapon, not a tool. But weapons are tools that got to be weapons by being misused. And Cain, who invented so many things—cities, culture, murder—also invented weapons, by starting with a tool.

But what tool was it? Versions of Cain's crime embrace the entire history of tools.

- It could have been a rock, the ur-tool of humans. The Apocryphal *Book of Adam* says a rock, as does Milton in *Paradise Lost.* Byzantine and Islamic sculpture and illuminations usually depict a rock.
- A club is shown on the Hildesheim doors in Germany, on a bronze door of San Zeno in Verona in Italy, in a fresco at the Camposanto in Pisa, and on reliefs in several Italian churches — the cathedrals in Modena and Orvieto, and San Petronio in Bologna.
- Agricultural tools are often pictured as the weapon, naturally enough. On a window in Chartres Cathedral it's a hoe, in a Paris manuscript a mattock (something like a pickax), in the Psalter of St. Louis a spade, and in many versions a sickle. In one Hebrew legend it's a rod — meaning, I suppose, a measuring rod, useful to farmers. These tools are anachronisms, by the way, since the Bible specifies that one of Cain's descendants, Tubal-Cain, was the first to fashion metal tools (Genesis 4:22). For this reason, one commentator suggests that the sickle be thought of as similar to those that archaeologists have discovered in Palestine: carved of wood, with serrated flint blades fastened like teeth along their cutting edges. They presumably date from Neolithic times. The same scholar claims that the most primitive sickle is a jawbone, as pictured in Egyptian wall paintings.
- This naturally leads to the jawbone of an ass, ethnologically correct because it isn't metal. But nonetheless curious — could it really be a sickle? More likely a plow. Looks like a boomerang in paintings. Hamlet, in the scene in which he addresses Yorick's skull, mentions as the murder weapon an ass's jawbone. The jawbone is mentioned in nearly every English mystery play, and pictured in countless illuminations, reliefs, paintings, and woodcuts

in Britain and northern Europe, including Irish stone crosses, many English psalters and Bibles, the Ghent Altarpiece, Master Bertram's Grabow Altarpiece, paintings by Van Eyck, etchings by Lucas van Leyden and Beham, and drawings by Rembrandt. Its popularity may well have stemmed from a confusion between Cain's story and that of Samson, who slew a thousand Philistines with the jawbone of an ass.

- *Beowulf,* which describes the monster Grendel as a descendant of Cain, says that Cain killed Abel with a sword.
- Lord Byron has Cain slay Abel with a branding iron in his verse drama *Cain: A Mystery.*
- A relief in Salisbury Cathedral appears to show Cain using a mason's hammer, no doubt a professional joke.
- In the modern camp song "Happy Sunday School," it's the leg of a table (rhymes with Abel).
- *The Book of Lecan,* a fifteenth-century Irish compilation, says the jawbone of a camel.

But my guess is the hammer—like the one I was using now. We'll say a primitive stone hammer, but hafted to improve the blow's power. The blow must have been powerful, because the Bible tells us the earth opened its mouth to receive Abel's blood, implying a great quantity. Unfortunately, no version I know of, except the relief in Salisbury Cathedral, shows a hammer. Still, what a weapon. Any of the tools above, in fact, could be misused as hammers. A hammer, then.

NUTCRACKER MAN

In 1959, when the Leakeys found a fossil skull they called *Zinjanthropus* (later rechristened *Australopithecus boisei*), Louis made the mistake, at a news conference, of mentioning a fracture in one of the parietal bones. The following day, headlines around the world trumpeted

"The First-Ever Murder." Australopithecines are a now-extinct genus of hominids who lived in East Africa with another genus, *Homo*, who became us. For more than a million years they shared the same world, before *Australopithecus* went extinct. The Leakeys found the skull in the presence of tools made by *Homo*, which suggested to the press not only murder but cannibalism: they'd killed the poor dimwit, dragged him to their lair, butchered him, and ate his flesh.

Cain too, in tradition, was said to have drunk his brother's blood. And Cain, unlike his brother, was a user of tools, which makes *Homo* his ancestor. *Australopithecus* had powerful jaws and a receding skull; anthropologists dubbed him Nutcracker Man, though the thinking now is that the jaws were for grinding tough, stringy plants, stalks and all. No one is certain, but the consensus is that *Australopithecus* was not a tool user. He didn't need tools, because of his monstrous built-in Jaws of Life, whereas his neighbor *Homo* invented tool use. Robust australopithecines may have driven *Homo* to other food sources for which the latter needed tools—such as meat. So our ancestors found an evolutionary niche requiring tool use, which in turn led to planning, control over the environment, intelligence, and, presumably, civilization.

Think of Abel as one of those big-jawed, large-toothed australopithecines. Maybe he had a sagittal crest—a sort of keel on his skull—to which his powerful chewing muscles were attached. Most australopithecine skulls have sagittal crests. Maybe Abel was Pan—half god, half goat, with a horn on his head.

And think of Cain, the tool user, as *Homo habilis*. He killed his brother with a hammer because, to make culture, first you kill nature.

THE MANDARIN

That Cain made culture and civilization is surely one point of the biblical story. Says the ancient historian Josephus, Cain "put an end to that simplicity in which men lived before by the invention of weights and measures: the guileless and generous existence which they had enjoyed in ignorance of these things he converted into a life of craftiness." So Cain with his tools initiated the rise of technology. Maybe future illustrations will show Cain slaying Abel with an oscilloscope.

Both Josephus and, after him, Augustus, make much of the fact that Cain built the first city (Genesis 4:17). "He was the first to fix boundaries of land and to build a city," says Josephus, "fortifying it with walls and constraining his clan to congregate in one place. This city he called Anocha after his eldest son Anoch." Augustus saw Cain as another Romulus, founder of the earthly city. Romulus, like Cain, killed his brother.

As a farmer, Cain plowed furrows; as a city planner, he drew streets. Drawing lines and mapping the earth are sure marks of civilization, says Oliver Wendell Holmes. The first misuser of tools, Cain killed his brother—and civilization flourished. Maybe Abel's murder was a sacrifice of the sort the ancients once practiced when building a bridge: a man was killed and buried in the foundation so the bridge wouldn't collapse. Maybe Abel's death was a *figura* of Christ's: through it, humankind achieved redemption. (A *figura*, in biblical exegesis, is an event that prefigures another.) But this isn't how early exegetes saw it. Civilization, as represented by cities—Babylon, for example—is not redemption but corruption. And the blood on its walls, seeping down through the centuries, is Abel's.

In *Civilization and Its Discontents,* Freud refers in a footnote to "Rousseau's famous mandarin." The mandarin in question, as he'd explained in a 1915 essay, "Our Attitude Towards Death," is mentioned in Balzac's *Père Goriot.* Rastignac asks his friend Bianchon if he's read Rousseau, to which Bianchon answers yes.

> "Do you remember the passage where he asks the reader what he would do if he could make a fortune by killing an old mandarin in China by simply exerting his will, without stirring from Paris?"

"Yes."

"Well?"

"Bah! I'm at my thirty-third mandarin."

"Tuer son mandarin," says Freud, has become proverbial for this secret truth: that we would all be murderers if the material benefits were sufficient, if we could murder by intention rather than deed, and if we were certain of never being caught. Clearly, the mandarin is a legacy of Cain — of the biblical myth, so powerful in its ripple effect, that the benefits of civilizations are built upon murder. The furrow Cain plowed was the first line he drew. The second was his murder of Abel. The third, his city's wall — in other words, the line between nature and something new and unique, civilization. Once drawn, this line converted nature into savagery as the defining antithesis of civilization. Now we had sides: us on one, and on the other, them. *Kultur* on one side, on the other, barbarism.

But the murderer Cain is the one who drew that line, in building the first city. And the murder of Abel reminds us as well that the barbarians are really us, the ones inside the walls, on our thirty-third mandarin — since it's we who made the walls.

MOW YOUR LAWN

Working like a machine, I cut the final tread and drove each nail straight, with two or three blows. I'd lost my innocence, I felt; I'd swapped roles with my brother. Had he still been alive, he'd be the pastoral gentleman now, and I'd be the tool user. Imagine Paul sitting on his new front steps and surveying his domain, a little wedge of New Hampshire. Some teens drive by, honking. "Mow your lawn!" they shout. He points to the mower's four flat tires and shrugs, both palms upraised. As they drive off, he waves. Then lights a cigarette. Chuckling to himself, he shakes his rounded shoulders. Bobs his bird-like head. Sudden unexpected frown. Bent posture, pursed lips, sad eyes, cheap shoes. His longing to belong—his instinct to withdraw.

BROTHER'S KEEPER

After the murder, God asked where Abel was—as if He didn't know— and Cain famously replied, Am I my brother's keeper? It's as if he were saying, I'm busy, I'm a farmer. I don't have the time to keep track of my brother. He's the keeper, not me—the keeper of sheep. I'm not a shepherd. You made me a farmer. See what you've done?

So God put a mark on Cain, making him, indelibly, Cain. God has the power to do this, to "burn Nature with a kiss," as W. B. Yeats puts it—and thus seal it. Byron's notion that Cain's murder weapon was a branding iron, then, has special force, suggesting that God's punishment was of the eye-for-an-eye variety. Perhaps God's mark ended evolution's diversity, by fixing things in their natures. Indelibility itself is the mark of Cain. It says, I am Cain and I'll always be Cain. You, you are Abel and you'll always be Abel. We are what we are by God's culture, which is nature. I killed you and I'm marked. That's why I did it. The tools that God gave me—they made me do it. I'll show you what I mean. I'll build a city and make human culture. Then nature can live outside with savages like you and the animals you love so much.

"I think I could turn and live with animals," says Walt Whitman. "They do not make me sick discussing their duty to God." This is the remark of a civilized man.

PAUL

But Paul was not alive and never was a country squire.

I lined up the last nail with my injured hand.

If he came back from the dead as I was finishing those steps and tapped me on the shoulder, what would I have done? In the grisly comic books of my youth, such things happened all the time. The corpse shows up at the door caked with dirt, trying to speak, but his lips are sewn shut—so the face rips around a mouth straining to open. His muffled inarticulate groans, like those we make in dreams, say what the guilty party knows already: You killed me, your own brother, by not showing me affection. You thought you were better than me, didn't you?

I swung the hammer with a vengeance.

III
BODY

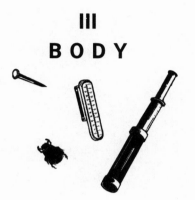

1

OUTSIDE IN

AT LAST I threw my tools in the van, drove back to Jud's Mobil, and called the real estate agent. I told his answering machine that the house had front steps but don't show it to anyone over two hundred pounds. On an impulse, I phoned the Red Roof Inn and canceled. Then I jumped in the van and drove home.

I'd get there between one and two A.M. It was stupid, I knew, driving home at night, exhausted. But I was desperate to get back. I pictured Hannah and our boys in upstate New York, where our house did not smell, nor had it been abandoned. Rather, it was filled with books and paintings, stuffed with boys' things — bicycles, basketballs, climbing magazines, Clearasil — and in my mind's eye it almost seemed to be breathing, set against its hill. Paul's house was a shell, but ours had a heart and lungs, vital circuits, beds for dreaming . . . front stairs too.

I was fleeing Paul, I realized, yet doing it in his car. So as I fled him, in a sense he surrounded me. It suddenly felt like bathing in his water. Some things come full circle, I suppose. Paul had died of an aneurysm; how would I die?

My thumb continued to throb in its Band-Aid. Overhead, the empty sky was a huge white sponge, absorbing all the light. Trees and hills had darkened, and the headlights of cars in the opposite lane were perfect little aspirins. Air cool and dry. I might even need to put the heat on pretty soon, so I code-checked the dashboard, the van being new to me. I felt like a fighter pilot, in control, then imagined that Paul, driving this van, must have felt the same way when he'd traveled this route to visit us. There was still enough light to watch the road slowly open, watch the screen of appearances split down the middle and curl to either side like shavings from a plane. Yet something in that screen continued to withdraw, to shrink from my approach. As the world opened up, something inside it, buried deeply, withdrew.

Then night came all at once, as though a door had slammed. Driving in darkness was more dangerous, I knew, than driving in daylight, yet it felt agreeable. It felt crustacean. The other cars now rinsing through my vision out there in the night were fellow bottom feeders. Their drivers were mostly alone like me, as far as I could tell. By now I was on I-93, a road marked by blood. Several years after this highway first opened, in the 1960s, when I was a teen, my father and I, returning to Boston from New Hampshire after visiting his chiropractor — chiropractic then being outlawed in Massachusetts — passed a fresh wreck at a bridge abutment in Methuen, somewhere close to here. People had pulled off the road to take a look. The driver's door was ripped off, and the body of a woman lay across the seat, her legs severed at the knees. Having just obtained my license, I was driving. "Just keep going," my father said. The males in my family never said, "Oh, how horrible," or "Are you okay?" Just keep going.

At home that night I wrote my first poem, "The Accident," and showed it to Paul, who lived with us now, after Grandma's death. Paul had been in the army; he'd seen the world. He lay back on his bed, lit up a cigarette, read my poem, and kicked me out of our room. You don't know a damn thing about life, he said.

Driving Paul's car, I listened to his music. His van had a CD player, a luxury my cars never had possessed. When the van became mine I inspected all its crannies and compartments, opened every receptacle. In a drawer beneath the passenger seat was a cache of classic jazz CDs, including one I've since played repeatedly, *Early Duke*. Somewhere on I-495 I slid it into the player and "East St. Louis Toodle-Oo" came on, from 1926. Ellington describes it as a portrait of an old man walking home after a hard day of working in the fields, and he and his broken walk are coming up the road, but you know he's strong in spite of being tired.

I followed my headlights flying down the road, listening to this number. Then I played it again, turned up the volume at the chorus of Steamboat Willy muted trumpets, and laughed out loud. When the ominous zoom-zoom line of the tuba and lower-register reeds returned, I thought of the proud gloom of the cellos and basses in the principal theme of Prokofiev's *Romeo and Juliet*. Ellington was similar but less ponderous. Pure unfettered joy with a cartoon shadow. I slapped my hand on the steering wheel and started crying. What a lost bright world, I thought, it will never come again. So why am I so happy?

I knew why. I'd gotten everything done and now was going home. I'd fulfilled my duties as reluctant executor and now could forget my brother for a while.

But I couldn't. I began to wonder about Paul's love of jazz, another corner of his personality I'd never understood. When I was a senior in high school, he took me to see Dizzy Gillespie at Storyland in Boston. Having been raised by Grandma in a country village, he never seemed to feel comfortable living in the city after she died. He'd served in the army, then moved in with us, sharing my room, but still called himself a country boy. Yet jazz was big-city music, was it not?

At the time, he was working in a South End warehouse. We saw Dizzy on a weeknight, weeknights being cheaper. I nursed a single ginger ale all evening, because Paul, who was treating, had warned me to order only one drink. I could tell the music filled him with pleasure, since he kept his mouth shut and smirked, to seal it in. Each time Dizzy's cheeks puffed larger than grapefruits, Paul wanted to laugh, just like me listening to "East St. Louis Toodle-Oo" now.

But no one laughed or shouted for joy or wept at Storyland; jazz, which used to be hot, now was cool. Between sets, Paul became nervous and withdrawn. He leaned back in his chair and his eyes scanned the room. The people in that club were hard to read, I remember — tough guys and hoods who talked like Kennedys. And the audience was racially mixed, a rare thing then in Boston.

Riding home on the bus, Paul shrank into himself. If I was seventeen then, he was over thirty. We were alone until the bus stopped somewhere on Broadway and a punk stepped on with regulation hair — ducktail and sideburns. He wasn't that much older than me, and on that empty bus he chose to hang on a strap directly over Paul, waving his knee back and forth, back and forth. My brother finally mumbled, "Let's go," and pulled the cord. We had to squeeze past the little hood, who wouldn't move. It was three or four stops before ours. We walked home in single file down Broadway to Summer Street.

Past Lowell, I switched on the cruise control — the traffic had thinned. Chrysler's little ghost in the machine held my speed constant at 63 miles per hour. One of Ellington's signature tunes came on, "Black and Tan Fantasie," 1927. After the bouncy intro, Bubber Miley's high opening B-flat extends for four bars, then explodes into yacky rain forests. Somewhere in the middle of this "magnificently structured melodic creation" (Gunther Schuller), Tricky Sam Nanton's plaintive trombone whinnies like a lovesick horse. The whole thing ends with a tag based on Chopin's "Funeral March."

The next cut was another version of the same, recorded two weeks later. Driving through the darkness, I floated on the music. My alpha rhythms seemed to have adjusted to the hum of the tires and the rise and fall of Duke Ellington's music, and were hypnotizing me into feeling eternal.

Then I thought it wouldn't last. I began worrying about auto accidents, about smashing up the car. The thought was phantasmic. It could happen, but probably wouldn't. Still, it could happen. Earlier, in twilight, that was the thing that withdrew as I approached it, buried inside the opening world—that ghostly potential of a violent smash.

How slowly it seems to unfold, when it does. There's always a skid, a wait lasting centuries. Once, with a friend who made an ill-advised left turn against traffic on Massachusetts Avenue in Boston, I calmly watched as a delivery truck skidded into the door beside me. Last year, driving at night outside Ithaca, I ran over a deer already dead in the road, and realized what a solid obstacle soft bodies can make. Part of the carcass got caught on the car's frame, which drove our dog crazy. I parked outside for a few nights, and it quickly disappeared—we live in the country.

The only line I remember from Anthony Burgess's novel *A Clockwork Orange* is the one about driving back to town, "running over odd squealing things on the way."

What would movies be without hard cars and soft bodies? The movie screen shows what the windshield mustn't, "images of the body in extreme circumstances" (Lennard Davis). Comforts of the movie house ape those of driving, but movies are safer—you're not flying through space. The multiplex is our Roman coliseum. You suck on greasy popcorn while bodies splash across the screen like forbidden fruit torn open—eroticized or mutilated bodies, bodies aroused or bodies riddled with bullets, bodies crushed in cars, bodies exploded, bodies chopped up, bodies thrown off roofs.

Coming home from Storyland that night, Paul sat slumped on the bus, his usual posture. Perhaps his body language invited aggression. Yet he'd enlisted in the army—he'd been schooled in bravado. I remembered how he looked upon arriving home, having served his hitch, when he first came to live with us. He'd been stationed in Bakersfield, California, and, he later told us, once was shipped to Nevada, to witness from a bunker an above-ground nuclear test with dark glasses issued by the army.

I'd just become a high school sophomore. We expected him that weekend, but on Sunday, not Saturday, and no one had heard the car drop him off. He burst into the kitchen in full uniform, then stood there saluting, and my mother squealed, "Paul!" "Blood and Guts!" I shouted—the name his platoon had christened him with, as he'd informed us in a letter. Even then I sensed their sarcasm, but really, who knew? It could have been affectionate, could have followed from his buddies' smiling acknowledgment of some unexpected pluck.

He looked sharp and smiled broadly and announced to Mom how he'd mop the kitchen floor once a week now, having learned to in the army. "You'll do it twice, then forget it," said Dad at the table. "How you doing?" he added.

It couldn't have been very long after that that Paul bought his microbus and we'd just finished washing it. Pride of ownership, neighborhood safekeeping, surplus army spunk—God knows what the cause was—but when a car ran the Stop sign at the corner, Paul stepped into the street and shouted as it passed, "Hey fella, that sign says Stop, not Slow Down."

Squeal of tires, slam of door. He stood above Paul, a tall boulder-bellied man with white hair and pale skin, crazed and cracked across his face, and thick black-rimmed glasses. He must have been twice my brother's age, well over sixty, but he inquired about his balls—would Paul like to keep them? My brother, I saw, did not know what to say. There was a code in our neighborhood. I knew it well enough to avoid, when I could, occasions to practice it, but Paul didn't have a clue. He was supposed to act puzzled and use words to this effect: How come your keeper released you, you crazy fuck? Then, for example, if he were Joe Pesci, he would have lunged for the carotid with his ballpoint pen. Instead, he wilted like a flower. "It didn't look like you stopped," he managed.

"That's none of your fucking business, is it?"

"Well—it didn't look like you stopped."

Behind some parked cars, I hung my head—like Paul—hands in pockets, from shame as much as fear.

"Get the fuck off the street," said the man. Paul did as he was told. "Mind your own fucking business after this, you little creep."

Paul said nothing.

Invigorated, beet-faced by now, the man jumped in his car, slammed the door, and drove off.

Somewhere beyond Littleton, I pulled off for gas and found myself in a Texaco convenience store, a red and black hallucination. Every car here was a sport utility vehicle, and most of the customers wore athletic shoes to match, with high wraparound soles and little trapezoidal air vents. When I walked inside to pay—past green, blue, and red twelve-packs of soda stacked shoulder-high in the glass entry—the fluorescent wonderland seemed full of exotic produce. They were merely human beings, I knew, but what grotesque examples! It must have been my mood. The store also housed a Baskin-Robbins, a Blimpie, and an A & W, and perhaps for that reason everyone in it seemed well fed. In fact, most were eating—burgers or cones—as they milled among the snacks, sunglasses, Tampax, refill mugs, aspirin, hairbrushes in plastic bubbles, and shrink-wrapped firewood. One little girl with a dolly-mop head seemed not to have a body so much as a stick. The rest were hewn solids, some squat as bowling pins, some tall with high knees, and nearly everyone wore shorts. Did that account for their strangeness? I saw body types, not people, and wondered how they saw me, with my grass-stained jeans still brushed with sawdust. They didn't seem to notice.

Two dolphin-shaped women with Red Sox caps and ponytails swinging from the caps' rear vents studied the thousand varieties of chips. Round faces, yellow eyes, straw-colored hair, rhino folds above their knees. A middle-aged man, squat like a tree stump, wore shorts that came down below his knees and a grandpa undershirt, without sleeves. Ropes of muscles seemed to torture his upper body, and the Lenin mustache and beard so black on his face looked pleasingly at odds with the gray stubble on his head.

There were hourglass bodies whose hips and shoulders billowed, and pear-shaped bodies, and torsos like drainpipes. The Scandinavian look: large bony ears, prominent nose, high cheeks, long neck, skinny body, small breasts, and big flat hands. One boy had pulled his arms inside his T-shirt and folded them there; he looked like a kitchen sink. His gold hair matched a small gold cross hung on a chain around his neck. My *Britannica* describes "physiognomy" as the practice of reading moral character through bodily and facial characteristics, but to me these people were all blank slates. I had no idea who they were. They were red and yellow photos, they'd flown into their casings, they were outsides without insides, yet had colorful feathers.

It wasn't that long ago that police and criminologists consulted charts of body types and head shapes in their work. So did eugenicists. The goal was not just weeding out degenerates, it was ensuring the tyranny of the normal, in Leslie Fiedler's phrase. According to Fiedler, social groups achieve this goal by arranging for the ritual slaughter of freaks. It must not have worked. At the beginning of the twentieth century, cries for fitness and health, anti-immigration sentiments, the eugenics movement, and proposals for the sterilization of criminals and other defectives had apparently failed, if the sideshow before me was any measure. One splendid specimen with a thick tubular neck walked around with such authority you could draw a straight line from the back of his head all the way down his shoulders to the small of his back. It was as though, for a brace, he were wearing a tire iron. With his large bony head and tiny baseball cap, sucking on a Tootsie Roll Pop—wearing white socks and Teva sandals—he was hardly an exception to the general menagerie, but part of the show.

I've noticed it often in nineteenth-century novels—the recourse to physiognomy. In Mrs. Gaskell's *Mary Barton* a man at a trial says of the accused, "I am no physiognomist, but I don't think his face strikes me as bad." And what signifies bad? According to Cesare Lombroso, in his *L'Uomo delinquente* (1876), the moral birthmarks, or stigmata, to look for in born criminals were receding foreheads, massive jaws, prognathous chins, heads lacking symmetry, long, large, and projecting ears, rectilinear noses, strongly marked wrinkles, thick hair on the head, scanty hair on cheeks and chin, feline eyes (cold, fixed, and glassy), a long span of extended arms, an ape-like agility, and superior eyesight, though the other senses generally lacked acuteness. What, then, was normalcy in such an economy? The neutral face, the average body? No such thing exists. Yet the urge to "read" bodies has proven irresistible, and may stem from a desire to find a "natural" language, both common and self-evident. Since we live in a fallen world, however, one sage's self-evident lexicon of body types is another's secret code. Robert Fludd, for example, in his *History of the Microcosm* (1620), said that large and fleshy feet mean foolishness in love, very hairy arms signify madness, a nose that reaches the mouth indicates a generous person, and baldness is a sign of perspicacity.

Where do such pronouncements come from? The roots of physiognomy lie in the ancient world, according to my *Britannica*. The earliest physiognomist was a man named Zopyrus, who analyzed Socrates' face and body and pronounced him to be oversexed, dull, and stupid. When Socrates' disciples laughed, the master stopped them. It was true, he said. That was his former character before he took up philosophy.

But my favorite is Aristotle. In his treatise on physiognomy (which may be spurious) he says that those with bulbous noses are piggish and insensitive, while sharp-tipped noses belong to the churlish — who are like dogs — and large, obtuse noses to the generous and leonine. Slender, hooked noses are signs of an eagle-like and noble character, retroussé noses of people who act like preening roosters, noses with notches of the crowish and impudent, and snub noses of the indolent and luxurious, whom Aristotle compares to deer.

I saw no notched noses in the Texaco convenience store, but did note a man with a crease across his head and a bulging brow, like a bufflehead duck's. The code's secret, then, was our link with the animals. From Aristotle's litany of snouts and beaks to Lombroso's apish and feline birthmarks, the common template describing human variety had been borrowed from the circus and zoo. What a key! Welcome to the monkey house. I saw octopal hips, avian eyes and chins, large thickets of hair, even sagittal crests. One overweight girl rounding an aisle flapped her hands like flippers, while a tall man behind her walked with delicate balance, flexing his body exactly like a giraffe's.

Then something kicked me in the chest. I'd just handed my Visa card to the boy behind the counter, and we were waiting for the okay. A snatch of conversation drifted by — "maxed out my 401(k)" — and a woman asked the clerk where the copy machine was. I swiveled my head and noticed three men emerging from an arched doorway leading to the fast-food booths. Behind them at a table sat my brother, hunched over a burger. His large nose and ears, his horn-rimmed glasses, his small and mousy head, and the way his gray hair lapped down over his ears — his baggy trousers, his gynecoid body type — all stamped him as Paul. I felt myself sinking. I was breathing through a straw. He must have seen me frozen there, openly staring, because he looked up and by the grace of God the resemblance passed like a shadow racing up the face of a cliff. The man became someone else, a subaltern Mr. Potato Head, perhaps. I hurried out the door, shaken.

Half an hour later I was speeding through Worcester, passing church façades lit up by spotlights beside the elevated highway. Fifty years ago, what the future would look like was elevated highways threading through skyscrapers twenty stories up. The future is always more modest than its simulacra, but this city interstate still had a certain cachet. Branches of streetlights whipped past below the highway. I spotted the night, solid as a girder, beyond the cloudy glow suspended over the city. The downtown lights were pretty bright to the right, but the darkness to the left was more familiar to me, where I-290 crossed the old Route 9 cutoff. I knew what it looked like even if I couldn't see it. Before this artery was built, when I was growing up, we'd taken that road every weekend of my life to visit Grandma and Paul, ten miles west in Wire Valley. It runs between railroad tracks and some raw-looking tenements stacked on a hill.

The song on the CD now was "The Mooche," another of Ellington's Cotton Club dance numbers. On this one, Miley uses a mute made from a bathroom plunger for his wah-wah trumpet. "I feel in this piece a conflict of two elemental forces," said a Dutch critic after Ellington's band played a concert in Utrecht—this is on the liner notes—"one the violence of Nature, which is an eternal struggle with the other, the force of Man, a more melancholy, restrained and mental force." Well. It does brood, that's true. It haunts you like a shadow straining to reach.

It was only nine o'clock and my back was getting sore. I had four or five more hours of driving to go.

2

INSIDE OUT

PAUL DIED OF an aneurysm. When my mother's neighbor told me on the phone, I remember trying to picture how it must have happened. It's quick, they say. A lot of people who have one never know until the end. Maybe not even then, especially if, as with my brother, it's low in the aorta.

He woke one morning at four A.M. with a numbness in his leg. The doctor told me later that was because blood had begun leaking through a fissure in the aneurysm, then trickled down and moistened the nerves. They took him to the hospital and performed extensive tests, thinking maybe a thrombus, or blood clot, had dislodged, a loose cannon in his circulatory system. His EKG was normal. They gave him a stress test. The numbness got worse—he had no feeling in his leg. They decided to ship him to another hospital, one specializing in vascular disorders, and wheeled him to an ambulance and sent him on his way.

They were pulling into that hospital's parking lot when the aneurysm burst and the heart emptied of blood. It had nowhere to go but his inner cavities, his fissures and canyons, slots and little craters. Bleeding to death inside one's body must be the worst form of claustrophobia. It had to feel like a great sinkhole in his body, the horizon of the world draining inside him. He was caught in a spiral of dizziness, I'm sure, so the crisis of panic— *What's happening? Oh my God* —most likely drained out as soon as he felt it, like those seemingly crucial things we forget the moment we think them as sleep overtakes us.

On the other hand, perhaps it took longer. And how long is long when you're dying, anyway? Falling from a roof might take only a second, yet it lasts forever. The reason for this is that time balloons, as arteries do—it swells with the surge. Of course, Paul was wired to monitors that must have shown what was happening, and maybe the medics were shouting "Paul, hang on!" as he faded, and pumping him full of electric current, and his body was jerking— "Are you with me, Paul?"—and all became a part of the spiraling dizziness, adding to the panic yet scattering it too.

When the sensation of spinning unclogged his brain, it also dislodged and cut loose his consciousness. His brain died first, starved of blood and oxygen.

Two weeks later, after the funeral, after I'd seen his house and learned what was in it, I woke up one morning feeling pains in my chest; they felt like heartburn, so I took some antacid. But they wouldn't go away. I taught a seminar on my campus, feeling increasingly short of breath. After the class, I had difficulty walking. I jog regularly and, in the summer, climb mountains on routes ten or twenty miles long. But I could hardly make it to the parking lot.

Halfway there, I turned back, and with my newly hatched festinating walk—stopping every few minutes to catch my fading breath—made it to the science library and looked up aneurysms. Severe heartburn feels like how I'd imagined an aneurysm would feel if it were pressing on the trachea or esophagus. However, I learned that most aneurysms were asymptomatic. Most? I sagged across campus to my car and drove to the closest ER.

In the hospital that night, the doctor told me that one of my lungs had collapsed. It might occur again in a week or two, perhaps in a year or two, or maybe never again. To reinflate the lung, he inserted a tube in my chest, which drained out the air caught in the chest cavity. One way that a lung collapses is by springing a leak—caused by a cyst or other weakness in its wall—and the more air that escapes into the chest cavity, the less the lung can inflate against the pressure. The lung leaks and air accumulates slowly, so it may take a while for it to fully collapse. Mine was fully collapsed.

The tube, going in, felt like being stabbed. As the doctor shoved, I felt it scrape a rib, felt each millimeter of tissue and nerve it divided. Once the air was released, my lung inflated as predicted, all at once, like an air bag. And *that* sensation is impossible to describe—something like an umbrella popping open inside you.

I lay there squirming, feeling little adhesive pains here and there, like new stars being born. Those, I was assured, were the result of the lung's readhering to the sticky pleura. Pleura? I was learning such interesting things about the body on whose shoulders I'd traveled all my life.

It does make you wonder about the various ways, while your body sleeps, that all its inner cauldrons can percolate and bubble, stirring plots to cause trouble, chaos, and confusion, planting seeds of death.

READING THE ENTRAILS

In 1945, in the village of al-Qaṣr in Upper Egypt, a night watchman named 'Alī killed a thief attempting to steal irrigation equipment from his clan's fields. The next morning, he in turn was murdered, by a member of the thief's family, a man named Aḥmad. Six months later, 'Alī's son, Muḥammad 'Alī, was digging above the Nile Valley cliffs for talus rich with nitrates, to fertilize the same fields. He came across a jar at the base of a boulder whose lid was probably sealed with bitumen, although we'll never know because he smashed it with his mattock. He did this with reluctance—it might contain a jinni, he thought. Then again, it might also contain gold, and in fact when he broke open the jar, yellow particles swirled out. They turned out to be fragments of papyrus. Inside the jar were books of the type made in late antiquity, when scrolls had only recently been abandoned in favor of stacks of flat sheets bound in leather. He wrapped them in his coat, hopped on his camel, and carried them home.

A month after that, a neighbor spotted Aḥmad, the man who'd murdered Muḥammad 'Alī's father, asleep by the side of a road outside their village. Beside him was a jar of unsold sugarcane molasses. The neighbor alerted Muḥammad 'Alī's family, who'd been urged by their mother to keep their mattocks sharp. They fell on Aḥmad while he was sleeping, hacked off his limbs, chopped him into pieces, ripped out his heart and ate it raw, sharing it among them—the supreme blood revenge.

Muḥammad 'Alī gave his books to the local Coptic priest, after being told they were Christian texts. His mother had already burned at least one when she ran out of firewood, and others had been distributed to neighbors. Some found their way to Cairo, where they fetched high prices, but when collectors and scholars asked their discoverer where he'd found them, Muḥammad 'Alī, afraid of an ambush by Aḥmad's family, only agreed to take them to the site under government escort and in disguise.

Ten years later, Aḥmad's teenage son opened fire during a funeral procession for a member of Muḥammad 'Alī's family, killing or wounding twenty people. Muḥammad 'Alī himself was shot above the heart, and displayed the wound with pride the rest of his life, since, being intact, he was living proof of unsuccessful vengeance.

The books turned out to be a large group of Gnostic texts from the first several centuries of the Christian era, now best known as the Nag Hammadi Library. In one of them, *The Apocryphon of John*, the creation of Adam is described as a kind of choral assemblage of factory parts, with a different angel or demon assigned to each limb and organ. So: "Eteraphaope-Abron created his head; Meniggesstroeth created the brain; Asterechme created the right eye; Thaspomocha created the left eye; Yeronumos created the right ear; Bissoum created the left ear; Akioreim created the nose; Banen-Ephroum created the lips; Amen created the teeth; Ibikan created the molars; Basiliademe created the tonsils; Achcha created the uvula. . . ." This goes on for several pages of the original codex. Angels and demons are appointed as guardians over each item, as well as over the bone-soul, the sinew-soul, the flesh-soul, the marrow-soul, the blood-soul, the skin-soul, and the hair-soul. By the end of the passage, Adam's body contains enough guardian powers to run a football stadium, each assigned to a fragment of the whole. There are demons to reign over heat, cold, and wetness, and others assigned to the senses, the imagination, the passions and emotions. Someone named Oummaa is in charge of "composition"—presumably a sort of batter taster.

The resulting soft machine called Adam has been literally articulated as a collection of parts inside a bag of skin, also a part. This was in the text a man had found before chopping his enemy into pieces.

What *was* the body for those late ancients? What secrets did it hide? One difficulty was that finding out—by dissection, for example— might release a swarm of demons. "He that toucheth the dead body of any man shall be unclean seven days" (Numbers 19:11). In 1300, the Pope issued a bull excommunicating those who cut up dead bodies.

Dissection by then had come to be regarded as a sinful prying into nature's secrets.

The more ancient ancients were not as squeamish about body parts, as anyone who has read *The Iliad* can attest. Yet Homer's descriptions — "Idomeneus stabbed Erymas in the mouth with the pitiless / bronze, so that the brazen spearhead smashed its way clean through / below the brain in an upward stroke and the white bones splintered, / and the teeth were shaken out with the stroke and both eyes filled up / with blood, and gaping he blew a spray of blood through the nostrils / and through his mouth, and death in a dark mist closed in about him" — while graphic, are curiously detached. They have a sort of stillness, like separate snapshots arranged to make a series. One feels, in Homer, that there's not much difference between the inside and the outside of the body. Inside, outside, public, private — the ancients saw them as continuous. Maybe that's why they regarded those mysterious human innards shrouded in darkness — the pipes and cisterns of the body, wrapped in bloody spaghetti — as hardly mysterious at all, being part of the world every bit as much as stones, birds, olives, and urns.

FLUDD REDUX

Skip ahead to Robert Fludd. In 1633, the same "Trismegistian-Platonick-Rosy-crucian Doctor" and "cacomagus" we met earlier, the coinventor of the thermometer, described looking over a physician's shoulder as he dissected a cadaver in London. The place was most likely the College of Physicians' house at the end of Paternoster Row, on Amen Corner, in the shadow of St. Paul's Cathedral, although Fludd doesn't specify. Both Fludd and the dissector were members of the London College of Physicians, and both were anatomists, so let's say Amen Corner.

The physician was attempting to prove that no passageways existed in the muscular wall between the right and left ventricles of the heart. Belief in such "intraventricular pores of the septum" went back at least to Galen, and probably resulted from dissections of miscarried or aborted fetuses. The fetus does possess an opening between the two sides of its heart, since its circulating blood is its mother's, and this blood bypasses its lungs, which of course can't function in the womb. When a child is born, the lungs inflate, and blood from the right atrium begins to flow through the pulmonary trunk into the lungs, from which it returns to the left atrium; and gradually the passageway between the two sides of the heart closes.

Four years earlier, the French philosopher Pierre Gassendi claimed to have witnessed, in a dissection at Aix, a surgeon named Payanus who probed with a spatula for such openings or pores in the septum of an adult—and found them. "Taking the spatula, he approached the septum of the heart to try the penetration. He attempted this not straight on as others do, but he first made the approach most lightly with the edge of the iron entered in beneath . . . and he explored the approach always further by twisting the iron up and down, and to the side, most patiently." Fludd, in his description of the dissection *he* witnessed, mentions this passage and upbraids Gassendi for failing to conclude the obvious: that the surgeon produced the openings he was searching for in the very act of searching. Those who have examined the heart with care, like the physician whose shoulder he peered over, says Fludd, have never found a septum with "pores." "Not in any one out of the many cadavers that he examined did he find such a septum; and neither I nor any others who with most acute and almost lynx-like eyes saw this when we examined the septum of the heart."

Lynx-like eyes to be sure. Fludd would have needed keenness of sight at such a dissection, or, as they were called, at the "mysteries" of an anatomy. In the house on Amen Corner, the dissecting table probably had a curtain around it, hung on a metal frame, to ensure the cadaver's decency before the cutting began. The physician wore white aprons and sleeves and a large white bonnet that probably dwarfed him, since this man was short. Light was surely a problem; wax candles were always provided, to peer into the body cavity. In this case, perhaps the heart was removed and carried to a window. Or maybe the physician simply plopped it on the table next to a candle and touched it with his silver-tipped rod—made of white whalebone—and let the others turn their lynx eyes upon it.

The cadavers at such anatomies were malefactors executed for felonies in London. Queen Elizabeth granted the College of Physicians four such bodies a year, a number James I increased to six.

Why would such mythical openings in the heart concern a man like Fludd? Because the doctor whose shoulder he was peering over was William Harvey, who had demonstrated to the world that blood circulates in the body, and in so doing had asserted that it moves from the veins to the arteries by means of the lungs. But according to the ancients, the lungs drew air into the body to cool off the heart, and the pulmonary vein carried that air into the heart. Therefore the blood passed from the right to the left side of the heart through pores in its septum. "I should like to be informed why," asked Harvey, "if the pulmonary vein were destined for conveying air, it has the structure of a blood vessel?" In fact, as he knew, the pulmonary vein conveys blood, not air, and the lungs close the loop of circulation by making a link from the veins to the arteries.

As for the other link, from the arteries to the veins, Harvey had to presume that it existed, since what we today know as the capillaries were too small to be seen without a microscope. And Harvey's work, says Steven Vogel, "antedated practical microscopes." Thirty years after Harvey published his findings, Marcello Malpighi provided the finishing touch, becoming the first to see capillaries with a microscope. But I'm getting ahead of myself.

FLUCTIBUS FLUXUS

Fludd, who liked to give his name as de Fluctibus, was Harvey's colleague and friend. As Fellows and Censors of the College of Physicians, they had the power to examine and license new doctors. Fludd was one of the first to acclaim Harvey's discovery of blood circulation, and he helped Harvey find the publisher for his book announcing the discovery: William Fitzer in Holland, who specialized in Rosicrucian texts. Yet Fludd was an enthusiast and a mystic, whereas Harvey, according to Geoffrey Keynes, with "a somewhat cold and secluded mind," was "eager for knowledge, but not burning to share it with others." Harvey thought that human beings were mischievous baboons and modern writers were "shitt-breeches." He was very short, with a brownish complexion, round face, small eyes, a little pointed beard, and a pudgy body. His temper was quick—he carried a dagger—and he had trouble sleeping, either because of the continual flux of ideas racing through his head or because he was one of the first Englishmen, says Keynes, to form an addiction to coffee.

He was always alert, skeptical and quizzical, and did not suffer fools. Is it possible to conclude from this description that Robert Fludd was not a fool?

Or was he patronized by Harvey?

We know that Fludd was there that day because he later published a book defending himself and Harvey against the attacks of Pierre Gassendi, who'd witnessed that butcher Payanus digging into a heart with, of all things, a spatula—and in it he cites Harvey's dissection. Later, after Fludd's death, Harvey went even further in demonstrating the impermeability of the heart septum: he tied off the pulmonary artery of a "throttled human being" (a highwayman) and pumped the right ventricle and atrium with water until they were larger than a football and ready to burst; no water passed from the right to the left side of the heart.

What went through Fludd's mind while looking over Harvey's shoulder? Perhaps the flickering candle, the pulley and hook hanging from the ceiling, the fire in the hearth, the smell of blood and body tissue, not to mention the heady odor of his fellow physicians crowding around, since no one in seventeenth-century England bathed very often — perhaps all this made him think of better things, of escaping that close, poorly lit room. The human body was a glory to Fludd, as it would be to William Blake two hundred years later. "The Head sublime, the heart Pathos, the genitals Beauty, the hands & feet Proportion" was the way Blake expressed it. Fludd would have concurred. In his book *A Philosophicall Key,* our old friend Pan — Fludd's Principle of Universal Nature — creates the human body out of "grosser elements" to house the "supernaturall splendour" of the "Aethereall spirit." I've modernized the spelling in the following long quotation. Pan is reporting the instructions he received from Demogorgon, the god of the earth:

> Then in his middle sphere shall thou erect a pavilion called the heart, which, like the sun in the greater world, shall send forth his essential beams circularly from his center, that thereby they may animate and vivify every member of this so well-erected a microcosm. Then also will I command, that Chronos or Time . . . shall justly guide and proportion the minutes of his life and days, observing carefully that the motion of his pulses be obedient to just measure and harmonical proportion, and that their Systole and Diastole do live together in peace and concord as man and wife. . . . In the which therefore thou shalt set to thy helping hand first to transmute by thy natural motion the chilly substance and cloudy vapors of the airy ventricle into crimson and ready blood, which thou shall conduct by the doubleguarded channels of the veins through every region of this earthly edifice, that thereby it may produce unto itself a universal fertility by successive and hourly nourishment, even as thy rainy influence make the whole earth of the macrocosm passing

fruitful. . . . Moreover the brackish torrents and wheyey streams shall trickle down from the mountains of the stomach, liver, and spleen, and kissing first in their current the scarlet and reeking billows of the greater veins, shall penetrate by a double conduit or channel quite through the stony and rocky caverns of the kidneys, as through the gravelly veins and sandy passages of the earth's mountain, and so by Time's direction shall fall soberly into the salt sea of the bladder.

The gray body Fludd observed over Harvey's shoulder may have possessed such a marvelous geography, but to see it would require more than lynx eyes — it would require, in Blake's words, looking through, rather than with, one's senses.

One can hardly imagine an odder couple than these doctor friends, the rational Harvey and the mystical Fludd. Yet *A Philosophicall Key* was written in 1619, the year Harvey says he formulated his notion of the blood's circulation. And as this passage shows, Fludd was simultaneously forming a similar concept: that the heart, like the sun, sends forth his beams — that is, the blood — "circularly from his center." In his *De motu cordis*, when Harvey places his discovery in the center of a chapter at the center of his book, in uppercase letters — "I began to think whether there might not be A MOTION, AS IT WERE, IN A CIRCLE" — he offers not as evidence but as bolstering atmospherics a series of Fluddian metaphors:

This motion we may be allowed to call circular, in the same way as Aristotle says that the air and the rain emulate the circular motion of the superior bodies; for the moist earth, warmed by the sun, evaporates; the vapours drawn upwards are condensed, and descending in the form of rain, moisten the earth again. By this arrangement are generations of living things produced; and in like manner are tempests and meteors engendered by the circular motion, and by the approach and recession of the sun.

So Harvey too used macrocosmic pictures to describe microcosmic realities, not unlike what I'm doing in tracing Paul's story. In Harvey's case, this method enabled him to emphasize two things. One, that blood, like rain, is preserved in its circuit — it's always the same blood. The old view was that blood, continually manufactured, was continually being absorbed by the body, since it was the "virtue" that nourished and warmed the whole body.

The other, that blood circulated, turned out to be one of the great paradigm shifts in science. It didn't depend just on lynx eyes and a scalpel-edged mind; it also required a new picture and model, that of the circle. Fludd was not the only one ever to say the blood moved in a circle, nor was his notion of circularity exactly that of Harvey. But he was there with his "well-erected microcosm" when Harvey needed a model. As Walter Pagel asks, "Could [Fludd's] idea about the circular motion of the spirit in the blood and its imitation of the movement of the Sun have left an impression in Harvey's mind and have in some way 'sensitised' him to the association of 'circularity' with the blood and the heart?"

FROGS

Geoffrey Keynes reports that Sir Richard Quain visited the Harvey family vault in 1868. William Harvey's coffin was a wrapping made of lead roughly shaped to the body, with a face carved on top. Other members of his family had similar leaden shells, some of which had sagged and contracted, so that their skeletons showed through. In Harvey's case, the lead had cracked, and Quain writes of being horrified when a large frog jumped out.

Maybe this frog was a descendant of those seventeenth-century martyrs to science who were tied down, stabbed, cut open, chopped up, injected with fluids, and boiled to demonstrate the blood's circulation. As one of Harvey's biographers points out, it isn't possible to demonstrate the circulation of the blood by dissecting cadavers, whose hearts have stopped beating. Living animals must be used. Harvey's great successor, Marcello Malpighi, said that in discovering the capillaries "I have almost destroyed the entire race of frogs." Harvey also cut open live frogs, as well as fish, pigeons, dogs, snakes, and chickens. "The examination of bodies of animals has always been my delight," he said. He once removed the heart from a frog and observed that the creature still skipped around. Another time, he chopped up the heart of a salmon and watched all the pieces continue to beat. He studied them closely; they were contracting, not dilating.

One of the most compelling passages of *De motu cordis* is Harvey's description of a dying heart. He'd already established that the heart is a muscle that pumps by contracting. The old view was that the heart and arteries both dilate and contract, and that the arteries, with muscles in their walls, pump as well.

> Last of all, drawing towards death, it [the heart] ceases to answer by its motion, and only by nodding its head seems to give consent, and moves so insensibly, that it seems only to give a sign of motion to the ears: So the heart first leaves beating before the ears, so that the ears are said to out-live it: the left ventricle leaves beating first of all, then its ear, then the right ventricle, last of all . . . the rest giving off and dying, the right ear beats still: so that life seems to remain last of all in the right. And whilst by little and little the heart is dying, you may see after two or three beatings of the ear, the heart will, being as it were rowsed, and very slowly and reluctantly, endeavour and frame a motion.

"Ear" in this translation (Harvey wrote in Latin) means auricle, Latin for ear — and auricle is another word for atrium. Harvey also describes moistening his finger after a pigeon's heart had stopped beating, then touching the heart. The warmth of his finger, he reports, encouraged the heart to recommence beating, "recalled as it were from death to life."

He describes experiments with live fish, in which he cut them open, tied off the aorta, and watched the heart fill to near bursting. Then he tied off the inferior vena cava, and the opposite happened: the heart became flat, almost empty, though still stubbornly beating. The aorta went flat too, receiving less and less blood, and soon none at all. What became of all that blood? After filling the veins it poured into the main vein and stretched it until it almost exploded. This proved the theory of circulation. The stream of blood went around in a circle, and no matter where he tied a vessel, an accumulation took place.

Then came Malpighi. He cut open frogs and observed the arteries running into the peritoneum (the membrane around the abdominal cavity) swell with each heartbeat and branch into smaller and smaller blood vessels. He filled the arteries in a dog's lung with mercury and observed its fine branches, like moonlit antlers. Harvey had boiled livers, spleens, lungs, kidneys, and other organs until their tissues "could be shaken like dust from the fibres or picked away with a needle," looking for the so-called anastomosis of the arteries and veins—the direct openings between them, posited by the ancients—with no success. There had to be what we call capillaries, he concluded, but they were too small to see. Malpighi saw them. He tied the artery running into a frog's lung, cut out the lung, hung it up to dry, and holding it against the setting sun several days later, looked at it through a single-lens microscope and made out its intricate network of capillaries, each one containing a thread of dried blood. He placed it under his double-lens microscope with a lamp and could trace with his eyes their labyrinthine curves and countless branches.

Pinning down live frogs, he cut them open and looked at their lungs, peritonea, and bladders; with the microscope he could see where the arteries rooted down into fine stringy nets of billowing capillaries, which gathered in bunches then fanned out as veins.

Malpighi, by the way, performed these experiments while experiencing severe attacks of kidney stones. Once he even cut open a kidney and saw what we know as the glomeruli, hanging on the arteries, as he put it, like apples on a tree.

I THINK I COULD TURN AND LIVE WITH THE ANIMALS

If any further confirmation is needed that human beings are no longer animals, it would be these explorations of the hidden body and of what used to be called forbidden knowledge. Harvey once demonstrated the heart's powerful pulse by tying down a dog and opening a proximal artery so that the blood rhythmically spurt across a room. Those who cut up living animals know they aren't human, of course. One can inflict disinterested pain only on that which isn't oneself.

Still, a part of us remembers the time when we were animals. The memory is a vestige, like the tail on human fetuses. Harvey's description of a dying heart, with its nodding head — as though falling asleep — eerily suggests a Victorian account of a fading pet's last moments. The odd combination of precision, objectivity to the point of bloodlessness, and the word "ears" (we think of furry little envelopes) creates for us today, no matter who we are — biologist, poet, cynic, sentimentalist — an unresolved tension. We flow back and forth, as perhaps Harvey did, between a mind that knows and a body that suffers.

Both Harvey and Malpighi died of strokes, or heart attacks — the distinction then wasn't always easy to make. So it turns out that both were animals after all. They were animals because their bodies could die, even if those bodies were a form of clockwork. Their contemporary Descartes, who called the body a machine, denied consciousness to animals, and his followers were said to make fun of those who pitied dogs for suffering pain. "They said the animals were clocks," said one

Frenchman, and "the cries they emitted when struck were only the noise of a little spring that had been touched." Descartes supported Harvey's theory, though with modifications. He especially applauded its mechanistic explanations. His followers were said by the same anonymous countryman to have nailed living dogs up on boards "by their four paws to vivisect them to see the circulation of the blood which was a great subject of controversy."

Today we at least anesthetize laboratory animals before cutting them open, although some insist this doesn't make any difference and we shouldn't under any circumstances cut open animals. Most scientists I know try to avoid causing any animal to feel pain. But sometimes, they say, it can't be avoided. Descartes was right in one respect: an animal isn't "conscious of" pain. But Descartes was wrong too. The attention pain commands weighs far too much to talk about consciousness "of." Both animals and humans *become* their pain. So pain, ironically, is one of those experiences that return us to our union with the animals.

This union, though, can be a two-edged sword. Consider my brother. He shared his house with a menagerie of pets and slowly reduced himself to their existence, to living in his own waste. He also abandoned those pets when he moved out, and the things I'd discovered in cleaning up his house told me what they'd suffered for that.

Meanwhile, poor Robert Fludd. He lost again. His notion of circular motion may have provided the model Harvey needed, but models are only models, and science isn't metaphor. The body is not the luminous landscape of visionary delight whose brackish torrents and streams of whey trickle down the mountains of the stomach and spleen, kissing the veins and penetrating the caverns of the kidneys. No, it is rather Harvey's soft machine of moving parts, of uniform substance, and of largely rational design, though just how rational is open to question. Evolution, for example, isn't rational—and it jerry-builds our bodies.

THE SQUID

Nearly one hundred years before Harvey, Andreas Vesalius, the first modern anatomist, got a lot of things right about our bodies and their basket of secrets, but not the heart and blood. That's why we needed Harvey. Vesalius like Harvey was convinced that there were not intra-ventricular pores between the two sides of the heart, but as to where the blood went from the right ventricle, he confessed to being uncer-tain. His account of the pulse and the arteries and veins was pretty much Galenic. Galen had shown, by inserting a reed into a severed artery, that the heart transmitted its pulse along the walls of the arter-ies, and that these walls actually contracted.

Harvey proved him wrong. It is the contraction of the heart that forces blood through the whole closed system, although it needs the help of either gravity or muscles by the time it reaches the veins. So, when we stretch, we squeeze blood through the veins, whose valves, discovered by Harvey, keep it moving toward the heart.

Still, the old view had accounted for an obvious phenomenon: when the heart beats, in a sense so does the body. The heart, says Steven Vogel, is a pressurized vessel. Like water pumped through a sys-tem of pipes, the blood retains the pressure of the system and responds to it at once. As the heart contracts, expelling blood, the pressure surge is immediately felt from the brain to the feet. Vogel points out that if the tubes and pipes in which our blood circulates were as rigid as the pipes through which our drinking water flows, we'd spring a leak with each heartbeat. The heart when it beats squeezes almost shut, and as it does so, blood surges out. The blood's movement through the system alone is not sufficient to absorb these repeated and powerful surges, since the system is closed and there are no pressure valves. Therefore the arteries have to swell or they'd burst.

Vogel asks why an aneurysm doesn't develop with every heartbeat. Because arteries, he says—elastic enough to expand with each pressure surge—are also resilient enough not to balloon out of shape while doing so. The elasticity comes from elastin, the resilience from collagen, two fibrous proteins often used in skin creams. The ligament running along the top of a sheep's neck is made of elastin. Without this substance in our arterial walls, the system would continually rupture at its joints.

Collagen, on the other hand, is less extensible than elastin and much more stiff. When the ancients used *ballistae* (slingshots) to throw ninety-pound rocks a fourth of a mile, they were using the collagen in a braid of cow tendons and relying on its powerful resilience. Without collagen, local expansions of blood vessels would appear like balloons up and down the artery walls—in other words, aneurysms.

As it is, the right mix of elastin and collagen enables our vessels to absorb the impact of constantly repeating pressure surges and reductions. That is, the system is designed to stretch to a certain point, then resist stretching—or increase stiffness—as distension increases.

Elastin is found only in vertebrates, as if one needed bones on which to hang this limp pasta. Cephalopods like octopi and squid have something analogous—an extensible protein—in their aortic walls. Their bodies are also elastic, with short muscle fibers running every which way across their mantles. Lacking bones, a squid makes its whole body a heart: it contracts to squeeze out water, then takes in more water when it reassumes its shape, and this is how it swims. How we swim is internally: we keep our salty ocean moving through our bodies. Squids keep their bodies moving through their salty ocean. The heart in human beings is the size of a squid.

STUDIES IN SCARLET

When Harvey showed that the arteries expand not because of muscles in their walls but because they're receiving the surge of the heart, his evidence came from a close friend to whom he refers twice in his writings on the heart and blood, though we never learn his name. He first came to Harvey with an aneurysm in his neck, "daily increasing in size." Its pulsations corresponded to those of the heart—that is, it swelled rather than contracted with each contraction of the heart. Also, Harvey could feel, presumably with his fingers, "large forceful pulsations" squirting into the aneurysm, while below it the pulse was weak. After the death of this friend, Harvey cut out his aneurysm, which he describes in a letter as having turned into a "pipe-like bone."

If he'd had a stethoscope (they hadn't yet been invented), Harvey could have *heard* the blood squirting into the aneurysm. Steven Vogel quotes the Sherlock Holmes novel *A Study in Scarlet,* in which Watson holds his stethoscope to a convict's chest, which seems "to thrill and quiver as a frail building." Inside it, he hears a sort of humming and buzzing. "Why," Watson cried, "you have an aortic aneurism!"

The American hero Kit Carson in his last years was diagnosed with an aortic aneurysm, which pressed against his trachea, causing spasms of the bronchial tubes and making him continually short of breath. He was told that when the aneurysm burst he'd die either of suffocation or from a hemorrhage. "He begged me not to let him suffer such tortures, insisting that death would be better by chloroform while attempting relief . . . than death by suffocation," said his doctor, H. R. Tilton. Tilton told Carson that a "grave symptom" would be blood in the sputum—that would mean the aneurysm was breaking through the trachea.

> He suddenly called out, "Doctor, Compadre, Adios." I sprang to him and seeing a gush of blood pouring from his mouth, remarked, "This is the last of the general." I supported his forehead on my hand, while death speedily closed the scene.

In other words, his heart drained and emptied, as had my brother Paul's.

3

ONLY THE LONELY

On the Massachusetts Turnpike, I stopped at a Roy Rogers and ate a rubbery sandwich, bought some coffee, then called home. Hannah thought I was crazy for driving home this late. She knew that I'd fallen asleep on the road once, before we were married. I'd been driving alone then too, and woke with the tires on the passenger side madly recoiling off hummocks of grass. I'd felt free to tell her about it because of my theory that it only happens once. If you survive, you never do it again. You find ways to stay awake—playing loud music, slapping yourself, twitching and jerking, pulling off to take a nap.

"Just find a rest stop and curl up and sleep," she said.

"I can't."

"Why?"

"I have to get home."

"Why?"

I shrugged, though of course she couldn't see it. I told her I loved her. I wanted to be home. To see our children. To sleep in the same bed we'd slept in for two decades, not in my brother's van.

I hung up and used the bathroom. Back on the turnpike, I began to develop a massive headache. Headaches used to be thought of as demons demanding release—hence trephination, cutting holes in the skull, the oldest surgical procedure we know of in human history. Many prehistoric skulls have been found trephined. I suppose it cooled the brain.

My headache, though, would keep me awake. I should have been thankful.

I'd exhausted Duke Ellington. In the drawer beneath the seat I rummaged blindly and found a Frank Sinatra CD, *Only the Lonely,* and popped it in the player. Plunging through darkness, thumb and head throbbing, it gradually struck me as nothing short of miraculous that I was hearing a voice without a body present. The illusion of presence is sometimes more powerful than the real thing. For example, I could turn up the volume louder than Sinatra could physically sing. But that would puncture the illusion. It would be like magnifying a picture until all you see is pixels.

Still, what a voice! During the high notes of "One for My Baby" it wobbled like someone balanced on an unsupported ladder. Not that he couldn't manage that register — just that the effort itself was the point. It *means* something to climb up there by yourself, he was saying, with your clown makeup on. The cover of the CD showed Sinatra's face superimposed on that of a clown. The saddest cliché: a smiling clown with a broken heart.

THE HEART OF THE MATTER

Who first thought of the heart as the seat of emotions? The first human being backed up against a cliff by a saber-toothed tiger, no doubt, whose adrenaline caused the threatened organ in his chest to kick into overdrive. Since this happens to animals too, the cornered heart may be still another link with our true ancestors — with dogs, like my brother's Rip trying to guard her little pups from young professors of English.

Heart in hand. Bleeding heart. Heavy heart. Heart in mouth. Heartstrings. Heartbreaker. Heart of gold. At the heart of.

Our emotions, it appears, are virtual machines jury-rigged by evolution as strained through human language and culture. Loneliness, for example, is most likely a vestige of the threat to survival in being cut off from one's group. Solitude and privacy, constructions of our culture, are never uncolored by loss or care, then. And the rewards of privacy—independence, self-sufficiency—are never unaccompanied by the risks of loneliness: depression and the sense of not belonging.

Was Paul's heart defective? Were his emotions out of whack? He had to be the loneliest man I've ever known. His whole body expressed it, especially in his later years, once he'd retired and cut himself off from the social world of work. Slouched and retractive, he moved through our house on his periodic visits as through a tunnel. I realize now he must have visited us because of Hannah, not me. Once Hannah grew used to him, she at least took an interest, in his travels, his ideas. I'd modeled myself against him all those years—not consciously, perhaps, but instinctively, for survival. My habits, my tastes, my posture, my clothes, became everything he wasn't. I don't mean to imply that my brother obsessed me. When he was alive I hardly thought about him, and never consulted a snapshot of Paul when I shopped for clothes. Yet I felt a sort of contamination if I wore baggy trousers.

Hannah, on the other hand, stopped regarding him as odd, at least when he was around. He warmed up in her company and even talked freely. In recent years she'd given him financial advice—start an IRA, don't use savings accounts, buy this or that mutual fund. When he took a buyout from his company and retired two years early, before Medicare kicked in, she told him about COBRA, how his health insurance would continue for so long, then he'd have to pay for it, until age sixty-five. She talked to him as though he were a normal human being, and spiced the talk with friendly advice. In return, he melted in her presence. They sat in two chairs at the kitchen table, facing each other. He laughed and expressed his opinions on voting, on politicians, on taxes. With Groucho Marx logic he asked, Why vote for someone who wanted *his* vote? As for taxes, he couldn't see paying for schools or libraries when he had no children and got nothing out of reading.

He sat with legs crossed, a hand between his knees, body folded forward toward Hannah. I remember thinking, How does one become a stranger to everyone yet so willingly respond to ordinary human warmth?

I could count those conversations on one hand. He visited us maybe once a year or so. When they talked, I tried to find something else to do, like washing dishes — something on the periphery.

THE MATTER OF THE HEART

Our bodies are webs in which we're hopelessly caught, and for all the primping and preening we do — the exercise, dieting, cosmetic surgery, conscious carriage — most of what we show to other people lies beyond our control. Often, like Paul, I recoil from the world and sink into myself. It's like breathing underwater. Our bodies are also palimpsests, and in acts of regression we recover older texts. We are Nutcracker Men or, even older, deep-sea creatures crushed inside a larger world. We in fact have two hearts, a right one and a left one, with no passageway between them, as William Harvey proved. And why two hearts? Because when our fishy ancestors emerged from the ocean and developed lungs, something had to pump blood to the body — the left side of the heart — while the smaller right side, inherited from fish, pumped it to the lungs, so it could be oxygenated. And our lungs, by the way, did not evolve from gills, as Steven Vogel points out, but from "outpocketings" in the esophagus, the same outpocketings that once served as swim bladders when we lived underwater.

STAR TREK

It was pitch dark outside. The traffic had thinned to big trucks and small cars, each its own universe. I felt strangely detached. Few everyday activities in modern life are more eerie than driving alone at night. The glow-in-the-dark instrument panels, like ancient phosphorescence — the anthropoidal arthropod machine — the movement through stillness, while still inside the movement . . . Night fills the car.

It feels like space travel. You hallucinate timelessness. Beyond the road, there's nothing to see: no hills, trees, buildings, or people, no flat or rolling distances, just the occasional light blinking past. You're at the edge of the world, or even past it.

What an illusion. I wonder what alien race devised it. Maybe it's a plot hatched by our genes to prepare human beings for real space travel, so that they, the genes, can colonize the universe. What else are we for but to carry our genes? The purpose of the heart is to circulate blood; the purpose of the circulation of blood is to transport oxygen from the lungs to the cells; the purpose of transporting oxygen to the cells is to enable them to burn the sugars or starch that make energy for the body, which, to close the loop, fuels the beating heart. My body is a self-consuming artifact. It's dispensable. And, thick with wonder, alone in a darkness without shapes or edges — omniscient, squirming, swiveling my head, reaching for things, listening and watching — I drive and suspect that whatever selfhood I possess, with its fears, joys, hopes, and black depressions, is also dispensable. Like my body, it's a gadget concocted by the genes to reproduce themselves.

WE ARE ALL MONSTERS

Men and women once were one, says Plato. Then the sexes split apart, and we were haunted by loss. So the genealogy of loneliness is loss, and the mark of loss is sexual difference. And when we struggle to mend that loss, it's as if, as Kafka said, we want a secret from each other — as if the other were a part of oneself, and to recover that part we have to claw through the obstruction.

Sexual difference means we're hung with body parts of comic inconvenience. The jerry-built body that makes us men and women has done so by deforming us. We're all monsters, then. Have a form and you're deformed. Females are failed males, and men failed women.

Each wears the other's sexual organs turned inside out. In the medieval fabliau "The Four Wishes of Saint Martin," a peasant takes home four wishes from the saint, as a reward for his devotion.

Give me one of the wishes, says his wife.

No, he says, you'd waste it. Women are stupid. You'd do something crazy. You'd wish that I be turned into a goat, or bear, or ass.

I promise you, she says, I'll never wish your shape be changed to anything else.

Okay. Have a wish.

I wish, she says, that you be covered with pricks, from your head to your toe, and all stiff as iron—then you'll know what a prick you are!

In the translation (from Old French) by Robert Harrison of this twelfth-century text, the transformation is described as follows:

> A prick leaped up on both his knees—
> keep listening and by God you'll hear
> of miracles—from out each ear,
> and right in front on high there now
> appeared a great prick on his brow,
> while downward to his feet the hick's
> whole body was a mass of pricks.
> From head to foot the pricks had sprung:
> he now was, one might say, well hung.

So maybe, we conclude, it's men who are stupid. But the story isn't over. The peasant is enraged, of course, and wishes in revenge that his wife be covered with cunts.

> She found, within a moment's space,
> two cunts were now upon her face,
> and on her brow, four, side by side.
> In front, in back, cunts multiplied,
> And there were cunts of every kind,

and cunts before and cunts behind;
cunts sinuous and straight, cunts brushy,
hairless cunts, cunts piled and plushy,
cunts both virginal and splayed,
and cunts well used and cunts well made.

That's two wishes down. The man and his wife now come to their senses and realize that in order to have one wish left, their fourth — a wish that will make them wealthy and happy — they'll have to use the third wish to rid themselves of these ornaments. So they wish them all away.

They glance down and see that their original genitals have also disappeared, gone with the third wish. No more sexual markers; the man and wife are neither male nor female. They must use their fourth wish to get back to square one.

I think of this story as the wise and clever triumph of our common straitjacket, dual gender. The nightmare of what happens, for the peasant and his wife, lies not in being covered head to toe by the genitals "appropriate" to each. On the contrary, it's the moment they have no sexual markers at all — the moment they're overwhelmed by sameness.

No wonder we rush toward each other through darkness, as I was doing now, just to come full circle.

But what about those for whom the body is a straitjacket wrapped around itself? Those reclusive human beings like Paul whose loneliness spawns repeated acts of solitude? Hung with sexual markers, they might just as well be as blank as mannequins. Neither same- nor opposite-gendered bodies exist for their embrace, since embraces would consume them.

Yet Paul's solitary pleasures in some respects aped the medieval story about the peasant and his wife, if the evidence I'd found was any indication. There were plenty of magazines and videos in his house—some buried in trash, some scattered about—mostly porno-graphic and of every variety. But certain themes emerged as dominant. My brother's taste seemed to run toward genital confusion. It was as though Paul combined in himself both the man and the woman in "The Four Wishes of Saint Martin," and therefore for his pleasure sought out embodiments of his own self-loathing. "He-women" said the video boxes, with their photos of long red shafts suspiciously pros-thetic yet glistening like intestines and sprouting in crowded groins beside what looked like rotted fruit. Pornography had apparently grown surreal in recent years. Other images displayed several bodies stuffed into one another in multiple ways by means of these excres-cences. The colors of the photos were like those in cheap cookbooks—red and yellow prevailed. I found them grotesquely comic and infi-nitely sad. If you were desperate, I suppose, they promised at least a kind of release. But release for someone so ferociously solitary can only crush that solitude, like mercury, into solitudes—into duplica-tions of the same.

SOLITUDE

I realize now why I drove home that night instead of waiting for morn-ing: to end my fussy loneliness. It made me feel creepy. I was cultivat-ing solitude, that two-edged sword. Minutes ago I'd been omniscient, in control. Now I'd begun to feel sorry for myself, trapped in a same-ness that never stopped unspooling. Space withdrew before my head-lights and piled against the distance, yet nothing seemed to change. The van, I thought, could be on a rolling tube simply driving in place. Something seemed to buzz—my fluorescent headache? Most likely my tires, whose soft running rip ran beneath everything, including Frank Sinatra's voice. It sounded like masking tape being pulled off a stage. It gave solitude a skin.

TOWER OF STRENGTH

I still have the same Time-Life book I had as a teen: *The Body*. It's a popular instructional manual in a series called the Life Science Library, with photographs, paintings, old woodcuts, and minimal text, in the style of the early sixties. In obvious homage to (or theft from) Renaissance anatomical woodcuts, especially those of Vesalius, our circulatory and muscular systems are portrayed throwing javelins in deserts or pole-vaulting on beaches, with ancient ruins and Tuscan villas dotting the background. One picture is captioned "The Skeleton: Tower of Strength."

All of this is noble and Adamic, and expresses a kind of Olympian pride in nation and race. In the section titled "Triumphs of Structure and Design," we learn that bone is the steel and concrete of the body. Photos of ball-and-socket joints are juxtaposed with those of TV rabbit ears, the spine is pictured beside a broadcast tower with its web of steel guys, the cranium beside a domed stadium, and so on. None of this is meant to suggest that the natural is unnatural — exactly the opposite. *We* are the triumphs of structure and design, and our bodies provide the foundational models for culture's designs.

There's another way of looking at it, though. All the prosthetic bodies we employ in our lives, from autos to backhoes to forklifts to cherry pickers, not only demonstrate the body's limitations but also illustrate how the body in time devised ad hoc means to adapt to new demands. During the slow gale of evolution, our bodies adjusted to bodies that had adjusted to entirely different climates and geographies. So the construction of the body, accomplished with whatever glue or spit was handy, was continually revised, subtracted from, added to, and propped up, with much straining of already existing girders and with improvised supports and odd hinges and joints, not all of which dovetailed. One thing we couldn't do was to strip it down and start all over and get it right once and for all. Our bodies are palimpsests because evolution could only modify an anatomy that already existed, and couldn't anticipate environmental upheavals, such as flooding and ice ages — it had to take them as they came.

For example, the spine. About six and a half million years ago, hominids began walking erect. Once we became upright the spine had to change, being previously suited to a horizontal position supported by four legs. How did it change? Among other things, the lower vertebrae grew bigger, to bear the new weight of the upper body. The pelvis rotated, and the iliac blades spread to make plates to hold the awkward bulk of the intestines. Still, we have lower-back pains and hernias, because of pressure on the disks between the vertebrae and because the heavy pudding of the intestines manages to find cracks to squeeze through anyway. And we have other problems, from aspirating food to fainting easily to varicose veins, all stemming from upright posture.

If the version of a monster in industrial society is of a creature constructed from spare parts of corpses, then, again, all of us are monsters, because as we evolved, old structures and parts became used for new functions. So the pores we use for sweating were originally holes through which our formerly more plentiful hair grew. And our sweat-producing glands were evolved from our ancestors' eccrine glands, used to prevent a creature's feet from slipping. Monkeys still have such glands on their palms, and when they sense threat or danger their paws become sticky to ensure a good grip in leaping for a branch. That's why our palms sweat when we're apprehensive.

And goosebumps exist because our ancestors puffed out their bodies and raised their hairs when cold or in danger. When we find ourselves doing the same, the vestigial hairs to which our erectile muscles are still attached don't emerge above the skin, the result being goosebumps.

And armpit sweat contains a vestige of the odor with which our primate forefathers attracted their mates.

And milk glands of women probably began as apocrine glands, which oozed the scented wax our foremothers employed to send sexual signals.

And the hymen is the vestige of a membrane in mammals whose function was to limit sexual activity to the period during which conception was likely.

And so forth. Our bodies may well be cultural constructions, as the feminist philosopher Judith Butler says, but their homemade parts and sedimented scraps can disrupt the most compulsory cultural activities, from cooking to dancing to eating to speaking. The matter of the body erodes or bursts through its cultural performances. The "heavy bear" we lug around (Delmore Schwartz's phrase) is not respectful of occasions. For example, our descended larynx—the product of an upright posture—means we're the only mammal whose windpipe is next to its esophagus. The result can be explosive fits of coughing guaranteed to snuff candles at the most romantic dinners. The locations of body parts are often full of inconveniences. "Love has pitched his mansion in / the place of excrement," says W. B. Yeats. Bad breath undermines eloquence, feet step on feet, noses subvert kisses, and farts punctuate bromides. Recessive genes and genetic mutations don't help. In one rare condition, the heart is reversed and appears on the right-hand side of the body. Just as faulty materials or unstable foundations throw buildings out of plumb, as in the famous Leaning Tower, so our bodies list or drag or keel over, or internally collapse, or wear due to friction.

Early Christian churches were often made from the ruins of pagan temples, and the churches in turn were sometimes retrofitted to become Islamic mosques. Just so, our bodies are made from parts we used to have when we were animals—a whole parade of animals—which is no doubt why, at certain moments, we still are.

ANGEL EYES

Sinatra was singing "Angel Eyes" now—a different sort of vestigial organ, I suppose—as I drove down I-88 past Cooperstown. Mothers tell their children that the shoehorn between the nose and the lip was made by an angel's finger. Shoehorn? It must have a proper name. Quick, my *Britannica*. "The upper or maxillary process grows inward more slowly, but at last joins with the fronto-nasal process, and in the adult the lines of union are seen on each side as ridges of skin which run down from the nostril to the margin of the lip, and enclose that slightly depressed vertical gutter to which the term *philtrum* is given." Volume XVIII, "Mouth," the only water-stained pages in all of my twenty-eight volumes. The brownish crackling paper feels as if it were drooled on sometime between the two world wars.

I'd be home soon. Good. " 'Scuse me while I disappear," says Sinatra's lyric. It was one A.M., and the traffic was so scant I could use the high beams for long stretches.

Angel eyes. Cherry lips. Tin ears, glass jaws, noodles, pussies, puds. There are times you'd think our human bodies might just collapse into a pile. They adjust to the ripples of time, both macro-time, the span of evolution, and micro-time, the segment we're each allotted. And they are the checkpoint crossings between inner dispositions and external circumstance, with the result that the emotional and social obstacles they have to hurdle during their threescore and ten can take quite a toll. Some do collapse back to their infant state of fragmented pieces lost without a home. Some erode, some distend, some tighten, some loosen, some sag, some sadden, some shrink and retire, some grow monstrous, scabby, scaly, or hairy. No wonder we're lonely. No wonder our loneliness is the one thing we share.

CHAP STICK

Five miles from home. The final cut from *Only the Lonely* had finished, and for the past half hour I'd been driving in silence. Wide awake, though. Thirsty, head throbbing. Thumb a dull reflex of low-amp pain. My lips felt inflamed but shriveled and hard, like cracked window putty. I'd seen some Chap Stick somewhere, and checked the little compartments in the dash. The small black and white tube lay behind a roll of quarters my brother had left there, I assume for paying tolls.

It slivered and caked on my lips unpleasantly. All at once it occurred to me that the last person who'd used this Chap Stick was dead. Molecules from his skin now smeared mine. It was almost like kissing him. I saw Paul in my mind, surrounded by flowers — face puddled in satin, soft eyes closed, lips slightly parted.

IV
CORPSE

1

ONE OF US

PAUL DIED in late February, three months before my long drive home in the dark. Peg, my mother's neighbor, phoned to inform me on a Tuesday afternoon. Mom was right there in the kitchen, too stunned to talk. I drove up to Boston the next day, to help with the arrangements.

The wake was scheduled for Friday. By Wednesday evening my mother and I were padding through the carpeted basement of the Flanagan and Roberts Funeral Home, where the caskets were displayed, each with its price discreetly printed on the back of a card on the stand before it. We whispered such comments as "This one's nice," because it seemed appropriate to keep our voices down, although the dead were not present—these copper, mahogany, and oak confections, holding silk and satin froth, were empty depositories.

I knew my mother well; she was following my lead, as I'd followed hers years ago. We strived for the proper mean between extravagance and cheapness, even though Paul was paying. Waste does not enter into these calculations, and no one pictures the fine pleats of silk a year or more later, crawling with mold and stained with nasty fluids.

We'd brought the undertaker a photograph of Paul, a pair of his glasses, his honorable-discharge papers from the army. We'd signed the contract and paid a deposit and endured Tobias Roberts' goodwill and well-oiled manner. He wasn't pallid, he glowed; he wasn't treacly but professional; and when we entered his "home" he behaved as if we were visiting a friend in Mr. Rogers' Neighborhood instead of South Boston. He was tall and barrel-torsoed and, leading us to his office, walked with a gentle roll. I remember thinking that if I'd met him in a grocery store, I'd know he was an undertaker. Unlike teachers, accountants, engineers, or secretaries, an undertaker *is* his profession, and good ones wear its indelible mark with ease and grace — Cain Lites.

Calling hours on Friday were from three to five and from seven to nine. When I pulled into the driveway with Mom and Dad, Tobias Roberts appeared out of nowhere with a wheelchair for my father. It had taken us longer than I'd anticipated to fetch Dad from the nursing home, and we were late. Not to worry; no one was there yet. Mr. Flanagan ("Call me Frank") wheeled my father up the handicap ramp, and I trailed behind with his oxygen bottle, until Frank locked the wheels and, without a word, took the oxygen from me and slid it into a bracket on the back of the chair.

He ushered us inside, where sweet music played through vents in the walls, ether for the ears. Paul was laid out in the casket we'd chosen, at the front of the room, safely distant from the rows of empty chairs. Hannah and the boys would arrive before five, having left New York at ten that morning. My mother's friends, too, would be drifting in soon, or so I supposed. Would friends of Paul's show up? Did he have any? I'd heard of one or two.

Time to say goodbye. Dad went first, with Mom at his side, but he couldn't see much, having slowly gone blind in the past decade. His sedimented illnesses each added to the crush: blindness, emphysema, an enlarged and thickened heart. Congestive heart failure, beneath all the rest, meant that his blood would not circulate properly, the pump being weak, so it backed up in the veins. This in turn forced fluid from his blood vessels into organs and tissues. The tissues swelled — his ankles were enormous — and his lungs, liver, and kidneys were waterlogged, choked with a kind of black rust. Dad was pushing ninety. Longevity was the curse of our family, at least of his generation — to be kept alive and fully conscious in order to experience all those ingenious shipwrecks the body has devised that nonetheless fail to sink you. When he breathed, he wheezed and rattled and glugged. Yet his mind was sharp. All the better to know exactly what was happening.

The blessing of his life was that he fell asleep often.

Frank Flanagan pushed him up to the casket, took away the kneeling rail, then pushed him closer. The occasion was designed to gently milk tears, the kind that serve as balm, and my parents submitted. Paul may have been halfway through his sixties when he died, may have been raised by my grandmother, may have been a recluse, but still he was their child, still got dragged into the world through both of their bodies, ripping flesh as he emerged. And the realization that your child has died before you, the being who'd cut furrows in your soul, whose birth had flushed you out with the deep joy of pain — who, in a sense, had been tied to you for life, especially since he'd never obeyed the biblical injunction to leave father and mother to cleave unto his wife — such knowledge is one of life's worst horrors for parents of any age.

My mother and father had never finished high school. They'd worked all their lives, and in what my father called their "golden years, hah!" had evolved a profound and religious fatalism worthy of Montaigne. Anyone who lives long enough develops a philosophy of life, and those of the educated and powerful are no more wise than those of the poor. My mother usually expressed hers this way: There's nothing I can do about it, so why have a conniption?

Even savvy resignation has its limits, though, when your firstborn dies.

Dad leaned forward in the wheelchair and reached into the coffin and touched Paul's face with the backs of his fingers, then slumped back. Frank pulled the wheelchair away and restored the railing to its place. Then Mom approached, appearing to shrink in the terrible wash of that cosmetic radiation. I reached for her arm, but she sank to the railing and bowed her head. I stood there and watched her shoulders heave, then glanced at Paul and thought, out of nowhere, The gods are present here too.

My mother seemed weak when she finally stood, but gradually regained her command. Her spirit was like four solid tires that would never blow out and whose tread would never wear. She had the soul of a survivor — that is, she felt things deeply, then went on to something else. Having been born long before the post-sixties questioning of women's roles, she'd served men all her life, especially my father, but never assumed the part of the martyr. Her devotion to duty and great capacity for love carried her through, plus her ability to laugh and the comforts of Catholicism. Before his death, Paul and I had finally convinced her she couldn't care for Dad anymore because it would kill her. She was physically incapable of dressing him, placing him on the commode, feeding and washing him, and Paul wasn't much help. In the two years since he'd moved back in with them, he'd spent most of his time sitting on his bed in our old bedroom, mired in various forms of computer solitaire. He'd purchased a Packard-Bell at Sears.

Now Dad was in a nursing home, Paul was dead, and Mom lived alone, but she had countless friends, including neighbors who watched her kitchen window every morning to make sure the light came on.

My turn. I kneeled at the casket and folded my hands and looked at Paul's face and drew a blank. It's true that they do a remarkable job now. No gray-white pallor, no toneless features, no shrunken, flat, or darkened crevices. His was the most inoffensive and natural dead body I'd ever seen, a triumph of the cult of the effigy. He actually looked more healthy in death than in life, having always been somewhat sickly and withdrawn. Because he looked more alive now, he didn't seem dead, just as when he was living he didn't seem quite alive. Have those who don't live, I thought, really died? Then I felt spiteful and arrogant for thinking it.

The thought rebounded. What about me? Have I really lived? And what did I know about Paul's inner life and its richness or poverty? Nothing, really.

The expression on his face was neither happy nor sad, the color of his skin neither sanguine nor pale, the puddled flesh around his jaw neither too soft nor too firm. The large mole between his left eye and ear had distended and spread in the last several years, as his face sagged, but even that looked oddly natural now. I don't think he'd gone to church in at least forty years, but they'd wrapped rosary beads around his folded hands. Tomorrow he would have a funeral mass, and it had taken the priest's most solemn assurances to convince my sainted mother that the Church does not ask questions anymore about the dead person's faith, and all are God's children and therefore welcome in His house.

I clenched my folded hands—he *was* a child of God. Then I told myself he was just a painted corpse, and I went cold as ice. He entered the world as a stranger, and as a stranger left it. He was one of us, I thought.

In the movie *Freaks*, by Tod Browning, the freaks dance around a woman they've horribly mutilated, chanting, "One of us, one of us, ooga-booga, one of us."

I controlled my emotions. Sadness, pity, fear. I stepped out of them as though out of a boat to kneel on the shore, and neither grimaced nor cried. Nor could I pray my usual "God, if you exist . . . ," feeling too hypocritical. Paul lay there, no longer a hermit, an oddball, or a prisoner of his flesh—no longer my brother, nor my parents' son, nor a human being anymore. I thought of his body as a honeycomb of cells from which he'd been released, having served his sentence. His genes were already pickled in formaldehyde, the genes he hadn't passed on. Procreation's the only way to ensure that the dead will resurrect, I thought. In the Gilgamesh epic, those who weep most in the nether-world are those who died without children.

We've all felt our bodies defeating us as we age—our spines curving, grip loosening, walk winded. When he was alive, Paul seemed to have lost every contest with his flesh. He'd always been small, with a head bent forward like a withered thistle on too weak a stalk, and the more he'd buried himself in isolation, the smaller he seemed when he came out. Yet he'd been flabby too, at least in recent years, and loved greasy burgers and fries and onion rings, for the way they stuffed belly and vessels, I assume. There'd been something almost subterranean about him. He often smelled of unwashed clothes, and of something else that reminded me of chicken feed. Yet here he was, presiding over this room as the center of attraction, though it was nearly empty. Already I pictured a few people coming, my parents being consoled, my mother talking with her friends . . . and Paul gradually forgotten.

If history is a vast granite wall a billion miles high and stretching from here to the farthest galaxy, Paul's life was the faintest scratch upon it, smaller than a hair. I'd always found myself, when he was alive, making amends for his strange existence. What was it like to live alone and have no one else to reflect your solitude? Like me, like all of us, he was cloistered in his selfishness, yet unlike most people he appeared to be incapable of joining it to a pack. Suddenly I pictured him in a sort of tilted heaven in which he couldn't stand upright but had to lean against the wall, and I almost smiled. Maybe he would come back to life, I thought, and fling those rosary beads across the empty room —wouldn't that be something! But what did I know? I hardly knew him. I'd been afraid of him, certainly, afraid of what his life had become. But in fact, what was it? I was not telepathic, and Paul's casket would not be provided with a phone (as Mary Baker Eddy's was) with which he could call and fill me in on the details.

When I went off to college, he mailed me a dollar a week for every week I didn't smoke. Fifty-two dollars a year, each arriving in an envelope with no note or message. I continued to smoke for two or three years while spending Paul's money and then, after he'd stopped mailing me the dollars, gave up cigarettes. He himself smoked unfiltered Kools all his life, until the day he died.

I too was tied to him, I realized, like my parents. He was flesh of my flesh.

When he was born, did the universe summon him? Did it create its own need for him out of itself, beckon his tiny organism forth from the ocean of space, entice and threaten and cajole him into existence out of pure nothingness? And if it did—if it habitually does this sort of thing—does it ever, spiritually speaking, leave the job unfinished, so that someone may be said to exist, but not exist enough? Perhaps the souls of some people are small, like their hands. It could be that some of us are dragged into the world like nets dragged onto shore with just a handful of fish. Some plants sprout already carrying the eggs that will become the worms that eat them. And for some human beings, perhaps a little bit of soul, like lint or pollen, clings to their meager drops of fat, but not very much.

Or are souls, like legal rights, not admissible of quantity?

Fullness of being guarantees immortality, thought Goethe. "If I work on unceasingly till my death, nature is bound to give me another form of being when the present one can no longer sustain my spirit." Yet poverty of being guarantees immortality too, Christ told us on the Mount. Eeny meeny miney mo.

Withdraw from the world, go ahead, Paul, I thought. Let it go to the devil. Throw down a challenge to the universe—notice me if you can. Try as hard as you can to notice me. You won't.

Well, there it was. I was almost crying now, despite my defensive irony.

There is no permanence, I thought, not even for those who withdraw and curl up and try not to change, and therefore not to die. The weary and old must be replaced by the vigorous and young, we all know this, because as Tennyson put it, we wouldn't want the world to grow moldy with age. So all of us are programmed to self-destruct, and someday I'd lay in a casket like Paul, although I'd already decided that cremation would be better.

I guess I should be thankful. If no one died, eventually we'd have to ensure that no one be born, lest the world grow too crowded. With a reproductive rate of zero, there could be no evolutionary change. Natural selection requires that variations be selected out, that they become extinct, but how can they be selected if there is no death? As Arnold Toynbee said, "Death is the price paid by life for an enhancement of the complexity of a live organism's structure."

All at once I felt the others staring at my back. How long had I been kneeling there? Just a few seconds, really. Time stops in such moments. It had stopped for Paul forever, but Messrs. Flanagan and Roberts had managed to prolong it with the science of their profession.

2

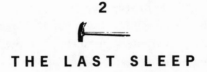

THE LAST SLEEP

ABRAHAM LINCOLN WAS shot on April 14, 1865, died on April 15, and lay in an open coffin in the East Room of the White House on April 18. On April 19, he was moved to the Rotunda of the Capitol, and on April 21 put on a train that traveled for 1,700 miles, first on a loop through Baltimore, Harrisburg, Philadelphia, and New York, then north through Albany, Utica, and Syracuse, then west through Cleveland, Columbus, Indianapolis, and Chicago. Its destination was Springfield, Illinois, where three weeks later he was finally buried.

Three weeks! He lay in state in various tents and public buildings at every stop along the way. Bonfires and flags lined the route, stations were draped in black, the train passed beneath arches of evergreens, and mobs held up portraits of the President wreathed in pine boughs.

It was a long and slow goodbye. By the time the funeral train arrived in Ohio, two weeks after Lincoln's death, reporters had begun to comment on the shrunken and decayed condition of his face. Some suggested that good taste required the authorities to close the coffin. Putrefaction had not set in, not completely, but imperfect embalming had. An embalmer who accompanied the train had "improved" the face several times, between stops, but apparently his improvements only made matters worse.

Arterial embalming had first been practiced about a hundred years earlier. But in the United States it hadn't been used extensively until the Civil War. Lincoln himself had charged a certain Thomas Holmes with devising a way to preserve the bodies of Union soldiers long enough to transport them north from southern battlefields. Popular histories call Holmes the Father of American Embalming, but he had plenty of competitors, some of whom claimed that Holmes's chemicals left corpses discolored. Whether this was one of Lincoln's problems isn't clear; the offended were discreet.

When he first lay in state, moreover, the tasteful were impressed. A reporter for the *New York World*, George Alfred Townsend, said of Lincoln's embalmer, "He has not changed one line of his grave, grotesque countenance, nor smoothed out a single feature. The hue is rather bloodless and leaden, but he was always sallow. . . . The white satin around it reflects sufficient light upon the face to show that death is really there." Townsend then described the embalming itself, a process that hasn't substantially changed since Lincoln's death; my brother's body had been similarly treated. His skull was sliced off and the brain removed, blood drained from the body through the jugular vein, and the empty blood vessels charged with a "chemical preparation" through an incision in the thigh. What this preparation was, Townsend didn't specify. Formaldehyde wasn't used until 1893. The pioneer of arterial embalming, William Hunter of England (1718–1783), used essential oils, alcohol, cinnabar, camphor, saltpeter, and pitch or rosin.

PURITY OF HEART

Thomas Holmes, on the other hand, was said to use zinc chloride and arsenic. He charged $100 each for embalming Union soldiers, and the war made him rich. He himself was said to be well preserved: lean and square-shouldered, with a full Prussian mustache, short wiry hair, and Rasputin eyes. A textbook exemplar of Kierkegaard's definition of purity of heart, he buttonholed others with the passion of someone who willed one thing all his life.

The one thing was to stem the tide of putrefaction that resulted from death. But in pursuit of this goal, he trailed behind him a wake of rotten corpses. He was kicked out of New York University's School of Medicine for leaving bodies around in inconvenient places—on professors' desks, for example—having walked off and forgotten them, he explained, in the heat of his studies. After his death a number of corpses were found in his cellar, and for a while police thought they'd discovered a nineteenth-century version of our John Wayne Gacy. But all were found to be wards from the city's orphanages, who were given to Holmes after their deaths for his experiments.

During his lifetime, he kept bodies in closets and bodies in cellars and displayed the embalmed head of a man in a glass case in his drugstore. The head and shoulders of a fourteen-year-old girl sat on his living room table. In the window of his drugstore, on a marble slab, lay a human arm, preserved, said a sign, by Innominata, his secret recipe for embalming. The sign also claimed that "invalids traveling by land or sea can now carry with them all that is necessary to insure the return of their bodies in a perfect state of preservation," thanks to Innominata, $3 the gallon.

During the war, he embalmed more than four thousand soldiers, but favored officers over enlisted men. Brigadier Generals Farnsworth, Rice, and Stevenson were all embalmed by Holmes, enabling public ceremonies to be held that turned out to be rehearsals for Lincoln's rite. Robert Wilkins, in *The Bedside Book of Death*, suggests that Holmes himself embalmed Lincoln, but the historical record doesn't bear him out.

When Lincoln was shot, arterial embalming may have been a novelty, but embalming itself was as old as the Egyptians. Herodotus writes that practitioners of this "distinct profession" in ancient Egypt removed brains by means of hooks pushed through the nostrils, and flushed out with drugs what they couldn't reach, the brain being considered an insignificant organ. They opened the torso and removed all the plumbing, then dehydrated the body by packing it inside and out with natron. Body cavities were then repacked with the viscera and stuffed with various ingredients, including sawdust, bundles of resin-soaked cloth, and sometimes onions and lichens. Then resin was poured in and the openings sealed with wax.

Arterial embalming, as proposed by William Hunter, simplified and improved this process by employing the body's inner meshwork of blood vessels. Hunter could not have devised his method without the work of William Harvey and Marcello Malpighi one hundred years before him. By chopping up frogs, they demonstrated that the vascular system included capillaries that permeated all the tissues of the body. So embalming materials now could work from the inside out instead of the outside in.

BEETLES

In his *New York World* description of Lincoln's embalming, George Townsend pointed out the obvious: this was not Lincoln anymore, but his effigy or replica. "All that we see of Abraham Lincoln, so cunningly contemplated in this splendid coffin, is a mere shell, an effigy, a sculpture. He lies in a sleep, but it is the sleep of marble. All that made this flesh vital, sentient and affectionate, is gone forever."

Effigy: a likeness, portrait, image. From the Latin *effigies*, something fashioned. To hang, burn, or execute in effigy is "to inflict upon an image the semblance of the punishment which the original is considered to have deserved; formerly done by way of carrying out a judicial sentence on a criminal who had escaped" (*Oxford English Dictionary*). So effigies represent absent bodies.

But they represent present bodies too, albeit bodies hollowed out by absence—by death. If a corpse is a presence embodying an absence, so are effigies, which makes embalmed corpses the epitome of effigies. Embalming began as the determined project to fashion from the dead a replica of the living. Not only was an Egyptian king emptied out—his brains and viscera removed—but his face was coated with resin and his body painted red with a mixture of ocher and gum. Artificial eyes were inserted in his sockets and, often, artificial hair attached to his head. The heads of early mummies were modeled with pastes or plaster; later, portrait masks were used. The idea was to make the corpse an idealized dwelling for the *ka,* the double or spirit, which had left the corpse behind. To reoccupy its body, the *ka* had to recognize it; if it did, then resurrection was assured. So it was wise to multiply one's chances. The corpse was painted and plastered, and the resulting mummy, wrapped in linen, was sealed up in several more effigies: one or two anthropomorphic coffins nested inside each other, as well as a mummy board, which covered the mummy and was painted identically to the coffins. The paintings showed the person inside, or his idealized effigy, eyes wide open, arms, like the mummy's, crossed at the chest, and robe covered with images and text from the *Book of the Dead.*

Among the prominent pictures on Egyptian coffins, one stands out: a scarab beetle pushing a disk of the sun. Real scarab beetles, we know, have been pushing balls of dung through the desert for millennia. Beetles born from seemingly lifeless dung naturally led the Egyptians to identify them with resurrection. And a beetle pushing the sun ahead of it often represented Ra, the sun god, reborn each morning in the sky.

In 1981, anatomists at the University of Bristol unwrapped a mummy whose coffin displayed the scarab beetle once above the crossed hands and four more times down the length of the body. Parts of the mummy were so well preserved that the Somerset police could take its fingerprints—but parts crumbled to dust as they were being unwrapped. The reason for the deterioration was insect damage. Three-thousand-year-old beetles were found perfectly preserved in the mummy's wrappings, and the Bristol scientists concluded that beetles had laid eggs in the corpse sometime during the embalming process, when it was exposed. In photographs, their carapaces make them indistinguishable from living beetles. They are as good an example of successful auto-effigies as anything we have from the ancient world, and—who knows?—with their body-length cases, they might have been the first inspiration for Egyptian mummies and coffins.

STUFFED KINGS

Some cultures set aside the corpses of their dead and fashion separate effigies, often stuffed with straw and intended for ritual immolation. When we think of effigies we think of straw, or wax. In ancient Rome, a wax mask of the deceased was worn by an actor during funeral processions. He imitated the dead man's mannerisms and gestures, while additional actors, also wearing wax masks, portrayed his ancestors welcoming the newly dead. In Sumatra, wooden dolls—effigies of the deceased—dance at their own funerals.

One culture that has left behind detailed records of its elaborate funeral practices buries its kings in three separate coffins: one for the corpse, one for the heart, one for the entrails. For a week, vigils and religious rites are held in the presence of these coffins (their presence being magical), then the heart and entrails are interred to the chants and songs of the tribe. Meanwhile, an effigy of the dead king is being made, a kind of stuffed doll. The limbs and trunk are made of wicker, and the head and hands are molded of wax, with hair attached by putty and face realistically painted. Mimetic realism was important to these people, and mimesis itself might therefore be thought of as based on death.

The effigy is dressed in linen and satin, with leg stockings of linen interwoven with gold, a cloak or mantle on its shoulders, and a large collar made of animal fur. Propped up, it presides in a sort of great hall for a number of days, and twice a day the nobility of the tribe assembles in its presence to eat. Then the king's effigy is removed, the coffin with the corpse brought in, and the hall of honor becomes a hall of mourning. Only now can the son and heir come forth to grieve for his father. He does so in his capacity as son, not successor. The son of the dead king in effect now rules; he issues orders and decrees, and directs all the arrangements for the funeral. But he wears purple instead of red —the king's color—and when he leaves the hall he terminates his unofficial mourning by ritually giving his purple cloak away. Furthermore, the son can't be present when the effigy is present, for the same reason that the effigy could not be in the same place as the coffin: because it is a legal and metaphysical impossibility for two kings to exist simultaneously. And the effigy, in fact, is king of the tribe until the son is invested as ruler.

Two days later, in the funeral procession, the effigy is back and the son and heir gone. The effigy is treated like the king himself marching triumphantly through the community, because that's what he is. Even in the procession, the coffin and effigy never appear together. The coffin goes first, amid trappings of a private funeral for a distinguished man, as opposed to those of a public funeral for a king. Representatives of the dead king's family (minus the son) walk behind the coffin in deep mourning. The effigy is carried at the end of the procession, arrayed in full kingly regalia and surrounded by retainers. And accounts of this ceremony all agree that the effigy cannot be distinguished from the "real" king by people just a few feet away.

This culture, incidentally, is that of early modern Europe. The tribe is the French, and the seven-week ceremony I've just described is the funeral of Francis I, in 1547.

RAGGED REGIMENT

"She looks like wax," we sometimes hear, or think, at wakes. That may be because wax has been used to "improve" her face. Lincoln's embalmer used wax. Like the French, the English for centuries displayed waxen effigies of kings and queens after their deaths. The English believed the king had two bodies, a natural body and a body politic — the latter not subject to decay and death — and this became the basis of their use of effigies at state funerals. When Henry V died — the English king who was heir presumptive of France — his effigy was paraded through France, whose people subsequently adopted the customs described above. England, however, never felt the need to spatially separate effigy and corpse, as the French did. The effigy was placed on the coffin, to be paraded at the funeral, then displayed at Westminster Abbey after the burial.

By the eighteenth century, when the practice had ended in England, the surviving effigies could be seen propped against the wall in the upper section of Bishop Islip's chapel in the Abbey, as though no one quite knew what to do with them. Horace Walpole described them as those "curious but mangled figures . . . now called the ragged regiment." By World War II, they'd made it to the basement, which was flooded in the bombing of London, and the wax, canvas, straw, and plaster became subject to the ravages of rot every bit as much as natural bodies.

The practice of constructing royal effigies ended in the eighteenth century because William Hunter's discovery of arterial embalming enabled royal corpses to become their own effigies. The old wax and straw effigies had accomplished two contradictory tasks: to delay a king's burial and to circumvent putrefaction. Delay was a practice often recommended to the sensitive, to reassure them that they would not be buried alive by mistake. Putrefaction provided that assurance, but was offensive to survivors. So: effigies on the one hand and sealed coffins on the other. Only arterial embalming could accomplish these apparently incompatible aims. Some doctors even recommended embalming as the ultimate insurance against premature burial, on the theory that the first cut would waken any comatose person.

Fear of premature burial seems to have mostly disappeared with modern medicine, but in centuries preceding the twentieth, and in most cultures, it was no laughing matter. Edgar Allan Poe exploited this fear in his story "The Premature Burial," and entrepreneurs in the nineteenth century invented all sorts of devices to guard against it, from nipple pincers to test fresh corpses; to waiting mortuaries, popular in Germany, in which corpses, smothered in flowers as they waited to be embalmed, lay with a finger attached to a string leading to a bell in an adjoining room, where a vigilant custodian listened for a ring; to the German Count Karnice-Karnicki's invention in 1896 of a tube leading out of a buried coffin to a box with a flag and bell in the cemetery above. The slightest movement of a buried person's chest would be detected by delicate machinery, which would trip the flag and ring the bell. The tube would amplify cries for help.

AUTO-ICON

Still, wax effigies never completely died out. Jeremy Bentham, who coined the phrase "the greatest happiness for the greatest numbers," lived with one foot in the eighteenth and one in the nineteenth century. He is best remembered as a founder of utilitarianism, and forgotten as the man who first proposed the Suez and Panama canals. In recent years, Michel Foucault has demonized Bentham as the inventor of the panopticon for the central surveillance of convicts, Foucault's chief image of the disciplinary society. Followers of Foucault who wish to vilify Bentham may do so in person, by the way—he was never buried. Bentham may be seen in a permanent display at University College, London.

Bentham's book on the preservation of corpses, *Auto-Icon*, declared that the human body, when dissected, "instead of being an object of disgust is as much more beautiful than any other piece of mechanism as it is more curious and wonderful." He envisioned future worlds in which burials would be obsolete, and preserved corpses, or auto-icons, would sit in temples of remembrance, their "habiliments" protected from decay by Indian rubber. By means of auto-icons, historical events could be represented and even reenacted, not by wax models, as in Madame Tussaud's museum, but by the historical figures themselves. "If a country gentleman have rows of trees leading to his dwelling, the auto-icons of his family might alternate with the trees; copal varnish would protect the face from the effects of rain."

It is a singular historical distinction to pioneer a social movement of one. Bentham became the first and only auto-icon. As directed in his will, his corpse was first publicly disassembled by a surgeon, Dr. Southward Smith, then his bones were wired together, his body packed with hay, seated, and dressed in Bentham's best clothes. The head was, according to Bentham's directions, treated "after the manner of the New Zealanders"—that is, desiccated, to be fastened on the effigy. But after standing it in a pan of sulfuric acid and using an air pump to draw away the fluids, Smith ruefully observed that all its facial expression had fled. Bentham had carried in his pocket for the past twenty years a pair of glass eyes, and these were mounted in the sockets, but unfortunately provided no relief from disgust. His dried head was not beautiful, curious, or wonderful, and was consequently placed between the feet. A wax head was made, and a capacious

Panama hat placed on top, and a cane wedged in one hand—then the auto-icon was installed in its glass case at University College. (The real head was later stored in a box in a university vault.) By Bentham's directions, his auto-icon was for a number of years wheeled in to be present at meetings of those societies formed by his friends and disciples, "for the purpose of commemorating the founder of the greatest Happiness System of Morals and Legislation." Apparently, he was also there for several meetings of the university's board, whose minutes note "Mr. Bentham present but not voting."

THE LAST SLEEP

Barbara Jones calls Egypt and the United States the "two great embalming cultures." She points out what many historians of American funerals do, that the Civil War created a class of skilled specialists trained in the preservation of corpses. With preserved corpses, ceremonies of remembrance for ordinary people could become mini-extravaganzas—compared to Lincoln's maxi one—and thus the "whole curious American funeral" began.

But she leaves out one step, as most other historians do. American wakes and funerals didn't take their present form until around 1900. In the thirty-five years between the Civil War and the new century, photography came into its own. The early years of photography coincided with the war, which cemented, in the photographs of Mathew Brady, Alexander Gardner, and others, the partnership between photography and death.

That partnership still thrives, as evidenced by books like Michael Lesy's *Wisconsin Death Trip,* Luc Sante's *Evidence,* Stanley Burns's *Sleeping Beauties,* Barbara Norfleet's *Looking at Death,* and countless others: collections of mug shots, crime shots, medical and posmortem photographs, shots of accidents and disasters, of battlefields and morgues, depictions of bodies and faces chemically bleached of the erotic, or silvered with sentiment, in the postures, both posed and surprised, of death. The wonder of it lies in the absence of wonder.

Photography creates stillness out of motion and repose out of violence; it snatches memory from the amnesia of time, and preserves in light what decays and rots and sinks from view back into earth's darkness. Its solutions, like the embalmer's, are chemical, and like the embalmer it makes effigies of bodies. In fact, the dead made ideal subjects for early photographers, who were spared the necessity of warning them to keep still.

Photos are not just representations, not mirrors, not the apogee of scientific realism; they are effigies, fashioned to replicate the dead and preserve them for the living.

These twin legacies of the Civil War, photography and embalming, worked in tandem to produce American funeral practices, especially the wake. In the second half of the nineteenth century, the postmortem portrait was one of a photographer's chief means of employment, like weddings today. For the wealthy, a tradition of summoning an artist to paint a portrait of the dead in a pose of restful sleep preceded such photos, as grotesquely dramatized in Flaubert's *Madame Bovary*. Photography was cheaper and quicker, and therefore less macabre. The Boston firm of Southworth & Hawes advertised miniatures of "Deceased Persons either at our rooms or at private residences. . . . We take great pains to have Miniatures of Deceased Persons agreeable and satisfactory, and they are often so natural as to seem, even to Artists, in a deep sleep."

Most people die with their mouths and eyes open, a phenomenon disconcerting to the living of all cultures. Traditionally, eyes have been closed to ward off the evil eye or to prevent ghosts from returning to the body through its openings. A face arranged with its eyes and mouth closed suggests sleep, of course, especially when the Deceased Person lies on a bed or is recumbent on a sofa. So "The Last Sleep" became a staple of nineteenth-century photography, and often served as the title of postmortem photos. For a time, photography democratized the effigy, once the exclusive property of kings and aristocrats. Photography enabled ordinary people to memorialize their lives too — it distinguished the undistinguished. The bedroom and the parlor were the usual settings for postmortem photographs, precursors of funeral parlors and their "slumber rooms."

Democratic practices often find themselves absorbed by a mercantile economy and the cult of the professional. By the time undertaking was professionalized, after 1880, and funeral "directors" replaced family members in laying out the dead, and funeral "homes" became common, the iconography and ideology of wakes and funerals were already in place, thanks to photography. "One idea should always be kept in mind," said W. P. Hohenschuh, author of *The Modern Funeral* (1907), "that is to lay out the body so that there will be as little suggestion of death as possible." The only alternative, then, was sleep.

Hohenschuh also advocated the use of clothes worn in life instead of shrouds or winding cloths, and the application of cosmetics to make the flesh look not only natural but healthy. Wakes and funerals as Americans know them today quickly took their present form, and strangely dovetailed with our hospital culture. Today we die in hospitals amid persons with whom we conspire to pretend we aren't really dying. Then, once dead, we're magically restored to the appearance of health, all the more significant in a society for which health is salvation.

Kneeling before Paul, I noted how rosy his cheeks appeared to be. Rouge had been applied, plus rose-colored lighting. His eyes were closed but the desiccated lids did not telegraph the pupils, thanks to eye caps. His mouth looked relaxed, with lips slightly parted, having been carefully sewn in this position. His white teeth, painted with transparent nail polish, positively gleamed, and his nostrils, stuffed with plastic pellets, hadn't collapsed as dead nostrils do. He really did look alive, or close enough to it. Of course no one at a wake actually thinks the dead aren't in fact dead. The wake is a fiction to which we willingly submit, a memorial tableau centered on an effigy. And the technology of wakes—the tissue builders, creams, the cotton padding in the cheeks, the "demisurgery" that restores a broken morphology—all contribute to an effect we know perfectly well is just that, an effect. The fear erased by embalming is not the fear of death but one conceivably worse, of being buried alive. In American wakes, this fear becomes aestheticized, and death's utter strangeness becomes a solemn cartoon—and those who grieve most may discover themselves also uncannily suppressing laughter.

Culture achieves the triumph of its power to inscribe the corporeal when we are dead. Bodies, however, don't always cooperate. Their biology can be a volcanic eruption overwhelming our modest cultural scribbles. So in the final battle between culture and nature, surprise—nature wins. American methods of embalming—combined with airtight coffins and waterproof vaults—usually result in accelerated decay once the theatrics are done, because anaerobic bacteria flourish in such environments.

We are, in life, walking, talking crematoriums and incubators. Cells in our bodies and bacteria just along for the ride continually die, while others, their offspring, are born and multiply. Microorganisms are dead when they've irreversibly lost the ability to reproduce. We're killing them all the time by washing our hands, by brushing our teeth, by ingesting antibiotics. They die so we can live; but when *we* die, they thrive. Like a clan of never-ending Snopeses, they throw a perpetual house party in our bodies, and inevitably wind up burning the place down. Decay produces heat, after all. Dr. Brouardel of turn-of-the-century Paris pricked his corpses with needles to let the gases escape, then set fire to the holes and watched the long bluish flames burn off the products of decomposition.

One more step toward the deep freeze.

3

TELESCOPE

HEAD STILL BOWED, I took a last look at Paul and stood without turning, secretly happy to be alive. Yet a moment later I felt guilty and depressed. Certain smiles begin inside—their stirrings are autoerotic, it seems—but the neutral, serious, protective frown that gives nothing away is a social practice learned over years. I composed my mouth into such a frown, then turned and walked back to join my parents, conscious of Messrs. Flanagan and Roberts hovering at doorways or gliding through hallways. Paul's coffin had plenty of flowers to sweeten it, some on top, some on stands. Twenty feet away, the rows of empty chairs began. All was subdued and tastefully dull, all carpeted and cushioned and curtained and softened, with a touch of wealth and quality—brown, black, and beige. At the back of the room, an accordioned wall could be opened for large wakes, but not for this one. A walk-in closet would have sufficed for this one. At last someone showed up, a cousin I'd nearly forgotten existed. It was almost four o'clock.

It hadn't occurred to me that relatives would come. I should have known Mom would call them. Most lived near Worcester, or in Maine or New Hampshire, and some I hadn't seen in decades. Once Hannah and the boys arrived we'd have a respectable handful. Actually, I thought, they should have been here by now. It gave me something to fret about. Meanwhile, at the head of the room, Paul lay there in effigy, claiming his fifteen minutes of fame. If you turned in that room you oriented your body toward his—shoulders perpendicular, shoulders parallel. He was not designed to be forgotten today. We would bury him tomorrow and so bury our sorrow, *then* resume our lives and forget him.

Spilling forward like a pot of spaghetti, Tobias Roberts approached.

He was very tall, six four at least, and rowed with his arms and paddled with his hands like someone in an inner tube strapped down with sacks of ballast. Since guests were now arriving, he suggested that my parents and I arrange ourselves in a reception line, to the Departed's right. First came Paul, then the table for spiritual bouquets, then at a proper distance Mom and I standing and Dad in his wheelchair. "And could you remind guests to sign the register in the hallway?" he asked.

"Why not bring it in here next to the body?" I suggested. "That way they won't miss it."

"Beside the Deceased?" He smiled and shook his head, as if pitying my ignorance.

"Why not?"

"We've never done it that way. These people have been to plenty of wakes. It would be unusual."

What people? I thought. But what I said was, "If they've been to lots of wakes, they won't forget to sign the register."

"There you go." He seemed suddenly indifferent. Clearly, this colloquy hadn't been important. It was something for him to do, as director.

My cousin, a retired schoolteacher from Weymouth, talked with my mother, who was becoming animated. Mom touched her arm, from which Mo's large purse hung. I caught Mo (for Maureen) sneaking glances at me, next in line, and I felt like a child about to endure the kisses of an aunt who would smell of talcum powder. All of my cousins were older than me, the baby of the family.

Like Paul, Mo had been a sort of recluse. She'd never married and, according to my mother, had once lived alone with three or four dozen cats. About ten years ago she'd gone off for work and left her electric blanket on. The cats piled on the bed, the blanket caught fire, and the house burned down.

I kissed her on the cheek. Hers was coarse with bristles. She asked if my family were coming today.

"On the way," I said, checking my watch.

"How long a drive is it?"

"Six or seven hours."

More people walked in, members of my mother's Women's Club. Mo pulled up a chair and sat beside my father. Mom, looking flushed, greeted all her friends. Her voice could be heard over everyone else's. "Where is she?" she shouted, then looked around blushing, hand across her mouth.

To my left, my father and Mo talked softly. Her square face and mannish lips reminded me of my grandmother. Faces are maps not of space but of time, each one imperfect, as though an ideal set of features lived somewhere behind them. Behind Paul, myself, and Mo were my father and his siblings, including Nancy, Mo's mother. Grandma, whose face now sits above my desk, was the distant continent all our features mapped, yet her face also charted others farther off, ones I'd never know. In the photo I'm looking at as I write this sentence, the map of Grandma's skin looks frayed and torn, just like my father's now. Their faces both resemble deflated parachutes that once billowed with time, but not anymore. They couldn't bear anyone's weight anymore.

My grandma has been dead a long time, but I remember her well. Once, when a child, I'd stayed with her for a week, though under exactly what circumstances I still can't recall. Were my parents on a trip? Working people then did not take long trips. Also, where was Paul? I can remember Grandma's house outside Worcester, in Wire Valley, remember her pulling me from closet to closet searching for something to occupy my time, a game or a book. She accused my aunt Liddie of stealing her Victrola, but it was right there in the bathroom on its own table. I can remember the town and how, out of boredom, in the middle of July, I found an old American Flyer sled in the barn behind the house and dragged it up Ash Street. Amused neighbors bent down to cute little me as though to a fishbowl and smiled in my face and said, Expecting snow?

But I can't remember Paul.

He must have been there. He'd been raised by Grandma. He was there when we visited every weekend of my childhood, but in a sense I can't recall him. I don't mean to imply he was chained in the attic. He was probably around, trying not to be noticed. In my memory now, his slumped and fading body blends into Grandma's, as if squatting in her soul, a frog on a chopping block. Their postures were similar. Her ghost imprisons his. Grandma was small and wore wallpaper dresses and blends into the shadows of all our old photos — in the shadows with Paul.

In high school, I was cool. In less than a year I went from an Elvis pompadour to a buzzcut, hooded sweatshirt, chinos, and what we then called desert boots. I habitually spent my weekends with friends drinking pints of Southern Comfort poured into quart bottles of ginger ale, and who in their right mind would give up such a life? That's why I cringed in the fall of my senior year when Paul made plans to spend the weekend in his microbus, to conduct his oracular ham-radio ceremonies, and my mother insisted he take me with him. Who knew for what reason? — parents too have their secrets — but I had to go along, and Paul had to take me, at least this one weekend.

He was going to New Hampshire, as it turned out, and beside me on Route 3 he hardly said a thing. Having recently bought my first transistor radio — which I hadn't taken along, since he hated rock 'n' roll — I asked him the difference between transistors and tubes. I'd spotted a box of tubes in the back, neatly stored on a shelf in the midst of his equipment.

"Well. They're both something like valves. They filter interference. They pass or block the current depending on, you know. But tubes get wicked hot and burn out like light bulbs and transistors don't, but they work just as good. They're small, they don't break. They last a lot longer. That's about the size of it."

I couldn't think of what to say. "They're just as good—transistors?"
"Your tubes pretty soon will go the way of the dinosaurs."
"So transistors are better."
"Of course they're better. That's what I just said."

In New Hampshire, he parked on top of a hill near an open shelter with barbecue pits, picnic tables, pit toilets, and a wide grassy slope open to the sky. Pine trees and birches surrounded this place, but their tops were all beneath us. No one else was around. It was Friday evening—we'd left just as soon as I arrived home from school. Fishbone clouds turned red in the sky and darkness leaked up from the universe around us while Paul pulled his generator out of the bus and set up his gear. With the bus's doors open and a Coleman lantern on the ground, he unfolded a card table and erected on its top a small city of equipment, complete with dials, jacks, buttons, switches, green and red lights, meters, and wires. On top of the bus he fixed a tall whip antenna, then sat on a folding aluminum chair, microphone in hand, and launched himself into the airwaves.

Meanwhile, I wandered through the parking lot and searched the picnic shelters and tried out the toilets. Once it was dark, I came back to the bus and sat in the driver's seat to practice shifting gears. Paul ignored me. Through storms of squeals and hisses, fading in and out, came amplified voices of solitary men, the cowboys of night skies, who sounded as though they were talking into tin cans. Some engaged in conversation with Paul, then faded out, then others took over, but how much of this was by design I couldn't quite grasp. He jotted down what appeared to be vital statistics in an open notebook. "Read you, EHF," a voice said. "Still can't get many local stations on fifteen meters. Guess it goes right over them. Over."

"Not much QRM on this end," said Paul. "Your Kenwood's knocking me out up here. So the rumor of hams in Vermont was true. I have a very solid copy. Over."

I opened the door and walked into the field. The stars were coming out, a storm of electric popcorn and discord, like the sounds of Paul's radio—which I couldn't escape—and like his generator's blare, both of which, along with the stars, I assume in retrospect were order in disguise. At the far end of the parking lot a few cars pulled in—no doubt teenagers going parking. How I envied them. It would be a cold night, I could tell that already. I'd never seen a sky so shattered by light, so large and overwhelming. Only three feet away, yet it was unreachable. In Boston we never had skies like that, not even while sleeping on neighbors' flat roofs in the dog days of August, or on City Point Beach.

"Anyhow, I wound up with a tech," I heard. "Do you copy? Over."

"Yeah, I read you," said Paul. "Sometimes I wonder how I ever made it. Band right now seems to be slipping. You didn't tell me your rig. Over."

"Still read you. Band won't hold much longer. HR Heath, HW 101 and full wave. Delta loop. Sounds like your XYL's making french fries. Could be that generator. Anyhoo, congrats on your General ticket, Paul. I tried last year but missed the code pretty bad. Far as I can see, that's a relic of the past. Who needs it anymore, I say. Over."

"I read you on that. But suppose they drop the Big One. Over."

"No need, no need. We're all radio active. Over."

"Har har *har*-dy har har. I'll tell that one to all my friends in Boston. Have to drive back Sunday, over."

"Hey, I might join you, my friend. Any jobs down that way? I'm close to busted. Can't feed catfish dogfood no more. Over to you."

"Much QRM on this end. Have to 73 soon. Please QSL. Over."

"Did you copy my address? Still read me? Over."

"Barely. Yes I did. These small towns up here—I know what you mean. I'm on a kick I call WATWOS, Work All Towns Without Sidewalks. Anyway, Clyde, you take care of yourself. Enjoyed the QSO and the jokes. Keep up the good work. Hope we can do it again the near future. I sure do enjoy chewing the rag. God bless. Over and out."

This last part was rattled off quickly, by rote. It was how he ended all

156 · A BOOK OF REASONS

his transmissions. Sometime later the moon rose, and sometime after that I retrieved my sleeping bag from the bus and found the very highest spot of the hill and threw the bag on the grass and crawled inside with my clothes on, and fell asleep on my back in the glow of the universe.

We pan-fried bacon and eggs the next day. Then Paul took off and left me there to mind his stuff. We'd slept until noon, and it was almost dark again by the time he returned, with burgers and hot dogs wrapped in greasy newspaper, and with a present for me. He held out a large paper bag. Said he'd driven all the way to Nashua to find it, knew a hobby shop there. I took the bag and looked inside. A telescope. Gee. I didn't know what to say. He'd never given me anything before, except the usual twenty dollars at Christmas. "Hey, thanks," I said.

He almost looked embarrassed. "I saw you out there looking at the stars." It hadn't seemed to me he'd even known I'd come along, let alone where I was. He stood there with a squeamish smile, mouth firmly closed, then turned around to refill his generator with gas from a container, leaving me to myself.

I felt strange about this telescope. It looked pretty expensive. Instinctively I knew that a gift like this wouldn't let me dislike him as much as I wanted to. And suddenly I saw a new side to Paul. He was naturally disdainful toward inferiors like me, his kid brother, but obsequious to superiors — his whole manner expressed it. So he gave gifts gruffly, having no other way to show his need to be liked. He never seemed to know what to say to me, as I didn't to him, and our conversations quickly petered out, unlike those he conducted on his ham radio. The message was clear: forget about me, enjoy the telescope instead. I willingly did. I assumed that's the way a gift should operate; it should erase the giver.

Later, I saw him hunched at his table in the light from the lantern, attached to his machinery by straps and wires like Mary Shelley's monster — or, I mused, like my mother in her beauty parlor. When I was a child and Mom got her hair done, I waited in a back room doing jigsaw puzzles. That night, instead, I examined the moon, looking through my telescope at its jigsaw shadows. The sound of Paul's equipment and of his transmissions had become a white noise rebounding off the moon—perfect silence, in a sense. The moon looked to me then like a flat communion wafer being nibbled on by mice. But I've since learned what the moon really is. It's where the dead go to live their porous lives, lives through which experience blows like the dust in ghost towns.

By consulting the instruction book and charts, I managed to locate a tiny image of Saturn. The telescope had a short tripod, and I had to bend down to look up through it. For relief, I stood straight and surveyed the sky with naked eye. I felt ridiculously happy, beyond all measure—thanks to Paul, I realized. Back and forth I went, bending down to the telescope, standing erect, expecting something extraordinary to happen—a flying saucer to zoom past, and a parachute to bloom from it. The universe revealed its hidden architecture, its anatomy, its secret insides. Yet I'd never felt more *outside* in my life, never more thrust up into the sky, on a promontory of Earth. Once, as I was emerging from the telescope, a shooting star chalked its line across the sky, and it stayed there awhile, written on the blackness like a photoelectric impression on a retina. I still wonder what I saw, the thing itself or its ghost.

At last Hannah and our boys showed up, the kids looking around and blinking in that room and generally disoriented like people gone snow-blind. They'd been driving for six hours, which rubberizes equilibrium, but also the boys had never been to a wake. Paul's death is what blinded them. They couldn't see to see.

Hannah, as always, looked fresh and beautiful in that room of sugared death. We kissed. She stepped back and peered into my face. I felt people watching. "You okay?" she asked.

I nodded.

I'd been watching our sons and had one of those moments of frozen terror far worse than reflecting on one's own mortality—instead, it was a zero-at-the-bone sense of my children's mortality. They were living—they would die. Life itself was the reason. Once you taste the fruit, you're doomed. But the fruit was life itself.

I felt divided from them; the feeling, after all, was mine, not theirs, and it seemed that if I brushed up against them they'd become *it*, as in a game of tag. To keep my distance was my sacrifice, I thought, as though I were offering my mortality for theirs. Paul, I realized, had never had such feelings, being childless. Did it make him more free or the opposite, more trapped?

Other cultures have stories to tell their children, not so much to help them make sense of mortality as to accustom them to its mystery. Here's one: Old Man has just created you from lumps of mud.

"When I was a lump of mud, was I alive then?" you ask him.

"No," says Old Man, "you were not alive."

"Then what do you call that state I was in then?"

"It is called death. When you are not alive, you are dead."

"Will I be alive always?"

Old Man doesn't answer. He's obviously thinking. "That hadn't occurred to me. Let's decide it right now. Here's a buffalo chip. Throw it in the river. If it floats, then you'll die and come back to life four days later."

"No," you say, "not a buffalo chip. The water will dissolve it." You feel very crafty. "Let's try this stone instead. If it floats, I'll live forever. If it sinks, I'll die."

Bad choice. You throw the stone in. It sinks. Well, after all, you're just a few hours old, you don't know anything yet. Old Man shakes his head. "Now nothing can be done about it. Now people will die."

So death was a poor choice made out of ignorance, according to this Blackfeet Indian story. It doesn't seem fair. But of course that's the point. How else do we account for the unaccountable?

The Shoshone also tell a story about death. Wolf and Coyote were creating the Shoshone, and Wolf said they shall not die. No, said Coyote, everything dies. Okay, said Wolf, there will be two deaths. After somebody dies, then he'll die again.

"No," said Coyote, the realist. "After somebody dies, he should stay that way."

"Okay," said Wolf. "It will be that way."

Not long after that, Coyote's son was sick and drew close to death. "I've changed my mind, Wolf," Coyote told his older brother. "I agree with what you said. We should have two deaths. That's a good idea."

"Don't be so stupid," said Wolf.

"Please change the rule." Coyote was weeping. "I didn't think my son would die right away."

"No, don't be foolish," said the resolute Wolf. "Once we make a rule we have to keep it."

The rule of all rules, then, is rules can't be broken. Rules like that are laws, and all laws pass through death, like water passing through a charcoal filter.

HOW TO SPOIL A GOOD WORLD

The smooth-tongued snake said to the first woman, "Did God really mean you can't eat from *any* tree?"

"Just the tree in the middle of the garden," she answered.

"What on earth for?"

"You can't eat it, you can't touch it," said Hava, the woman — in other versions, Eve. "If you do, death will touch you."

"Nonsense," said the snake. "Death will not touch you. God knows if you eat it your eyes will fall open and you will be like gods, knowing good from bad."

So she ate the fruit, and gave it to her husband, and he ate some too, and as a result pain entered the world, also copulation, difficulty in birth, farming—and death. "Dust you are, to dust return."

In all these stories, the line between knowledge and ignorance appears impossible to cross. How can we who die know about a time when death didn't exist, though we brought it on ourselves? We can't go back to what we never knew, since knowledge is one result of our act. Adam and Eve knew what they'd done only in the light of its consequence—death.

So death is the thing we look out of, not at. And knowledge of death is like a heavy chunk of lead in the center of our dreams.

MEET THE STRULDBRUGGS

None of these stories are satisfactory. They don't give us what we want. Parents want for their children—and so for themselves—individual immortality, the survival of a separate identity and consciousness. It's not enough to say, with Walt Whitman, that "the smallest sprout shows there is really no death," or with Lucretius or Giordano Bruno that we change our aspect, even disperse throughout the universe, but the atoms live on. We want to be translated to a higher spiritual plane with our unique selves intact. We want peace and well-being, tunnels and white lights, reunions with loved ones—all those things reported in near-death experiences. Elisabeth Kübler-Ross, after having spoken to more than a thousand people who had had such experiences, declared that she "knows for a fact there is life after death." Philippe Ariès, on the other hand, calls death "a biological transition without significance."

Knowledge is shared culture. Our shared culture, however, has been Balkanized by the authority that our shared culture gives to personal experience. I for one have had no experience of immortality. So I'm a skeptic. But if others have had personal experiences of leaving their bodies and meeting dead relatives and entering the light, who am I to be skeptical? Aren't all claims to knowledge equally valid?

So our knowledge swings wildly, in this stage of world culture, back and forth between skepticism and credulity. We are skeptical about things we haven't experienced, yet we examine the experiences of others with a hunger for truth inherited from the time when shared knowledge meant survival.

I stood there in that funeral home watching my sons gaze into Paul's casket, and thought that maybe we ask the wrong questions. Not why do we die, but why do we live? Would my sons waste their lives? Have I wasted mine? Perhaps the wish to live forever is just a desperate hope that a life not be wasted. The Sibyl of Cumae wished for immortality, but neglected to ask Apollo for youth to go along with it. So she aged and shriveled up and still didn't die, and was hung in a cage as small and dried out as a withered cicada, and when children said, "Sibyl, what do you want?" she replied, "I want to die."

Cain was also cursed, in some versions of his story, with the inability to die, as was Pontius Pilate's porter, named Cartaphilus, who, when Jesus was dragged out of court, struck him on the back and said, "Go faster, Jesus, why do you linger?" In this account (by Matthew Paris, in the thirteenth century) Jesus answered, "I indeed am going, but you shall tarry till I come"—meaning, this loudmouth would wander the earth until the Second Coming. In some accounts, Cartaphilus changed his name to Joseph, but in all he became the Wandering Jew.

Vampires too are unable to die yet famously long to. Their attachment to life becomes a helpless addiction, for which we pity and admire them and drive stakes through their hearts. The latter activity is akin to tricking thieves by slashing their purses.

In *Gulliver's Travels,* Swift describes a race of immortals called the Struldbruggs, the most opinionated, short-tempered, greedy, morose, self-centered, garrulous, and cold-hearted humans poor Gulliver's ever met. "Whenever they see a funeral, they lament and repine that others are gone to a harbour of rest, to which they themselves never can hope to arrive." At the age of ninety, they lose their teeth and hair, yet still live on, although dead to the law. Their heirs have already claimed their estates, so they exist on charity. They still contract diseases, but must continue living in order to fully experience their afflictions — as my father does now. They forget the names of things. "The language of this country being always upon the flux," and the Struldbruggs clinging to its dead versions, they can't talk with each other or with mortals except by means of a few vague words. "They were the most mortifying sight I ever beheld," Gulliver tells us, in Swift's ironic pun.

Yet, like Gulliver, they still cling to life, and as his Luggnaggian interlocutor says, any mortal with one foot in the grave holds back the other as long as he can. No wonder immortality is not knowledge but conviction, not faith but a demand. "I believe it, uncle, believe it fervently, passionately," says Sonya in Chekhov's *Uncle Vanya*. As Paul West, speaking for his mother, puts it, "No sensible world . . . offers approximations to an ideal that cannot exist." And as the old crone Sesame Weichbrodt insists at the end of Thomas Mann's *Buddenbrooks*, we will see them again, all those loved ones who have died. "If only it were so," replies Frau Permaneder, who began the novel as the irrepressible little Antonie. At which the hunchback Sesame stands on her tiptoes, all forty-eight inches of her, raps the table with her fist, and shouts in defiance, "It is so!" — the same words I wanted to scream at my boys as they walked back from Paul's casket.

It is so!

But I didn't.

One friend of my brother did show up at the wake, and this made my mother happy. She introduced him as Woody, one of Paul's fellow hams. He was thoughtful and soft-spoken and held my mother's hand between both of his, but when she left us alone, all he did was ask me questions. He was curious about Paul's ham equipment—what would I do with that? As it turned out, Woody lived in Haverhill, not far from Paul's house. What would happen to the house? he wanted to know. Would I put it on the market? I told him I'd only driven by it once—it looked in pretty bad shape. That's okay, he said. I'm real handy with a hammer. You could save a lot of hassle by selling it yourself. What price were you thinking?

No idea, I said. I'll have to have it appraised.

How about we meet? You can show me the place.

I felt ill at ease. This friend, it appeared, had turned out to be a carrion eater, but he looked like a nice guy: beaming face, yellow mustache. I told him I'd be back in a few weeks to go through my brother's house, and would give him a call.

V
HOUSE

O God, I could be bounded in a nutshell
and count myself a king of infinite space,
were it not that I have bad dreams.

— *Hamlet*

1

THE MESS

THREE WEEKS LATER I was driving out of Haverhill on my way to meet Woody at Paul's house in New Hampshire. I'd walked through the house by myself that morning, for the first time — the parts I could walk through — and still felt coated with slime. I'd tried phoning Woody to cancel the meeting, but no one had answered. After the funeral he'd sent me a letter reiterating his interest in the house, and I had the letter with me, so I drove the twelve miles across the state line to Haverhill, found the return address on the envelope, and knocked on his door. No response.

The world seemed flat and odd. Woody's street was a catchall: old houses, three-deckers, a 7-Eleven, a brick warehouse down the road, another across the street. Then I took a second look and saw the warehouses were churches. I'd been inside plenty of industrial-era New England Catholic churches, and knew that each of these could have contained its own exquisite cosmos walled against the outside world, with hand-carved hammer beams, domes of pure blue flecked with gold stars, and Gothic stone baldachins. Designed to fit the cubes of empty space between cotton mills, the churches had been built as retreats from the world their façades appeared to duplicate. But now they were probably three-quarters empty on any Sunday morning.

I climbed back into the van. Down the hill, across the river, the narrow streets of downtown Haverhill, the mill buildings and warehouses, inclined toward where I was parked, like a medieval map. Behind me, up the street, stately old white houses and quaint saltboxes curved toward a Church of Christ with regulation white steeple and, opposite its entrance, a green common at a crossroad. Woody's street was more or less a transition between the grimy and the picturesque, the two sides of New England. Actually, since the mills are old now—their power looms long gone, some converted to shopping malls—they qualify as picturesque too. Choose your route to nostalgia: the Saltonstalls or the Murphys. More than two centuries ago, the Wasp founders of Haverhill owned lots in town, on which they built houses, and commuted to farmlands in surrounding hills. Later the mills came, attracting Catholic and ethnic laborers, and genteel people removed themselves out toward their ancestors' fields, and Haverhill became a sinkhole walled by wealth.

I'd been going through Paul's papers in Boston for the past few days. As executor of his will and one of two legatees—Hannah was the other—I was legally accountable for his possessions, including his house. Accountable for his debts (though I hadn't found any), for the things he'd left behind, for his assets and even his life, it seemed—for his blister of existence, now broken. I'd heaved tons of junk mail; he seemed to save everything. There were certain papers crucial to find—his insurance policies, his IRA beneficiary designations, his stock certificates, maybe even his last wishes—and not having had luck at my mother's in Boston, I thought they'd be in his house.

Fat chance. I took one look and fled. How on earth could I show it to anyone? But I couldn't find Woody and he'd be there at noon, so I had little choice.

Cities like Haverhill are cobbled together by successive generations across planks of time—jerry-built, like the human body—so the old and new stand side by side, oblivious of each other. Driving through this stone soup was like driving through a ragged sequence of minds with their meshwork of plans and eccentric bookkeeping. Below me, downtown Haverhill looked rubbery and squeezed, as in those pre-

Renaissance paintings where three sides of some buildings are visible at once, and a roof tipped toward the viewer threatens to spill its cow, but doesn't. It occurs to me now that I wasn't just driving through a corner of Massachusetts but through a cultural screen that sifted out the material. I saw volumes and planes, not streets and buildings. A waffle-iron space held crosses of air between its gridded cubes, making grooved streets and alleys. I was driving through ancient Greek and Roman city plans, through Euclid's geometry, Renaissance optics and perspective, Newton's concept of space as an empty container, and grids set down in American frontier ordinances.

Haverhill's either a small city or a large village, hard to tell which. On its outskirts, it was impossible to know whether I was in the suburbs or the country. Transitions were subtle—a field, a patch of woods. I crossed the state border into New Hampshire, and here everything backslid. Strip malls, gas stations, car dealers, stores. Massachusetts has a hefty sales tax and New Hampshire has none, so the border between them, on the New Hampshire side, is thick with such weedy commercial growth.

At last, the road to Kingston ran past white pines and even some stretches of unmended stone fence. I drove past Jud's Mobil and turned up Twist Run Road. It wasn't that long ago—a hundred years at most —when only farmers lived in the country. Then came automobiles and rural electrification and the machinery of domestic comfort, and the country gradually lost its status as the city's antithesis. By the 1940s, suburban ranch houses like Paul's were being built on country roads. His road still had a few empty spaces, still showed relics of its rural past—barns, chicken houses, an apple orchard and a field—but all were abandoned.

Two people, not one, were waiting outside. With Woody was a friend named Alex, who lived down the dirt road that ran behind the house. As it turned out, Woody wasn't the one interested in buying Paul's house, Alex was.

Woody'd known Paul for ten or so years. Until a year ago, he'd lived in Kingston; they were fellow hams, and both had volunteered at the town fire department, Paul by manning the two-way radios, Woody on the ambulance crew. Stocky and short, with a pipe-bowl face and padded eyes and smile, Woody seemed the sort of person anyone could like. I felt bad that I'd seen him at the wake as a venal opportunist. His face was very ruddy. Both of his meaty hands shook my one. I understood this as a reference to Paul's death. "How you holding up?" he asked.

"Fine. You?"

"Terrific." He introduced Alex, a tall, jumpy enthusiast with a handlebar mustache and navy cloth cap, who explained that he'd never known my brother, just seen him to honk at when he drove past and Paul was mowing the lawn.

"Hasn't been mowed in two or three years," I said.

"I know."

"He was living with my mother," I explained. "He more or less abandoned this place."

Woody beamed, Alex fidgeted. We were low on the property, where it dipped toward a hollow outside the drive-in basement. The March day had grown warmer, and the sky was now blue with a touch of whitewash, but the air still felt crisp. Old weeds and thorn shoots lapped at the garage door, which apparently had remained shut for decades. Pieces of aluminum antenna lay on the ground or were propped against the house. To our right, twenty feet away, a rusty barrel with holes around the bottom stood on cinderblocks—the rural incinerator. Beyond it, underneath a white pine, sat Paul's old Dodge van and his ride-around mower, each on flat tires. The van's windows were broken. Three more junk cars were parked in the brush in a neat row down behind the van.

A padlocked door beside the garage was the only way I'd found to enter the house. It lacked a doorknob; instead, a clothesline snaked through the hole, looped to a spike on one of the antennae leaning next to the door. I fooled with the padlock hanging from a hinge bolted to the sill—the key was hard to turn. "I have to warn you," I said. "The place is really a mess. I've never seen anything like it." They stood there nodding and smiling, uncomfortable. Why did I think they were acting guilty, that they'd been inside the house and already knew?

The whole house heaved with a large hollow sound, like a dying whale, when I pushed the door open. The basement's dirt floor smelled wet and vaguely rotting. In the fading light admitted by the door, we made out water pipes and octopal heating vents and heavy-duty wires stapled to the floor joists. Deeper in the basement, running into the darkness underneath the joists, the only thing that caught the light was the central heating's cold-air return, its sheet metal ripped open. Directly in front of us, open stairs rose to a landing, turned, and disappeared.

I switched on the light. A kind of alluvial fan of empty orange and white milk cartons spilled down the stairs to the basement. Also, empty green bags of dog food, and red ones of cat litter. We looked around the basement. Bed springs in a stack. Mildewed cardboard boxes, an old bookcase filled with rags and soiled underwear leaning back against a pile of junk. Hubcaps, motors, a weed whacker, count-less plastic bags of trash, junk wood, good wood—two-by-fours and lengths of painted hardwood with nails sticking out. Piles of angle irons. Junk TV sets and insides of radios with their cities of tubes, plastic basins, metal boxes. To our right, nearly buried in trash behind the garage door, sat a white sports car pitted with rust whose cloth roof hung in ragged strips. Perched on its hood was a wet cardboard box and, of all things, a new Sears shop vac of red and black plastic. Woody waved the back of his hand at the car. "MG," he said. "Might still be worth a penny or two."

We walked up the steps on a path through empty milk cartons and bags of pet chow. The kitchen door hung from one hinge. Through it, we squeezed inside the house.

Woody muttered "Jeez," shook his head, and smiled. Alex said "Whew!" and kept scratching his chin. His exclamation may have been prompted by the smell or by the sight—it was hard to know which. Maybe I was wrong, I thought, maybe they hadn't seen it before. The smell seemed even worse than it had that morning, but people were with me this time. That made everything worse.

On the other hand, the fact of other people seemed to absolve me. It wasn't me who did this, my expression said. I too shook my head.

Dried grayish logs of excrement from large cats or small dogs were piled along the walls, especially in corners. The kitchen sink was filled with cat shit to its rim. More empty bags and cartons, more rags and magazines, more dirt and filth everywhere. Oily black threads of cobwebs hung from the ceiling and walls, and moved as we moved. The stove and refrigerator had been pushed to the middle of the room, and the refrigerator door gaped open. It was filled with food—rotten meat spilling over a shelf, still pinkish but withered and dry, cartons of milk, jars of salad dressing, cans of soda and beer, jars of mustard and mayo, all with faded labels. Something yellow and black the size of a chestnut on a box of butter may have been half an onion.

The smell in the house was also yellow and black. It was dirt, moldy towels, urine, excrement, and fine living dust, almost like pollen, and it seemed both wet and dry, both ripe and dead, and kept peeling off every wall and every surface. The house felt cold—the cold of the dead. The boarded-up windows made it feel like a cave. "Jeez," Woody muttered again. Alex met my eye and smiled and shook his head. I caught his cue. "I never knew he was like this," I said. "My grandmother raised him," I added. "I didn't know him that well," I said, and felt myself backing off, as though from a car wreck. Alex, meanwhile, nodded as if to say, We're all tourists here.

The way to the back porch was clogged by mounds of trash—no

sense in even trying. Instead, we climbed into the hallway toward the bedrooms, me switching on lights as we proceeded. The house seemed to drip, although everything was dry. Walking in this hallway was pretty difficult. Piled on a one- or two-foot layer of excrement were hundreds of discarded Pepsi bottles—the kind that look like carafes —and we had no choice but to walk across them, like eggshells. Each bottle was crammed with cigarette butts.

I couldn't open the bathroom door, there was so much trash behind it.

One bedroom door also was blocked, but someone had ripped it in half—vandals, no doubt—so we could see inside. "One cannot speak anymore of being," Samuel Beckett once said in an interview, "one must speak only of the mess." This room, wall to wall, was five feet deep in trash bags, milk cartons, boxes of documents, empty cartons of Kools, Pepsi bottles, empty bags of cat food, a Hitachi TV, eviscerated radios, model airplane kits, audiotapes, over-the-counter medication—Dayquil, Alka-Seltzer, Dimetapp, Bayer aspirin—and small, ubiquitous cardboard boxes of videotapes with red and yellow photos. This was the room whose walls had been covered by the previous owner with carpet remnants. Their zigzag designs and faded colors emerged above the trash. "Hey, put that light off again." I switched off the light. Woody and Alex were breathing down my neck. "What's that?"

"Clock radio, it looks like."

"Still plugged in."

I switched the light back on. The radio sat at a cockeyed angle on a pile of trash, its cord like some sort of hellish umbilical worming down into the depths. "Fire hazard," said Woody.

"It was like that this morning. I guess it's been on for two or three years."

"You ought to turn off the main."

"Good idea."

We talked like normal people planning reasonable acts. Backing out of the doorway, our feet caused the Pepsi bottles to rub and scrape against one another with a sound something like fingernails on blackboards.

I suddenly remembered Paul washing his microbus outside our house in South Boston, and felt my throat form a fist. He'd worn an old sock on each hand and dipped them in solvent to clean off the engine. What happened? Why were there hundreds of bottles filled with cigarette butts, why all this filth? I'd been standing off from things as much as I could, but now the horror came back, and I pictured Paul transporting objects, new things and junk, the useless and the useful, in a diabolical parody of intimacy and security—transporting them back to his house and pressing them in place with his back, arms, and chest, like a mother robin building a nest.

Reasons do have a limit. Shall I offer a history of the Pepsi bottle, the cigarette, the milk carton, the rag? A history of bad smells? Even now, in memory, I feel buried like Paul, trapped in his house, surrounded by a waste of unexplained things. To be fully conscious of *everything*, of course, from the rivers of microorganisms we breathe in and out to the history of the shoehorn, would be a form of insanity. "It would be like hearing the grass grow and the squirrel's heart beat, and we should die of that roar which lies on the other side of silence," said George Eliot. Fortunately, she added, "the quickest of us walk about well wadded with stupidity."

I reached into the second bedroom and switched on the light. This one we could just squeeze inside. The trash bags made a mountain at one end, but left a passageway to a desk piled with ham equipment. Here, ceiling plaster had fallen on everything, making it difficult to distinguish the equipment from the junk. It was all junk, I knew: the Morse code clicker, the mikes, the maze of wires and antenna leads, playing cards, a globe, empty packs of Kools, pennies, keys, magazines, a photo of Grandma—the one on my desk now—coffee cups, doo-dads, little boxes of screws, damp envelopes, more Pepsi bottles stuffed with cigarette butts. The desk was a board across two filing cabinets whose drawers I'd pulled open that morning. In them, and in the dozens of mildewed boxes piled nearby on the floor, were every bank statement, receipt, electric bill, oil bill, phone bill, pay stub, every QSL card, every letter and birthday card (some unopened) Paul had received while living here — more than twenty years' worth. I despaired of ever going through them all. Everything was damp and mildewed, everything soiled, all of it smelled.

Beside the desk, a mattress lay on the floor with some blankets. Old paper bags crushed shut were scattered here and there, on the floor, on the desk. I'd found similar bags in his van outside, stuffed with underwear, socks, sometimes pants or pj's. I realized later that each represented a trip he'd taken.

The mountain of trash bags, cardboard boxes, videos, and Pepsi bottles seemed almost . . . composed. Some bags had burst open, and the junk spilling out wasn't very different from the junk in the room, though cigarette packs seemed to be in abundance, also the usual eggshells and coffee grounds.

Some bags on top, knotted shut, displayed Wal-Mart logos with yellow happy faces.

"Looks like he started cleaning it up, don't you think?" asked Woody.

"You mean because of the trash bags?" said Alex.

"Yeah."

No, I thought, it looks like he gave up, let everything go. But I had nothing to say. Some emotions go beyond words, and maybe beyond human feelings too. I felt a powerful impulse to crawl out of sight and huddle in a corner. Paul hadn't begun to clean up the house at all. Just the opposite: his home was the place where he threw things away, as if lining his nest with his own waste. And he'd been doing it for twenty-odd years, since moving into the house. Some of the stuff he bagged as he went along, some he just left where it was.

As though reading my mind, Woody said, "Looks like he couldn't throw nothing away."

Alex raised his eyebrows. "Just the other way around," he said. "He threw it all away."

"Then lived in it."

"Yeah." They'd forgotten I was there, it appeared. Then Alex turned to me. "Did he live here like this?"

I shrugged. "Beats me."

But I lied. That morning I'd found a little diary he'd kept, in an appointment book. It was dated two years ago, just before he'd moved to Boston. I remembered he'd been hospitalized then for a bronchial spasm and heart palpitations. The diary detailed every pill he took, every hour he didn't sleep, every symptom and worry. Never in my life had I found anything more painful to read.

I AM NOT GETTING MUCH SLEEP! WORRYING TOO MUCH I GUESS, ABOUT EVERYTHING!! I DON'T EAVEN KNOW IF I CAN MAKE IT OUT OF THE HOUSE TOMOROW BY MYSELF?? I HAVE TO GET OUT, BY HOOK OR CROOK. TO GET MALE & FOOD FOR MYSELF & CATS!!
I HAVE TO GET RID OF CAT'S!!
TOOK 2ND THEODUR PILL @ 6:30 PM

02/21 SUN. AM.
TOOK ONE EACH OF PILLS @ 9:30 AM APROX. I AM FEALING BETTER BUT STILL TAKING IT AN HOUR AT A TIME! GOT SOME SLEEP LAST NIGHT, BUT NOT A HELL OF A LOT!!

02/22 MONDAY
TOOK ALL THE PILLS I NEED TO TAKE. NOTHING TASTES GOOD EXCEPT ICE COLD WATER, AND SOME FLAVORS OF ICE CREAM! CANT SLEEP GOOD UP

TIGHT AT TIMES! PILLS? NO SMOKING? MABY SOME
OF EACH??
    I AM HAVING SOME WILD DREAM'S!! DUE TO PILL'S,
I SUPPOSE??
    WHY DID THEY TAKE THE PATCH AWAY?? WHAT
HAPPENED THAT NIGHT MY HEART STARTED
POUNDING?

02/24 WED
    DONNT FEAL GOOD, WEAK, CANT BREATH GOOD,
BUT I DID NOT SMOKE YET TO DAY! 48 HOURS PLUS,
AND COUNTING.
    I HAVE GOT TO DO SOMETHING ABOUT GETTING
HOUSE CLEANED UP!! I DONT KNOW WHAT??

It went on like that for nine or ten pages, then abruptly stopped. He'd moved out of the house by the end of it, I guessed. I couldn't begin to imagine the depth of depression it suggested, the fear and horror and something else—self-loathing and disgust. I stood there that morning next to his desk, reading this diary, alone in his house, feeling more and more like an animal in a hole. When I closed the thing up, a piece of paper fell out. I bent down and retrieved it. I was shaking, I realized, partly from the cold. It was that newspaper clipping of nine-year-old Paul holding a branch of half apples, half blossoms. The branch had excited much talk in the town, said the little article underneath the picture; no one had ever seen such a thing before. "Miracle Blossoms," the caption read. A fragment of the page above the photo gave the year: 1938.

Later that morning I phoned Hannah from Jud's Mobil station. I had to tell someone about the house, but broke down sobbing. It was one of those gut-wrenching inside-out cries, in the back of Jud's store, near the coffee and bathrooms. I faced into a corner so no one would see me. "What's wrong?" she kept saying. "My God, what happened?"

When I started describing the house, I gradually stopped crying and regained some control.

Now I stood in the same bedroom with two strangers, wondering why I'd agreed to meet anyone here. I'd made the appointment before seeing the place, a stupid mistake, I realized now. I tried moving on, and started for the door. But it wasn't so bad. I was like them, I made myself think—like Woody and Alex, not like Paul. I was normal, like them, though I didn't even know them.

The boarded-up windows in this room were broken, and the window frames rotten. I'd found among his papers in Boston a letter from the Kingston town board warning him that his house had become a public nuisance. That's when he hired someone to board it up.

"What's this?" Alex asked. We were back in the hallway. I knew what it was but pretended surprise. We stood there looking down and shaking our heads. An old suitcase with straps lay floating like a raft on the Pepsi bottles, and on it sprawled the corpse of a cat. It looked mummified, head larger than the body, the skin on the face stretched tight and thin as nylon, making it resemble an underfed child. The torso, however, was rags made of dust.

As we walked through the house we found other corpses, most of them cats. One was a bird or very large bat. One could have been a puppy. Two or three lay in the living room, which in contrast with the bedrooms was fairly empty of trash. Although not of excrement. Here the yellow rug reeked, the couch boiled over, a pool table was covered with dirt and fallen plaster, and an old-fashioned cast-iron bathtub had been lined with bright pieces of carpet and opened on one side to make a kind of love seat. It too was filthy.

Woody tried the thermostat on the wall. "Doesn't work," I said.

"What about the plumbing?"

"You saw the sinks. Filled with dirt."

"Filled with cat shit."

I noticed scratch marks on the wall. They were everywhere in the

living room. In the kitchen too, as I'd seen that morning, not register-
ing what they meant right away. Now I put two and two together, and
the house suddenly struck me as a torture chamber.

Looking down at a dead cat, Woody said, "Guess we didn't get them
all out."

"We?"

"Like I told you at the wake, we took him to the hospital."

"Who's we?"

"The ambulance crew."

"You were with the crew that took him to the hospital?"

"I told you at the wake!" Woody's face was glowing red. "Bronchial
spasm. He couldn't hardly breathe. Never called us neither. He used to
show up every Tuesday, Wednesday, and Thursday nights at the VFD."

Alex leaned between us, waving his hands. "Volunteer Fire Department."

"When Thursday night comes and still no Paul, me and the crew get
together and come here," Woody said. "None of us was ever inside this
place before. We had to force the door. Found him on that mattress in
the bedroom, took him to the hospital. Come back and tried to round
up all the cats, but I knew there was quite a few that we missed. Some
run off, some was hiding wherever. Jeez, what a stink. Some of the
guys, they wrote him off right there. He never came back to the station
after that."

"He moved to Boston after that," I said.

"We put him on oxygen. He was pretty disoriented. Guess he pulled
through okay. This aneurysm wasn't related, was it?"

"I have no idea."

2

THE RATIONAL HOUSEHOLD

80 B.C. A Roman entrepreneur, Sergius Orata, is sued by the government of Naples for using a lake to raise fish and oysters for sale. The lake is public water, the suit alleges, not his private fish farm. The suit may have arisen from resentment of Orata, a wealthy man whose wealth is suspect. A businessman, an inventor, a cunning real estate speculator, he is considered a vulgarian by his neighbors. Those defending him are mistaken in thinking that by keeping him away from the lake they can deprive him of oysters, says one report: "for, if he was prevented from catching them there, he would find them on the roofs of his houses." This odd remark refers to one of his inventions, a tank built on posts for raising oysters and fish, which, in the winter, was heated by hot air from a fire made to circulate beneath it. Eventually the tanks were brought down to earth and the heat passed through ducts, and Orata discovered that selling country houses fitted out with heated bathrooms was more lucrative than raising fish. His followers learned to apply the system to a whole house, and central heating was born.

Actually, it might have been born in Turkey as much as a thousand years earlier, according to excavations done in 1954. Galen describes efficient heating systems constructed for country houses at Pergamum in western Turkey. But the idea never spread. And with the fall of Rome it died. Only in China did a tradition of central heating extend continuously into modern times. There, a room called the *kang* became common—one containing a raised platform heated by pipes underneath and covered with mats, cushions, and bright carpets. The *kang* was where guests were welcomed and where members of the household slept at night.

Once Orata's invention was forgotten, Europeans kept warm with braziers on tripods, until fireplaces became widespread in the Middle

Ages. But fireplaces were not central heating. It took a long time for Europeans to rediscover what the Greeks and Romans had evolved: houses with multiple rooms and central heating. The poor in the Middle Ages lived as the poor had always lived, in one-room hovels, but strangely enough, the bourgeois and the moderately wealthy also lived in one room. Even two-story houses in cities weren't broken up into rooms—rather, one large chamber, called the hall, served as living quarters, a meeting place to conduct business, a dining room, a kitchen, and a bedroom. The furniture appropriate to each of these functions was moved in and out of the hall as required, or pushed back against the walls. Family members mingled with lodgers, servants, apprentices, and other merchants, and people slept or made love behind screens or curtains while business was conducted ten feet away. In villages, too, prosperous farmers lived in houses whose single room was a kitchen, dining room, bedroom, and barn. That is, the cattle and sheep shared the house with the family, animals at one end, humans at the other. This one-room house was also cellar and attic: cheeses were hung beside beds to dry and age, salted meats suspended from the rafters, and there were no closets. Rather, chests held family possessions and clothing, and bins contained flour and other foods, including leftovers and grain for the animals.

Privacy did not exist. Communal sleeping was common, and the beds in any case were in the common room. One might think of this domestic arrangement as a sort of forced intimacy, but intimacy is not the same as proximity. The ancient Greeks and Romans lived in houses with many rooms—often arranged around an inner courtyard—but in the history of dwellings this appears to be a relatively brief interlude. Only in recent centuries have we resurrected the subdivided house with multiple rooms used for multiple functions, with cells of privacy and closets galore—and central heating. The norm throughout history is instead the house with one communal space, often shared with animals. It undoubtedly smelled, though the smell was fresh—like barns today. Not like Paul's house.

I THINK I COULD TURN AND LIVE WITH THE ANIMALS

Early houses retained the curvilinear shapes of caves, nests, shells, and beaver huts—from the beehive houses of the Scottish islands to the thatched wood and grass huts still seen in many parts of the world. Does this mean that early humans lived at one with nature, picking fruit off trees and finding shelter when they needed it? The line between a found place—for example, a cave—and a made place such as a hut is blurry at best. Some caves were made, like those at Puye in New Mexico, excavated from soft volcanic tuff. And some at Puye were not only excavated but walled in with blocks, and this by the same people who would later construct houses of stone ingeniously adapted to rock shelters high in the sides of sheer cliffs.

Conversely, some made places—trees tied together at the tops and covered with bark, or pits enlarged, or skins thrown across bushes— were first found and adapted to use, then soon abandoned, then found again by others.

Who made the first dwelling? Who first folded something over space and created an enclosure and lived inside it? Books like *Homes Without Hands* and *Architecture Without Architects* romantically suggest that humans came to this practice belatedly, and have lost the simple purity of those animals that wrap the natural world around themselves as a home. Only gradually (meaning tens of thousands of years) did humans "correct" nature—that is, create inner spaces whose primary purpose seems to have been to exclude the outer world rather than embrace it. So our dwellings developed rectilinear shapes instead of rounded ones. This meant that materials had to be processed, cut to uniform sizes. Once houses were made of wood, not trees, or of brick, not mud, or of cement, not stone, then the distinction between humans and animals became absolute. Cain murdered his brother, who lived with the animals, then built the first city to wall out savagery— that is, to divide himself and his kin from their own animal bodies. But the biblical myth compresses a slow and erratic history into a brief story, and it wasn't until the Scientific Revolution of the seventeenth and the Industrial Revolution of the eighteenth and nineteenth centuries that humans at last saw animals as objects that could be subjected to assembly lines, like any material. Just as trees contained wood, so animals contained meat, and were equally capable of being processed.

The first house, then, is seen in retrospect as "made" only when people are surrounded by processed materials. As Joseph Rykwert points out, for centuries the Romans displayed a replica of the thatched hut of Romulus on the Palatine, as a reminder of their humble origins. And many peoples — Greeks, Romans, Jews, Egyptians, Japanese — have practiced ceremonies in which "primitive" huts are ritually constructed, again to remind them of origins. Succot, the Jewish Feast of Tabernacles, is a good example. But so are log cabins reconstructed or preserved in American towns, familiar icons of founding pioneers. Thoreau's hut at Walden Pond, Theodore Kaczynski's shack in Montana, pop-up tents, blankets thrown by children over chairs, all ape that first act of unfolding an interior then enclosing it, which we can never quite forget and never quite recover.

BUSY BEES

Something in sixteenth- and seventeenth-century Europe — some growing sense of life's complexity — urged people to begin subdividing their houses and to segregate activities into smaller, more private rooms. My suspicion is that it was the terror of space, the sense that the very small (seen in microscopes) and the very large (seen in telescopes) were so linked to infinity that — God forbid — cracks could appear in our little towns and homes through which unlucky people might endlessly drop. The Western world had grown during the age of discovery; other cultures, languages, skin shades, foods, practices, and memories had begun to invade and subdivide its uniformity. The universe had grown even larger, with its planets and stars on the one hand, and its capillaries, fleas, butterfly wings, microorganisms, and germs on the other. So proximate spaces were needed: intimate and private rooms that could reproduce the security of the nest inside the spaciousness of a house.

Historians generally agree that the growth of capitalism, with its emphasis on individual initiative and consumption, also encouraged new concepts of privacy. Yet merchants and businessmen are the least private people I know—their lives for the most part are fully absorbed in work and its social lubrications, and even today our stereotypes portray them (unfairly, no doubt) as lacking inner resources. It would be more accurate to say that the division between public and private went hand in hand with a new organization of labor, and multiroomed houses were a logical result. For one thing, merchants no longer conducted business in their halls. Work and home separated, the family became more isolated and child-centered, and—as so many heroines of nineteenth-century novels complained—men operated in the public world while women were confined to the domestic one. One can see the same splitting cells and branching networks in the evolution of house plans: first the medieval hall divided into bedroom and kitchen, with sometimes a wardrobe and storeroom off the bedroom, and eventually separate quarters for servants. Most houses with more than one room still had no internal corridors, let alone heating ducts; each room opened into the next, and to go upstairs, or to one's workshop or the privy, one had to step outside.

By the eighteenth century, though, the interior spaces of houses had subdivided further, so that corridors and internal stairways became necessary. Bourgeois homes, those beehives, now evolved dining rooms and bathrooms, common rooms, reception rooms, breakfast rooms, libraries, studies, galleries, billiard rooms, conservatories, nurseries, schoolrooms, and closets; some even had antechambers—curious parasitic cells between larger rooms. Private spaces split off from public ones; gentlemen and ladies no longer received guests in their bedrooms, but in salons or reception rooms. In many houses, common rooms were downstairs, bedrooms up, making private spaces that much more off limits. Upstairs and downstairs became two separate worlds; one wore different faces and clothing in each. So, for example, in nineteenth-century Amherst, Massachusetts, Emily Dickinson, painfully shy, could converse with guests in the downstairs hallway only from behind her half-closed bedroom door upstairs.

Circulatory networks naturally accompanied this multiplied complexity of space: not just hallways and corridors, entry halls and stairways, and back stairs for servants, but bell cords to summon servants, indoor plumbing, dumbwaiters, ventilation ducts, and eventually heating ducts and wiring. The house came to mimic the human body, whose various circulation systems fuel its soft engines, and whose division into inside and outside lays the groundwork for all such divisions. Today houses are networks of distribution and dispersion with inputs for fuel and outputs for waste and little pockets of privacy and memory and storage, so that now, for example, the furniture stays in one place and people move around, whereas in the Middle Ages the furniture had moved around and people stayed in one place.

A BRIEF HISTORY OF THE CLOSET

American readers who skip the editor's footnotes may become confused by Samuel Richardson's *Pamela*, first published in 1740. Most of the novel takes place inside houses, where Pamela, a sixteen-year-old servant, is held in semi-captivity by her master, a man we know only as Mr. B. Pamela's sole outlet is writing letters, and she does so in her closet. Mr. B., meanwhile, hides in other closets to observe the lovely Pamela while she undresses. Like the cross-dressing Norman Bates in Alfred Hitchcock's *Psycho*, he emerges from closets in women's clothes and attempts to seduce his servant by sleeping with her as a fellow servant. Those who picture these transgressions would be wrong to assume that Mr. B. is like Brother in E. L. Doctorow's novel of two-hundred-plus years later, *Ragtime,* who bursts out of a closet fully erect in mid-crisis. Brother was hiding in a tiny space for storage. Mr. B. hides in "a small room of privacy and retirement," as Dr. Johnson's *Dictionary* defines the closet.

In the Middle Ages, people stored clothes, blankets, plate, and personal possessions in chests and baskets. Later, as houses began to subdivide, wardrobes and cupboards became used for storage. But in the seventeenth and eighteenth centuries, "closet" did not mean a place for storage; rather, it meant, both in England and the United States, a small room adjoining a larger one — usually the bedroom — used by a single person for private activities, such as praying or writing letters. With the Industrial Revolution, this usage gradually changed in America. By the time Catharine Beecher wrote her groundbreaking *Treatise on Domestic Economy* (1841), "closet" meant exclusively a place of storage, too small to pray in, let alone write letters. In a sense, one could say that the need for storage created by the Industrial Revolution and its processed goods — its ready-made clothes, its hats, shoes, and domestic implements — caused the European cupboard and European closet to mate and produce the American closet, which exists to store things yet still manages to connote secrecy and privacy, as in phrases like "skeleton in the closet" and "come out of the closet."

PAUL

Closets today are a selling point in houses — at least in America — due to our abundance of things to store. We are, in this respect, still the favored children of the Industrial Revolution and its compulsory bounty. What would Wal-Mart or Home Depot be — or, for that matter, Hoover, NordicTrack, Samsonite, and Milton-Bradley — without consumers whose homes have closets and garages, which for many people are their most important rooms? First came closets, then the Industrial Revolution, which altered the meaning of closets to that of places for storing things. Private possessions have always been hoarded, of course, but never to the degree made possible by America's embrace of the mass production of goods. The Industrial Revolution set in motion a system of storage and distribution that mimicked the private storehouses and exchanges of individual consumers. In turn, the house, itself a product, became a cornucopia of ever more products, each of them brighter and cheaper than the last.

In a sense, then, my brother's house had become one enormous closet, not unlike the comic staple of cartoons, movies, and *Fibber McGee and Molly:* one opens the closet door and a nightmarish trash heap cascades out, a flood of all those products you've ever wanted, including those you weren't sure about, those you forgot, and those you thought you threw away—cascades out in a landslide that buries the person still clinging to the doorknob.

HEAT

Modern Western culture grew in warm houses, like mold in petri dishes. Just as bodies must maintain their temperature to live, houses too ceased being cold, and clever people rediscovered Sergius Orata's hypocaust—his system for heating multicelled houses. Fireplaces couldn't do the job, not even the more efficient ones invented in the eighteenth century. For a time, stoves seemed to be the answer. In the sixteenth and seventeenth centuries, stoves with glazed tiles gave their names to heated chambers, especially in northern Europe—the German *Stüb*, the French *poêle*—and sometimes these stoves were placed between two rooms, one the more or less public space of the parlor or kitchen, the other the private bedroom of husband and wife. During the severe Bavarian winter of 1620, while nested in such a warm inner space—a *poêle*—Descartes conceived of his model of outer space governed by a complicated mathematical architecture. He wasn't literally inside a stove, however, as the novelist Paul Strathern has it. Yet the picture seems appropriate: René Descartes hunched in a stove, dreaming up the universe. Warm houses, warm minds.

Later, stoves were moved into basements and became known as boilers. By the time central heating was reinvented in the West, fifteen hundred years after Rome's fall, houses had already evolved both circulation systems of great complexity and pockets of privacy. Interestingly enough, in the nineteenth century, notions of the healthy effects of circulating air by ventilation—especially in America—preceded widespread acceptance of the comforting effects of central heating. In other words, cold-air returns led to furnaces and heating ducts, not vice versa.

A CLEAN, WELL-LIGHTED PLACE

In a similar manner, a whole paradise of domestic implements and appliances preceded the availability of electricity. Once an electric network was in place, we merely had to invent little motors to run our many gadgets, then plug them in.

First came the Argand lamp in 1783, which greatly improved the brightness of rooms. Later, gas lighting made them still brighter, and now managers of households could see the dirt that needed cleaning. Drawn from cisterns in attics and coils behind the kitchen stove, hot and cold running water made cleaning easier by eliminating the necessity of transporting water by hand into the house. Running water also made bathing easier and, with the invention of the water closet, eliminated the necessity of carrying out waste by hand—or worse, going out to a privy in the frozen night. Americans had the bright idea of combining the water closet and bathtub in one room. Add heat, and the inner life blossomed. It blossomed because there was less and less need to venture outside to discharge one's . . . burdens. Light, heat, and the elimination of waste could be experienced at leisure in a house, and families in winter could live in a bubble effectively sealed off from the outside world.

Around the same time, as Siegfried Giedion points out, machines for cooking, cleaning, and laundering were invented, all before electricity. "The principle of the domestic vacuum cleaner based purely on suction was invented and clearly formulated by 1859," he informs us. It was mechanical, yes, and ran by wheel power, but operated through suction. Hand-cranked dishwashers were available by 1865, and washing machines by 1869. The gas iron was invented in the 1850s, and a whole series of related mechanical aids trundle across the nineteenth century, from the 1830s to the 1870s: egg beaters, clockwork fans, apple paring and coring machines, mechanical churns. Even after electricity was available, water-powered machines, based on principles going back to Hero of Alexandria, were briefly rivals of electric power. One described by Giedion attached to a faucet and ran a vacuum cleaner, massager, and hair dryer.

Then came light bulbs, electric service, and the small electric motor. First to be electrified, in 1889, was the fan. The fan not only cooled housewives in summer (and their husbands at the office) but made central heating feasible in winter. Hot-air heating systems throughout the nineteenth century had been cheaper to construct than steam or hot water, but as Witold Rybczynski points out, they weren't very popular, because air would rise through ducts only if heated to a very high temperature, as much as 180 degrees. As a result, many American doctors and, more important, our first domestic gurus, such as Catharine Beecher, considered hot-air central heating unhealthy.

But a simple fan, installed at the source, could blow heated air mixed with fresh through a system of ducts at a moderate temperature. The modern house was born.

THE BEECHER BUZZ

A housewife must arrange "ten thousand little disconnected items," said Catharine Beecher in her *Treatise on Domestic Economy*. It made sense, then, to find ways to connect them—that is, to rationalize the construction and management of a household. The history of the modern American house in what we might call its classic phase—say, from 1850 to 1950—is the history of the application of rational principles to an avalanche of change. Part of this change came about because of the disappearance of servants. Beecher devotes considerable space to the "servant problem" in both of her books on household management, the 1841 *Treatise* and its expanded and reconfigured version of 1869, *The American Woman's Home*, written with her more famous sister, Harriet Beecher Stowe. The servant problem, in a democracy, means that domestic service requires subordination, a relic of feudal times, Beecher said. She correctly saw that "Abhorrence of Servitude [is] a National Trait of Character," as one of the chapter headings of the *Treatise* declares, and a decade before she and her sister took up the abolitionist cause, she noted that many domestics equated "servant" with "slave."

Beecher understood that domestic service would all but disappear in the United States. Therefore housewives must learn to do themselves those things that servants have always done. She did not make the further inference that "housewife" meant "slave," and in fact never questioned one fundamental assumption of the evolution of private life: that a woman was the center of all domesticity, from cooking and cleaning to raising children. As Witold Rybczynski says, "Beecher did not dispute that the woman's place was in the home; what she did assert was that the home was not a particularly well-thought-out place for her to be."

Catharine Beecher was the oldest child of a Calvinist minister with "an almost total lack of organization in his private life," says her sister's biographer. His religious enthusiasm created chaos at home, and his mode of operation, according to Harriet, was contained in his pet name, "Turn to the Right Thwack Away." Catharine inherited some of this zeal, and one suspects that scientific household management meant for her barely corseting her never-ending activity and projects — what her brother-in-law Calvin Stowe called "the Beecher buzz." "Whenever Kate makes her appearance in the house all my distresses are multiplied a million fold," he told his wife, Harriet, in a letter, "because she has a million times more buz than you." This was the woman whose formal portrait shows a square face and jaw, prominent nose, wire-rimmed spectacles, penny-roll curls, and more fabric wrapped around her — more crinoline and hoop skirts, more folds of drapery, in the style of the day — than a Victorian window ever suffered.

In *The American Woman's Home,* she and her sister organized the work flow and layout of a kitchen by basing it on the cook's galley of a steamship, which, they pointed out, contains every utensil needed in cooking for two hundred people "so arranged that with one or two steps the cook can reach all he uses." Their house plans and kitchen designs call for well-lighted, continuous work surfaces at a height that requires neither stooping nor reaching, with shelves and drawers above and below them to hold everything from towels and cleaning powder to the implements and mechanical tools designed to save the housewife time. The Beecher sisters were also bears for ventilation, which, as Rybczynski points out, was a nineteenth-century idée fixe, not unlike "organic" foods today. So, *The American Woman's Home* has two entire chapters on ventilation, one titled "Scientific Domestic Ventilation," in which Catharine and Harriet declare that every house should have a central air shaft with connecting branches in each room to vent "vitiated" air. Each adult, she pointed out, vitiates thirty-three hogsheads of air a day, and in a closed house we all breathe this poison. Rybczynski details the flawed science on which this analysis was based, but grants that Beecher was ahead of her time in one important prin-

ciple: comfort in the home could be achieved by technology and rational planning.

HOUSEHOLD ENGINEERING

Such planning reached the status of scripture fifty years later, with
Christine Frederick's *Household Engineering: Scientific Management in
the Home*. Frederick based her book on data surveys and motion and
time studies conducted by the same efficiency engineers who were ra-
tionalizing assembly lines at the factories of her husband's business
associates. For example, by moving a pot from the pot closet to a shelf
adjacent to the sink, hanging a knife on a nail beside the sink, and in-
stalling a garbage pail on a shelf beneath a countertop with a hole,
a housewife can prepare boiled potatoes in two minutes instead of
five, using eight steps instead of nineteen. Frederick also initiated the
system that plagued both my and Hannah's mothers: keeping recipes
on index cards alphabetically arranged by category— "Beverages,"
"Breads," "Beans"— in a little file cabinet, or "recipe file," on a kitchen
shelf. "All these cards should be punched with a small hole in the center upper edge. Then a small hook should be screwed in the shelf at
about eye level, and as a card is taken from the box, it is to be hung on
the hook, where it can be easily seen and read." She also suggests cards
with celluloid tabs, so they won't become soiled or bent by frequent
thumbing.

Such scientific management of a household sounds quaint to us today. Much of it is undoubtedly useful, and some has become such
accepted practice that we hardly give it a second thought. Still, one
can't help imagining efficiency engineers in white smocks and gloves
calculating the trajectory and velocity of a flying plate when a housewife or househusband throws a temper tantrum. Should they stand
eight feet away from the wall or six? Actually, today's efficiency experts

might recommend an inefficient kitchen as an opportunity for both upper- and lower-body exercise. One could cook a meal while achieving cardiovascular happiness, thus efficiently fulfilling two duties simultaneously.

In the late nineteenth and early twentieth centuries, the passion for rational planning sprang from the same impulse as statistical surveys of intelligence, the morphological organization of criminal faces, and the management and care of normalcy. The Zeitgeist seemed to demand such optimistic practices. Knowledge, after all, would soon erase the unknown. By the turn of the century, professors of physics were warning students to pursue other disciplines, since the future of physics would only consist in searching for one more decimal place.

One prescient writer understood the horror beneath such attitudes, however — understood how the resolve to gain control over one's living arrangements, to manage one's environment, to organize and plan with reason and logic, can all come unhinged of its own momentum. In Kafka's story "The Burrow," the domestic concerns of such household engineers as Beecher and Frederick are presented in the context of a devoluted home, one that recovers our link with the animals and their intimacy with nature. The narrator, a sort of gopher or mole with human thought and language, methodically describes his underground burrow, its smells, its ventilation shafts, its food storage, its entrance, and its arrangements for security. He's a technocrat, a problem solver. Should he distribute his stores throughout his burrow or keep them in one place? One place is best: "self-conceit suffers if one cannot see all one's stores together, and so at a glance know how much one possesses."

Yet he lives in a world of mounting anxiety. The security he's achieved is never enough, and his burrow requires continual repairs, perpetual vigilance, unending work. What a powerful nightmare this burrow becomes, with its combination of womb-like security and increasing demands for management and remodeling. Anyone who lives in a home can sympathize, but especially those who live alone. Kafka's burrow is the secret shadow of the rational household; the two go hand in hand. It's the story of being overwhelmed by one's arrangements and their manifold duties. As things grow worse, piles of dirt clog the narrator's tunnels, and he shovels them back then runs off, but the soil trickles into the passageway again. And all of this seems to be happening to *him;* every time a grain of dirt slides down a tunnel's walls, he experiences a kind of spiritual erosion.

At last he gives up. Exactly like Paul. Standing in that house with Woody and Alex, I saw Paul in his bedroom as though in a burrow— lying on his mattress, facing the wall, knees tucked beneath his chin, eyes wide open.

3

THE REVENGE OF PRIVATE LIFE

ONE THING ABOUT a smell—it gets inside you. Inside that house, it penetrated my privacy. I wondered if Woody and Alex felt the same. We crawled, it seemed, back to the cellar door, down the steps, outside. We emerged into the light as if stumbling from a cave. But something held me back. I'd shared a smell with Paul and would never forget it. The sheer revulsion I felt, the inner stain, seemed like some sort of polluted communion. As I blinked in the light, as I took a deep breath, I knew there was no way I'd ever purge that smell. Particles of it would always be with me. Also, it seemed that a miniature Paul was huddled up somewhere in a corner of my soul, and as I squeezed the padlock shut the picture grew clearer, nearly overwhelming me. He was part of his house, the house was part of me, so I was part of him. I almost felt I understood him. Paul had reversed the evolution of dwellings, from a modern ranch house with all the conveniences back to an animal's nest. Like the narrator of Kafka's story, his inner world had spiraled out of control in concert with his outer—which also was, in relative terms, an inner world, a burrow sealed off from the daylight outside.

So inner and outer finally merged. He walled himself up against the outside world, he listened for a flutter, a whistle, a murmur—any harbinger of death, the faintest would do—and he never really knew if it came from his body or the walls of his burrow.

At least, I told myself, my brother had escaped—he'd fled his burrow and managed to live for another two years. It must have been the shame of being found in his house by people he knew—Woody and his ambulance crew—that gave him the impetus. He'd fled our house in California years ago for a similar reason, after overhearing Hannah and me talk about him. By some labyrinthine logic, Paul had convinced himself that others hardly noticed him. But when they did, I suspect, he felt like a boy caught hiding by adults whose only solution was to run and hide again.

His last years in Boston were hardly an improvement. He withdrew more than ever, to my mother's dismay. On my visits I tried to avoid walking past his open door, but the apartment was small. I slept on the couch, since he'd appropriated every inch of space in our old room. There, near the door, he sat on his bed, staring at the computer, mouse in hand and tray on his lap. He looked up only if I stood in the doorway, and eventually I did—out of fraternal duty or to torture us both, I'm not sure which. He was my brother, I told myself. He'd been generous to us. He had a decent heart. He took my mother shopping, took her to visit Dad at the nursing home, and her gratitude enabled a white lie to grow without ever being told: that he'd moved in to help her. I hadn't seen his house then, of course, so didn't know what he was hiding, sitting on that bed. He did drive to New Hampshire once a week to pick up his mail. I asked why he didn't rent out the house, but he shrugged off the question.

Standing at the door, I tried some small talk about his computer. It doubled as a television set via the cable connector in the wall. He could freeze pictures from his favorite programs and store them on disks, he said. On his shelf over the computer were dozens of boxes, each with dozens of disks, each filled with such stills, filed by name. He'd printed out the files. He handed them to me. I leafed through them, trying to muster whatever he expected—interest, appreciation. "Boy on a horse." "Yellowstone Park." "Little girl in a pool." "Kathie Lee."

Boxes of junk mail on the floor beside the bed. Dirty clothes in paper bags.

Looking back now at him sitting on that bed, he seemed to be still living in New Hampshire. The clock radio glowing in the dark back in his house on a sea of trash was the soul he'd left behind, his little winged psyche, still trapped there. He was still one with the house he'd abandoned. And at the end, after two years in Boston, he died like the house did, his conduits and pipes fouled, clogged, and split open. Like the plumbing and central heating in his house, Paul's circulatory systems broke down completely.

Was his life a waste of life? I've asked myself that question countless times and still can't be certain of an answer. Thoreau said he went into the woods so that when he came to die he wouldn't suddenly find he hadn't lived. But he also said that most people live lives of quiet desperation, whether in the city or the country. Despair is barely concealed, he pointed out, even under our amusements. Especially under them, I would add. I'd seen Paul's amusements—ham radios, pornographic videos—those of solitude and boredom. Wastes of time, they became literal waste, just as most of his clothes became rags on his body. Until he moved back in with my mother, I don't think he ever washed his clothes, just bought new ones at discount stores and left the old to rot where they lay.

We've all read about houses like Paul's—those discovered to be filled with trash or cats when their owners died—but reading about it and being there yourself are two different things. The most famous example is probably the Collyer brothers on Fifth Avenue in New York. One was blind and never went out, the other emerged as seldom as possible, to buy food for himself and his blind brother. In March of 1947, the police received an anonymous phone call that someone was dead in the house, and found all five floors of their brownstone, attic to basement, stuffed full of trash, to every room's ceiling. Tunnels had been burrowed through this garbage, with clever booby traps to keep out intruders. They found the blind brother dead on the second floor, but it took them nineteen days to find the other one—in the same room, it turned out—buried beneath one of his own traps.

So I should have been thankful. Paul's version of the revenge of private life was, by comparison, mild. This was not consolation. It could very well be that small horrors, those experienced alone, are the worst. The Collyer brothers had each other, after all. And I pictured Paul's life, in my despair, as having endured alone its own erosion grain by grain by grain, yet having continued its diminished existence immersed in the remains.

Tall, gangly Alex was jumping up and down, swinging his arms. None of us, it seemed, could quite look at each other. To say the fresh air outside felt good would be like saying it was quite a relief to come back to life after having been dug up. "It's worse than I thought," Alex finally said.

"Me too," said Woody. "That night we came and got him, it was pretty much dark. It was bad, I remember, but not as bad as this."

"Maybe vandals made it worse," I offered.

"There you go. That's it. They would, wouldn't they?" Woody was nodding.

"I'm thinking I'll have to get it cleaned out before I put it on the market."

"Or you could sell it as is." Alex raised his eyebrows.

"Who would buy it like that?"

"I got two strapping boys, we could clean it out ourselves," Alex said. "Do it on weekends. They're both Boy Scouts. Must be some merit badge. Rent a dumpster. Family project." He was getting excited and seemed out of breath. A lumberjack turned cabinetmaker. His hands wouldn't stop moving. More and more, his face took on the startled expression of someone falling backwards down a hole. The cloth cap made it rounder, his face. "We'd work on it weekends. It wouldn't take long. Take it off your back. No fuss, no muss. Hell, you don't want to be burdened with this place. You going to clean it out yourself?"

"Thought I'd get some estimates."

"Who from?"

"Cleaning services."

"What, a bunch of maids? They'll take one look and run screaming down the road."

He did have a point. We were standing near the van in a little patch of sunlight that didn't warm the air. The van, stuffed with junk and trash like the house, deepened in color in that patch, if white can be said in any fashion to deepen. Every scratch and burr was visible. This was not the Plymouth van Paul drove before he died—not the one I owned now—but an older Dodge box, delivery-truck style.

Bouncing on his toes, waving his arms, Alex looked around and out of nowhere said, "How much you want for that mower?"

"That thing?" We regarded it, next to the van. All the metal parts were pitted with rust, but most of it was plastic. Four flat tires. "Fifty dollars," I said.

"Sold!" He took out his wallet and handed me a fifty.

"What about that MG?" Woody piped up.

"Make me an offer."

"Five hundred dollars."

"Six," I said.

"Sold!"

We were giddy, it seemed. For a while we just stood there. Woody explained he'd have to meet me here later — would tomorrow be okay? With a tow truck, he added. He'd bring the money then.

"Look," said Alex. "If I buy the house as is, you won't have to clean it out, won't even have to put it on the market. I got two strapping boys. They can do the work."

"Maybe you better let them see it first."

"They've seen it already. Most likely," he added. "We live just down the road."

"I get the impression everyone in town's seen it. How much were you thinking?"

"Say, thirty thousand dollars?"

I looked at Alex. He tried to smile.

"Nothing's working," he said. "No plumbing, no septic, no heat."

"The lights work," I said. "The water and septic haven't been used in a couple of years. You don't know they don't work."

"Look at this," Alex said. He walked around the van and pointed to a concrete collar sticking out of the ground with a thick concrete lid. "That there's the water supply. That's his spring," he said. "I don't know if you noticed, but in the house, inside? If you look in the basement? The septic pipe goes through the foundation right around up there." He nodded toward the back porch, up the slope behind the house. "See them thorn shoots and bushes? That's most likely the leach field. How far would you say you got from here to there?"

"Fifty feet?"

"I'd say thirty-five. And it's upslope from this, and this here's the water supply, and it's a spring. Get my drift?"

"So someone will have to put in a new septic, and maybe dig a new well. I expected that."

"And clean the place out and rip out the walls and rewire and so forth. Might as well burn the place down."

"I've thought about that too," I admitted.

"You got insurance?" Woody asked right away. He'd been thinking of it also, it appeared. Beside him, Alex raised his eyebrows. We looked at one another. The Volunteer Fire Department, I thought.

I nodded, then shook my head and tried to chuckle. "No thanks," I said. They extended the moment, watching me, then shrugged, almost in unison, as if to say, Okay, we tried.

"You could tear it down and sell the land," offered Alex.

"I thought you wanted it," I said.

"Hell, I'm looking for a challenge. It's a nice location. I can do the work myself!"

You and your strapping boys, I thought. "I'll think about it," I said. "Thing is, I have to get the house appraised anyway."

"What for?"

"Probate court."

"You want a quick sale, it could save a lot of trouble. Thirty thousand cash."

"Got the money on you?"

"I could get it. Just like that!" He snapped his fingers, throwing his hand back. But the snap seemed limp. He could tell I wasn't budging.

"I don't have much choice. The probate court mandates an appraisal right away. They have to determine the value of his estate as of the date of death."

Alex raised his eyebrows and smiled. "Thirty thousand dollars!"

It was tempting. But another part of me had made the decision without consulting the rest: to get the house cleaned out, whatever the cost.

VI
ORIGINS

1

C L E A N

MOST OF THE cleaning services I phoned weren't interested. The housecleaners said to call an industrial cleaning service, and the industrial cleaning services thought I needed a housecleaner. Dirt R Us never called back, JB's Krew took one look and declined to give an estimate, Royal Custom Cleaning left an estimate of $6,800, then called me in New York a week later and said they'd changed their mind and didn't want the job. I was driving back and forth from upstate New York every other weekend, with little success. I had no intention of cleaning it myself—it would have been impossible—and actually began to feel some relief, as though the responsibility were slipping through my fingers. There was nothing I could do. I realized that must have been Paul's conclusion too. It was like holing up in a small protective cave inside a mountain of despair.

Maybe I could hire Alex's two strapping boys and their teenage friends. But Alex never got in touch with me again.

I made most of the calls to cleaning services from Jud's Mobil station, and the third or fourth time I borrowed his phone book he asked what I was looking for. So I emptied my story right there in his store like a bucket of slops. He knew Paul's house well, drove by it every day. Knew the town had been having trouble with teens breaking into it, he said. Knew Paul himself a little, knew he smoked Kools, had sold him many cartons, stocked them mostly for him. I did not tell him where they wound up, as one-inch butts stuffed inside a thousand Pepsi bottles.

Jud spoke with a slight hesitation and stutter, and asked obtuse questions, such as, How come you wanna clean it out? I explained that I thought I'd have a better chance to sell it. He wrinkled his brow. Tall and thin, sandy-haired, hook-nosed, he was slow to react yet quick and efficient as he went about his business. And capable, it seemed, of doing several things at once—of talking with me, ringing up sales, pumping gas, and answering the phone, all, as it turned out, while his gears turned. He possessed the disconcerting trait of glancing off to the side as he talked, not once or twice but every few seconds. His eyes blinked a lot. One ear was pierced and displayed a silver bead. He gave me the name of the town scavenger, the man who would haul off anything for anyone, and who always had two or three friends in need of work. But still he seemed preoccupied. Then he stammered, What the hell, I could use an extra buck. I got some friends who could too. How about I take a look?

It took several months to go from talk to an agreement. We even drew up a contract: he and his crew could have anything they found, except ham radio equipment, important papers, and cash. I told him even though I'd be around, still I'd have to rely on his honesty. He said that I should ask around town, ask anyone at all, and they'll tell you I'm straight. I stick to my word and keep my agreements, he said. But I never asked.

Our arrangement was that he'd hire and pay the crew, order and pay the deposit on the dumpster, then I would pay him on completion of the job $1,275. I'd also pay for an extra dumpster if needed. Jud and friends would empty out everything, basement to attic, and leave it broom clean. They'd do it in three days. The question of workers' comp or health insurance would have been shrugged off, I realized. But who knew what sorts of hazards lay buried in that trash? One reason I wanted it cleaned in the first place was my fear that the county health department would sooner or later come sniffing around. Be sure to wear masks and gloves, I told him.

The day before they started, I removed whatever boxes and files of personal papers I could find. My plan was to park outside the house and sit in the van and go through them while they worked. Then I wandered the house one last time with plastic bags and gloves and bagged every cat and dog corpse I could find. They were stiff and mummified, some flat as road kill, though the flat ones generally stuck to any surface from which I tried to peel them. Those had a tendency to pull into pieces.

It was May already. Little green bat wings had begun to unfold from deciduous trees and bushes outside, and the day was drizzly—as my cousins in Maine used to say, it was spitting out. But I was inside trying to save my dead brother that much more shame, though I knew it was really me who'd be ashamed. Buried in his house, climbing through debris with a sack across my back, I cursed the absent gods for not striking the place with lightning long ago. *What are you waiting for?* I felt myself drawing a line in my soul beyond which forgiveness for Paul would not cross. His life had slowly contaminated him, leaving him helpless. He'd become a man tormented by the same compulsions that were medicine for his torment: the need to hoard, the inability to throw things away. For this existence—for its sadness and waste—I'd filled, drop by drop, day by day, since his death, with a numbing cold sorrow. It seemed to come from far away, from a spring inside the earth.

But for his treatment of his pets, all I felt was anger. Couldn't he have left a door or window open? Does feeling so abject excuse anyone from a modicum of feeling for other living creatures? I pictured them roaming the darkened mounds of trash, searching for scraps, ripping bags open, climbing and clawing at the walls, while all the time— summoning up a thin wire of strength—they protected shifting territory and slashed at each other. They probably died of thirst, not hunger; every corpse was desiccated. Then something strange happened. As I stood in Paul's kitchen, paper mask on my face and rubber gloves on my hands, my own feelings of rage, like a chemical solution, catalyzed to abjection. I noticed bits of fur and leathery skin clinging to the yellow gloves, and something drained inside me. This entire business was crazy and disgusting. I felt emptied out, almost dizzy. Everything, I thought—cleaning out the house, selling it, being a responsible fiduciary, in the probate court's language—was all a crock of shit. Why not go ahead and burn the place down? At least that would purify it.

But what would purify me?

So I finished the job, tied up the bag, and went down through the basement. A poem by Philip Levine began to haunt me. In it, a pig being led to market pictures his innards released from his body and shaken out "like a hankie." *Not this pig,* he thinks, but he trots along anyway on his owner's leash. Above all, it was the title that kept running through my head as if on a loop: "Animals Are Passing from Our Lives." But they take their revenge, I thought, they pass away but pile up. Meanwhile we remember, as in a dream, far back, the time when we shared a life with animals. And our myths remember too, from the Shoshone stories of Coyote and Wolf to the ancient Greek legends of Leda and the swan.

Today, however, our myths are neuroses, and our stories "cases." Two of Freud's most famous patients have come to be known as the Wolf Man and the Rat Man. Apparently, the animals' revenge takes the form of haunting our inner lives. The Wolf Man experienced an intense fear of wolves, identified, says Freud, with a primal scene in which his parents copulated like ferocious beasts. The Rat Man thought if he did something wrong, rats would eat their way into the anuses of his father and a woman he loved.

Freud wrote of other animal phobias—fear of horses, for example. I'd experienced mild dog phobia myself after Paul's dog, Rip, had bitten me on the leg: dreams of ferocious dogs in dank cellars, fear of approaching them. . . . But they diminished over time. It was only after

Paul's death that I discovered Freud's suggestion, in *Totem and Taboo*, that animal phobias were a characteristic disturbance of our age. I came across this idea in trying to understand my brother—in a search for reasons. Why was Paul the man he was?

The case of the Rat Man became the central one in which Freud discussed, in our lingo, obsessive-compulsive disorder. He called it "obsessional neurosis." Howard Hughes, for example, was obsessive-compulsive. He insulated and darkened his room with paper towels and tissues. Fearing contamination, he stopped wearing clothes. Yet he never washed, never cut or combed his hair and long beard, never pared his nails, which curled back as they grew. Before handing him a spoon, his Mormon attendants wrapped the handle in tissue paper, sealed it with cellophane tape, and wrapped a second piece of tissue around the first. Hughes then took the spoon, discarding the second piece of tissue, and used it with the handle covered by the first.

It should come as no surprise that Freud traced obsessional neurosis back to infantile anal eroticism, and identified its etiology as severe toilet training, an explanation not generally accepted today. The three character traits of anal eroticism, he said, were orderliness, parsimony, and obstinacy, all learned by means of the infant's control over excretion. The infant takes pleasure in keeping back and postponing, in holding in his feces as long as possible, and then, once they're out, not letting them go, but playing with them instead, smearing them around. The impulse to gather, collect, and hoard, say the Freudians, stems from an arrested anal eroticism. Ernest Jones: "All collectors are anal-erotics."

Freudianism has always been a species of informed speculation, of course. Its explanatory power is more metaphorical than biological, though Freud himself often suspected that biology was the true answer. In the continuing war between culture and nature—between world-historical explanations, say, and those that refer all character traits to hardwiring in the brain—no one walks the fence between the either/ors as well as Freud did. For one thing, his explanations have passed into the lexicon of popular culture. Everyone knows what "anal" means: those with a mania for cleanliness and order. Yet few psychologists today would dare suggest that animal phobias are symptoms of a discontent of our age.

What would Freud have thought of Paul? Was it really toilet training? I sometimes imagined frightening scenes between Paul and Grandma, whose methods, I knew, were of the old school, and included rubbing sheets wet with urine in the face of the accused. I know because, to my mother's dismay, she'd once done this to me.

Yet my brother possessed no mania for order, and surely not for cleanliness. He did hoard and collect with a sort of passive passion, with the carelessness and haste of an unconscious person fulfilling a need. What he hoarded was his trash.

I wonder if he even saw what he'd accumulated. Most of us don't. That's why we keep accumulating. Think of it this way: the duty to be orderly, obscurely felt as disturbing, unravels from within. You begin by tolerating neither waste nor disorder. Where does waste come from, anyway? From throwing things away. Therefore, do not throw anything away. Retain everything instead, even if it piles up. Over time, you won't notice. You'll look right through the mounds of trash, brush them aside as inconvenient obstacles. Gradually, then, out of the impulse toward order and control, the debris of order blossoms — waste and filth. It can take a long time, twenty years or so. One day you wake up as though shaken from a dream and look around and see it. I suspect the big change came with Paul's retirement, three years before his death. He no longer had work to occupy his mind and time. How does it feel to open your eyes and see that your life has piled up around you? "I HAVE GOT TO DO SOMETHING ABOUT GETTING HOUSE CLEANED UP!! I DONT KNOW WHAT??"

It could be at this time that the animals around him first became a burden. He tried giving them away—"Want a cat?" he could have asked Woody—but they clung all the more. It's like shattering a mirror—it just produces more reflections. "I HAVE TO GET RID OF CAT'S!!" he wrote. Exactly when it was impossible, it became necessary to get rid of everything. Filth is the excluded, says Julia Kristeva. Filth is defilement; it can come from the body, expelled by the body— spit, blood, shit, piss, sweat—but once it crosses the frontier of skin, it must be thrown away. Why? To establish the self as clean and pure. Filth, in other words, is matter out of place, as Mary Douglas says, matter in the wrong place. Cat shit in the sink. If it's not thrown away, I am not clean and pure. To say the same thing, I'm thrown away myself, I'm abject. Abject: *ab* plus *jacere,* "away" and "cast." I'm cast away from life. I've thrown everything away yet at the same time I haven't, because I've managed to hoard it. Because I've thrown it away, I've done my duty, but because I've hoarded it, I've covered my bets. I'm clinging to myself. I'm the person given the impossible job of saving the very things I throw away. I both retain and exclude them—I foul my own nest. I'm a castoff. An animal.

The solution, then, is to leave the filth behind and move back in with mother.

At the door to the basement, I threw the plastic bag in a pile of trash, peeled off the rubber gloves, the paper mask too, and tossed them after it. But locking up the house I remembered something, and pushed the door open and climbed the cellar steps to get it: the photograph of Grandma. Paul'd kept it all those years on the desk beside his mattress; I pictured it now as the eye of his hurricane.

I was a pimply adolescent the year she died. Four years earlier, both she and Paul had lived with us in Boston for a whole summer, I'm still not sure why. Her roof in Wire Valley was being replaced, or her wiring, or her plumbing. Or maybe my father was keeping an eye on her—she'd been acting strange lately. Once, in his Chevy, she'd opened the door of the moving vehicle, and Mom had to grab her. After that, someone else always sat beside the door.

That summer in Boston she grew even more troublesome. She

sometimes left the house and wandered the neighborhood, forcing Dad to search for her. He tried locking the apartment, and this resulted in struggles between him and Grandma, frightening to remember. They happened in darkness. Her strength, he said later, was surprising, even shocking.

I was sleeping on the couch, and lay there and listened. Grandma had been given my bed and shared my room with Paul—the same room, several years later, I would share with him. As I've said, our place was pretty small. It seemed odd to hear my father first negotiating with Grandma, then pleading and cajoling, at last ordering her to bed. She rattled the door, kicked it, and they scuffled. He called her "Ma." That may have been the first time I realized she was his mother, not just my grandma.

The next day, she knelt at the living room window—open to the street—and prayed as loudly as she could: "Forgive my son his trespasses, as we forgive those . . ."

Later that summer, she crept up behind me at the same window and gripped my arms by the elbows with the strength of steel clamps. "Lean out," she said.

I didn't, of course. I tried to lean in.

"Lean out, you stubborn child."

We lived on the second floor. It was twenty feet down. "Take a deep breath. Lean way out." My arms felt like pencils in her tight grip. The top half of my body began tipping out the window, at the mercy of her strength. Then she pushed.

I barked helplessly, "Oh!"

She yanked me back in, limp as a rag doll. "There. Are they gone?"

"Are what gone?"

She wasn't listening. "My own mother cured me of the hiccups that way. Nothing beats a good scare. When I was a child I had the hiccups once for four days running." She'd turned me to face her. Her round black eyes, her peanut-shell face, her masculine nose, and lips thin as liver sliced with a razor blade—all had relaxed into a kind of nectar. No one could be more sweet than my grandmother, yet she'd just terrified me for no reason. "Hiccups wouldn't stop," she continued. "I slept with them, ate with them. Stuck my head underwater and counted to a hundred. Held my arms above my head and panted like a dog. Nothing worked. Then Mama snuck up and pushed me from behind at the window to my room. She grabbed on, just like I did with you, so I was safe. But I thought my heart would stop. My own mother! Thought creation was against me."

"That's what I thought too!"

"After something like that, you cherish every breath you draw. No more wishing for the evening if it's morning, and wishing for the morning if it's evening. It don't work unless you're trusting."

Trusting? I remembered the time I'd lived with her a week when I was five or six years old. She accused all her children of stealing her things. Liddy had taken the Chinese checkers game, Madge the lawnmower, Winona the window fan. We rummaged in closets, in the cellar, in the attic, looking for clues of these crimes against nature, against the debt of love and gratitude owed to a mother. My most vivid impression of Grandma is seeing her bent into a closet, searching through boxes, paper bags, and shoes, while I stand behind on tiptoes craning my neck. The closet recedes like a pop-up book back into its folds as the door swings slowly shut, gathering Grandma into its dark wings . . .

In Boston, she once consoled me for some injustice I felt, some perceived martyrdom — not being allowed to watch *I Love Lucy* on television, I think, even though it was summer.

My mother'd told me that when she and Dad were newlyweds living with Grandma, Aunt Liddy often visited from Maine. Aunt Liddy had committed a terrible crime: she'd married a Methodist. She began having children and one by one brought them to visit in Wire Valley, without her husband, Uncle Jason — and one by one, Grandma took them to St. Patrick's to have them baptized by a priest.

After that summer with us in Boston, she returned to Wire Valley.

But each succeeding weekend, Dad found more evidence that her world had gone centrifugal, like beads whipped off a necklace and scattered everywhere: social security checks in the trash, windows left open, pipes frozen, no heating oil. Paul couldn't help much; he had a job by then at the little airport in Wire Valley. The job paid for his car, which he needed to commute from Grandma's house to the job.

Within a year, Grandma had moved in with Aunt Winona, and Dad told stories of her taking off her clothes and sitting in protest on the living room floor. Six months later she was in the senile ward of the state hospital in Worcester, a house of horrors so terrible that my father left Mom and me in his Chevy, parked on a road beside a high brick wall, when he went to visit her. Meanwhile, Paul joined the army. She died when he was stationed in California. He couldn't come to her funeral, but once his hitch was over he moved in with us in Boston.

By the time I arrived the next morning at eight—our agreed-upon hour—Jud and his crew were already working. Trash was strewn across the yard. It turned out they'd come at sunrise, and had torn off the shutters, opened the doors, and removed the back windows, beneath which the dumpster sat.

But why all the cars? The whole town had shown up, or so it seemed to me. People watched from the road. Children ran around, more cars pulled up and parked, rap music blasted from a pickup truck. Several television sets sat beneath a tree, also some chairs, a microwave oven, sorted piles of videotapes, and a telescope. Then I noticed the sign, spray-painted on the back of a shutter and propped against a tree: *Yard Sale Today.*

Sunlight slanted through trees. The new leaves had perked up. Birds flocked about, singing happy songs, and townspeople honked at their friends as they passed. I felt caught in a nightmare.

Men tossed plastic bags out a window of the bedroom with the carpeted walls. Most landed in the dumpster. I crawled through a window in the other bedroom, where several teenagers were pawing through the ham equipment. Jud was in the hallway, his two helpers in the bedroom. One of them was up to his neck shoveling trash into a bag held open by the other, who averted his face. All three had shovels the size used by cleanup crews behind the elephants at the circus. They wore masks and gloves, at least. Only idiots wouldn't. Dust filled the air and floated lazily everywhere. It colored the light yellow and brown and made the place feel underwater, like a giant cup of tea whose bag had ripped open.

"What's this?" I shouted at Jud. In the hallway, he shoveled bottles and shit into a bag.

"What's what?"

"All the people!"

"We're clean — cleaning out the house."

"I told you I didn't want anyone in the house except the crew. You agreed to that. It's a liability nightmare, for one thing. What's with the sign?"

"You got a problem with that?"

"*Yard Sale?* Are you serious?"

One of the helpers burst out of the bedroom, chased by the other holding up a centerfold. I realized they'd removed all the doors. Jud introduced me. "This is Ray, this is Eric." Ray closed up the magazine, pulled off a glove, and removed his mask. He reached to shake my hand. His arm looked like a leg. Wrapped in each sleeve of his white T-shirt was a pack of cigarettes. I wanted to tell him not to smoke in here, but too much was going on. I felt overwhelmed. In the tea-colored light he looked menacing: crewcut, pirate earring, stubble of blond beard, muscular torso. He was clearly a dedicated lifter of weights. He shook my hand firmly.

Eric, on the other hand, held back. He'd gone from a kid being chased by a friend to a somber adult in an instant. His eyes were dark, whereas Ray's were blue. His shoulder-length hair looked mostly

214 · A BOOK OF REASONS

black, but the cobwebs and dust made it hard to tell. I should have told them to wear shower caps, I thought. He'd begun to cough, and while Ray slapped his back, he glared at me, it seemed. He blamed me for this job he'd gotten into. Get men who will not walk away from the job, I'd emphasized to Jud.

Jud seemed to be ducking in the hallway. I realized his head was almost to the ceiling on that thick floor of cat shit and bottles. All at once he asked his crew, "Who painted that sign?"

"I did," said Eric.

"Take it down." Eric left. Then Jud looked at Ray, who walked back into the bedroom. He turned to me, and for once hardly stammered or shifted his eyes. "You want us to do this job? You said we could keep what — whatever we found."

"I didn't say you could sell it."

"What the hell else did you think we'd do, give it away?"

"I meant not today. Didn't I say nobody in the house except you and your helpers? There's two kids in there going through the ham equipment."

"Ray's two boys."

"I don't care. It's too risky. I can't have a mob of people in the house. And those people outside. You'll have to ask them to leave. Also, we agreed the ham equipment's mine."

"They're just look — looking at it. Here, do me a favor. Hold up that bag. I keep missing it." He drove the shovel with a fury into a hardened crust of excrement. A bottle flew past my foot down the hall. When he dumped it in the bag, a mushroom cloud rose, and we both turned away. "One more," he said, and I held out the bag.

When it was full he tied the thing shut and gestured me to follow. We walked through the bedroom and climbed out the window. He threw the bag into the dumpster.

On the ground beside the dumpster were fifty or sixty rolls of plastic trash bags. Also wheelbarrows, rakes, more shovels, and a toolbox. The dumpster seemed almost the size of a boxcar, and trash was spread around it—scraps of paper, bottles, wounded umbrellas, crushed boxes, magazines.

I looked out toward the road. The music had stopped and there were fewer people now—at least so it seemed. Full plastic bags flew out the window of the other bedroom. Jud took my arm and we walked toward the dirt road. "I called up the guy who hauls away the appliances. He says there's a charge of fifty bucks each for the air conditioner and fridge. EPA regulations."

I shrugged and looked away. What choice did I have? I felt tongue-tied. "Fifty bucks each?"

"One thing you—you might want to do? Take all the ham equipment you want to keep and put it in that closet." He gestured at the house. "Then it won't get mixed up. You okay?"

"Yeah, sure." I couldn't stop coughing. I'd been brushing off my clothes when suddenly it felt as though someone'd jerked a rope knotted to my stomach and running through my mouth.

Jud watched me. "You ought to wear a mask."

We stood in the sun. Today would be warm. I finished my fit, gulping air, catching breath. "I brought some soft drinks in the van," I gasped. "I'll go get the cooler. You and your crew help yourselves anytime."

"Hey th-thanks. We brought some too."

For the rest of the day I sat in the van going through Paul's papers and throwing most of them in trash bags. Jud came and went in his pickup all day. Every now and then a car or truck pulled up, and someone approached the bedroom window and drove off with a bundle—of what, I couldn't tell. I didn't really care. The dust from the house had left my insides swarming with pestilence. All day I kept coughing, the swampy tissue in my throat seething as if it had been shot full of needles. Also, I realized I'd never been a boss. This was something new to me. I taught college students how to think and write, but didn't make them sweep the floors. I began to feel guilty for sitting in my car while

Jud's crew worked. One time Ray shot out the back door screaming through his mask. He looked at the sky, tore off the mask, took a deep breath, then swaggered back in.

They took breaks to smoke or drink sodas, but not for very long. Was Jud paying his friends by the hour or the job? They had only three days. Had he promised them booty? Made them think they'd find a treasure? I never did ask what they did for a living. What wormholes of fate and space-time, I wondered, put them inside the house and me outside watching? I'd parked beneath a tree down the dirt road, with the house in full view up an incline before me. They were younger than I was, but no different from the friends I grew up with in Boston, in my neighborhood and high school. Every now and then, one of them on break snuck a peek in my direction. Sometimes I got out and leaned against the car or walked around the house. I watched dust drift out the windows.

When he wasn't gone or working, Jud sat in his truck making calls on his cell phone. A small man built like a fireplug pulled up in a dump truck, and he and the crew wheeled out the appliances—two stoves, the refrigerator, air conditioner, washer, old water tanks from the basement.

The extra charges mounted. I imagined Paul warning me: They'll walk all over you, better be careful. Sitting in the car, I mentally reasoned with him: No one else would touch the job, I should be grateful, I couldn't do it myself. Fuck the extra charges. I feel so weird, I said— or imagined saying. I feel like an outcast.

You? snorted Paul.

In the late afternoon, Jud strolled down, swinging his arms, glancing left and right—every way but at me. He said they almost had the bedrooms cleared out, but the whole thing was taking longer than he thought. And that dumpster was outside the bedroom windows, so when they cleaned out the other end of the house they'd have to carry or wheel everything to it.

I pointed out to him that there wasn't as much in the other end of the house.

"There's a shitload," he said. "What—what about the basement?"

I shrugged. "What about it?"

He looked around, then snapped his fingers. "I got an idea."

The idea was, he had a friend with a backhoe. He thought he could get it. They could throw things out windows into the loader and drive it around and dump them in the dumpster. They could load up right at the entrance to the basement.

Sure, I said. Sounds like a good idea.

It's seventy-five bucks an hour, he added. Plus a hundred to bring it to the site.

Sure, go ahead.

He pulled out his cell phone, extended the antenna, and walked back to the house.

Meanwhile, I sat and went through Paul's stuff. Once in a while I found something of interest. An annuity contract. Two or three stock certificates. I found his large cache of sketches, memos, and notes about reinventing the notch filter. I also found letters Hannah and I had sent him years ago, before we moved to New York. In one, we thanked him for forgiving the loan of a thousand dollars to help buy our first house.

But mostly it was all unrelenting sameness. Its sheer tedium wore me down. Why save every phone bill you've ever received? Why, for that matter, did I feel the necessity to go through each one, thinking something might be there? I had to, I felt. It was my duty. Doing so brought me closer to Paul, to the life of the recluse who was my brother.

I asked for a wake-up call at the Red Roof Inn, rose before dawn the next morning, stopped at IHOP in Salem, and made the house at first light. A man I'd never seen before was dismantling the tall radio antenna bolted to the chimney. From high up on the aluminum tower, he asked me to help him. Could I tie on that wrench beside my feet to this rope?

He lowered the rope. I tied the wrench on. "You from the Volunteer Fire Department?" I asked.

"Sure as hell am not."

"Who said you could do this?"

"Fellow inside. From the Mobil station. He sold me the antenna."

"How much?"

"Six hundred bucks."

I crawled through the window. Jud and Eric were ripping up the rug from the living room floor. Ray hadn't arrived yet. "I need to talk with you," I said from the door. Jud gave the rug a last violent yank and walked into the kitchen. "That antenna outside. You told me you'd give it to the Volunteer Fire Department."

"They didn't want it." His expression was different—hard yet neutral. He held back from expression and didn't stammer at all.

"That guy on the roof says you sold it to him."

"You got a problem with that?"

"I've got a problem with everything."

"What is it this time?"

"We agreed you could keep anything you found except the ham equipment."

"That's not ham equipment."

"Of course it's ham equipment."

"Ham equipment's the radios and mikes and things."

"And tower and antenna."

He looked at my mouth. "So fire me."

"Okay."

He neither frowned nor smiled. His face did not move. It became a mug shot. Then he broke into a self-reflexive smile and shook his head, looking down. "Whatever."

I waited. His mannerisms came back: swiveling his head, shooting glances here and there. Outside, a loud machine bubbled up, and we heard a triumphant whoop. Ray with the backhoe. Eric and Jud ran through the dining room and jerked the front door open.

Hadn't I just fired them?

Later, Jud walked down to the car with a box full of papers he'd found in the basement. Looked like they might be important, he said. He rummaged in the box. "Passbook. Pay stubs. This here looks like an insurance — insurance policy."

"Thanks."

"What about those cars?" He gestured toward the three junk cars in the brush behind the house. "I could get rid of them for you," he said. "Won't charge you nothing."

"Fine. Sure. Whatever."

He'd won. Yet relief washed over me.

The day soon grew hotter. By mid-morning, Jud and his crew were working shirtless. As the dumpster filled up, they used the loader on the backhoe to crush it down. Ray chugged and spun and maneuvered the machine like a cowboy on a yellow palomino. He positioned the backhoe with the loader raised beneath a living room window, and Eric and Jud stuffed the rug they'd ripped up through the narrow window, and it puddled in the loader. As he sped back and forth from the garage or front door to the dumpster out back, his tires left ruts like huge unzipped flies. Meanwhile, Paul's house poured out its junk like some diabolical, mocking cornucopia. I had no idea why I insisted on keeping the ham equipment, incidentally. I must have thought it would be a memento.

The same man who'd come yesterday with the dump truck showed up with a flatbed and hauled off the three cars.

Gradually I began to feel lighter. I realized why I was going through this nightmare: to cleanse and renew *myself*, not Paul — to exclude the filth he couldn't exclude. In the dumpster, the trash made a giant mound, but Ray packed it down with every new load. They were almost finished, Jud announced. No sense ordering another dumpster. Each time he packed it down he gained another foot. Then another inch. Then nothing.

They were done.

It was nearly dark. They'd finished in two days. I shook their hands and tipped them twenty bucks each. Jud and I settled up. The overcharges came to about a thousand dollars, including the max extra weight for the dumpster. Total, $2,335. I happily paid, and watched them leave. Then I walked around the house with a plastic bag and lawn rake, and cleaned up debris. Inside, I took up the bathroom rug myself, since they'd neglected to. Underneath were little checkerboard tiles, white, green, and pink. They looked brand-new.

Our agreement had been to leave the house broom clean, but that was a laugh. *What are contracts for?* I smiled and shook my head. The next morning I bought a shop vac at Sears, though I remembered there'd been a new one in the basement; the crew had taken that. I vacuumed the house, including all those oily threads hanging from the ceilings. I checked the attic — empty except for a couch they apparently couldn't squeeze through the door.

I was loading the ham equipment into my van when the man from G & C Container Service arrived and had what my brother would have called a shit fit. "Christ almighty," he said. He asked where Jud was. I told him to try the Mobil station. No, he said, he'd stopped there. Jud wasn't around.

"What seems to be the problem?" I asked.

He waved at the dumpster. "What seems to be the problem is I can't take it like this."

"Why not?"

"Suppose to be level with the top."

"We couldn't get another dumpster." I tried not to panic. "It was Sunday. Nobody answered the phone." This was not the whole truth.

He walked around picking up things. Threw a piece of cardboard on top of the load and it slid down and struck him on the shoulder. Threw it up again. "An inch don't make no difference. Hell, a foot. That shit's three or four feet over the top."

"We had to keep packing it down with the backhoe."

I bit my tongue. Don't tell him that!

"You the owner?" He hadn't looked at me once. He kept climbing on the dumpster and pushing at the trash with both arms.

"Yes." With his back to me, he looked out at the road in his blue jumpsuit. It wasn't clean. "I already paid the extra weight," I said.

"How the hell did you know what the extra weight is before somebody weighs it?"

I shrugged. Crossed my fingers. He walked to his truck and spoke on the two-way radio in the cab.

"Look," I said when he came back. "I know it's a pain. Here," I said. "This is for your trouble." I held out two twenty-dollar bills.

He waved his hand in disgust. "Forget it." Already he'd begun unfolding a tarp. He threw it over the dumpster, walked around to the other side, reached for the rope, and pulled it down. He walked around the dumpster again, straightening the tarp and tying it down on hooks beneath the rim. When he was finished, the canvas tarp was stretched tighter than a corset. It looked like a shroud in a morgue for pregnant giants.

He climbed into the cab and backed up the truck. "Another inch," I shouted, gesturing with my hands. He wasn't paying attention. The pneumatic beam resting in its steel frame was just about to kiss the front of the dumpster when I raised my hand and shouted, "Whoa!" But he'd already hopped out and started working, stomping back and forth. I stepped out of the way. He hooked a steel cable onto the dumpster, then pulled a lever on a box behind the cab. The steel frame of his truck rose into the air on huge shock-absorber legs. He pulled another lever and the cable tightened. The engine whined so loud I thought its gears were stripping. The dumpster didn't budge.

Then it heaved and lurched forward. The slot in its bottom clumsily fitted itself on the beam, and this seemed disturbing—an act of sexual congress performed under duress. It lurched forward some more, tilting to one side. For a horrible moment I thought the whole thing would tip and crash and spill its contents.

But it slid up the beam with a sound of screaming steel. I felt it in my teeth. As the dumpster inched up, the beam slowly lowered on grasshopper legs, which folded in half and tucked themselves away with apparent haste. I could see why. The dumpster slammed down and the whole truck shook. He turned off his winch.

He drove off without a word, the truck slowly swaying with its awful weight. I feebly waved as it labored up the road. I was giddy with joy.

Then I hopped in my van and drove down to Wal-Mart and bought the thermometer with which this book began.

2

WASTE OF LIFE

WAS PAUL'S LIFE a waste of life?

The redundancy of the question decoys easy answers: "waste" sandwiched between two thin slices of "life." Sawdust and glue inside rosewood veneer. If his life was a life, it wasn't a waste; if it was a waste, it wasn't a life.

Was it a waste?

Careful. Go slow. Some questions blow up in the formulator's face. Don't we all waste our lives to some degree? Leave this question alone. Leave it tied and double knotted, the inner voice says, the same inner voice that masks its temptations with icy calm.

Did he waste his life?

The safe thing to say would be that no one can know. Certain questions can't be answered. But unanswerable questions go on spilling poisoned sweets, go on asking themselves over and over, rising all at once in a thousand dry bubbles, like boiling sugar. In the scale of the infinite silences that terrified Pascal, aren't all lives a waste?

No. Some are not.

Reverse the logic. In the hands of a loving God, don't some unnoticed lives slip through the omnifingers?

Yes. Some do.

This is not the received wisdom, by the way. "Either life is always and in all circumstances sacred, or intrinsically of no account," says an English journalist quoted by Annie Dillard. He was trying to understand Mother Teresa's Sisters of Charity in Calcutta. "It is inconceivable that it should be in some cases the one, and in some the other," he added. Yet the inconceivable happens all the time. Some lives transcend their given limitations, some never get the chance to. Some accumulate a soul, some wind up as empty skins, as though the very process of life and death had washed right through them. Paul slumping forward in a crowded room, having pinned himself against the wall. Paul staring straight ahead, his blank face sagging and drained of expression, yet upholstered with hopelessness — fists in pockets, trying to act casual, making little clucking noises in his throat. Paul inside his boarded-up world. On the edge of his bed in my mother's house, mouse on a tray balanced on his knees, watching the computer screen, playing virtual solitaire, freezing television images. It sounds like a washout, a complete surrender, a waste of every heartbeat and breath.

But he'd tried introspection. I'd found diaries and notebooks. He dreamed, he invented. He designed a notch filter for microwave broadcasts. Introspection gives weight. It grants existence to a soul. It's not the same as self-knowledge, which takes coy brutality, but it surely is a start. It lifts the volume a peg, it means someone notices you — yourself. The introspective man may very well fail to see his own world piling up around him, may look out of, not at, it. His concern with himself—with his health, bowel movements, symptoms, inner twinges—doesn't, in other words, rule out living on a dump he can't even see. In thinking of himself, did he feint and dance around—go for the underbelly—miss the obvious, seize the odd—sprinkle ashes on his soul? Did he grow too comfortable with the flavor of his consciousness? Nibble at edges or, however blindly, search for the jugular?

Did Paul waste his life?

Under pressure of work and the patriotic duty to consume, my obliging brother may have decided that introspection itself was the waste of time. To not waste one's life in the global marketplace is to be "productive," to work every day, to observe a routine, and to reward oneself with products. When a recluse retires and work is over, however, his personal avalanche of commodities and goods may freeze in the very act of crushing him. Then the unwasted life devoted to work, to productive citizenship, itself becomes the waste. A nightmare like this is not the exclusive destiny of working stiffs, either. A virtual life in a supermarket culture, a life of simulations designed to numb feeling, can happen to anyone: managers, professionals, poets, congressmen, Indians, housewives, teachers, and hockey players. Now and then one such person snaps awake. "And Richard Corey, one calm summer night, / Went home and put a bullet through his head" (Edwin Arlington Robinson).

There is an alternative. In America we talk a great deal about "making a difference" and "touching other people," perhaps because we instinctively know that we ourselves are also other people and could use a little help. "Only connect," insisted E. M. Forster. "Never stop doing good!" urged Ivan Ivanovich in Chekhov's "Gooseberries." These desperate injunctions sound like clinging to a life raft. So they are. How else survive? The most surprising thing I'd found after his death was a letter to Paul from a woman in Kentucky. "Thank you, Thank you, Thank you!" it began. "I can't thank you enough! We paid our phone bill off, paid the utilities before they got shut off and went out to eat with the kids. For us, that's a major splurge." It was signed Dori Burns, dated a week before he died. I showed it to my mother, who told me that Doris Burns was one of two sisters Paul had befriended in Boston years ago, daughters of a neighbor. One now lived in Kansas, the other in Kentucky. He'd kept in touch all his life—or they had, apparently. He sent them money. Later, going through his papers in Boston, I found a stock certificate with the other sister's name listed as joint owner with Paul. Directory assistance in Kansas City gave me her number. Phoning her, I felt like Publishers Clearing House. It wasn't a lot of stock—118 shares of Loral Corporation, worth a little over two thousand dollars. Still, she squealed with joy. Then remembered herself and expressed her condolences for my brother's death.

They'd been nine or ten years old when Paul befriended them. Their father had mistreated his children, that's what my mother thought. Cute little girls, she said, pictures of innocence. Later, as teens, they ran away from home, and phoned Paul, not their parents, when they wanted to return. He drove all the way to Kansas to get them.

Innocence, I thought. Reminders of childhood. We all have our ways of clinging to hope even when life seems to be a waste, when we're just getting through it. The getting through lurches back and forth in our souls from a burden to a glory, and may result in crushing failures. So fail again, said Samuel Beckett. "Fail again. Fail better."

This is what a recluse thinks, having given up on life. This is what he remembers from his own childhood: a ragged line of maples, lilacs, and underbrush between Grandma's and Mrs. Whitcomb's house—a seesaw sky, wet ashes in the driveway, a bicycle with solid rubber tires to register every pebble and stick. He remembers discarding the bike and creeping around the trees and bushes looking for toads in the underbrush and diamonds in the dirt, shirtless in the autumn heat that follows rain. One unruly shoulder blade plows up through his back— he can feel it. He remembers pretending to be a drunken fool in solitary play, and flopping about in the huge lilac bushes with an empty bottle in his hand.

It's almost October, yet the leaves in the trees between his house and

Mrs. Whitcomb's still hold great masses of ungloved moisture, not yet the dry yellow-green leaf scraps of early fall—not yet and, who knows, maybe not ever, judging from the weather, from the freak of climate and nature, which has managed to suspend a long drop of time, stretching an especially robust summer two, three, four and more weeks past its normal breaking point.

Mrs. Whitcomb's house beckons. There she is on her porch. The massive white wedding cake of her house, atop its hill of lawn—with columns and black shutters and a double-wide porch and matching balcony above—dwarfs Grandma's little cottage this side of the trees, for this spot is the portion of Ash Street where houses suddenly become the central New England equivalent of plantations. And Mrs. Whitcomb herself exists in eternal contrast to shriveled Grandma, who always wears black, summer and winter—black dress, black hair, black shoes, black stockings. Mrs. Whitcomb's mauve clothes—or pink, or blue—spread, in her chair, across the ocean of her age, and counterpoint nicely the white wicker furniture, her cauliflower hair, the down on her arms, her white soft hands, the lumpy ripples of her face. She always sits. People come to *her*, especially children, for, from her sheeny folds a plump arm will telescope, producing at its tip— wrapped in wax paper and square as a button—a pale green mint julep, which awaits its Chosen One.

Not today, though. Today she simply points down across her lawn. Paul, all bladed shoulders—all skinny freckled arms and sunburnt wrists, with warts between his fingers and a gash of black hair loosened on his forehead—cranes toward where she points, then glances back with longing at her tent of a dress, to spy a stray green viaticum. Like a loyal dog, he won't look at her face. Then he does—her pillowed features have formed a question mark around white and round eyes.

A white scar of sky shaves the porch's far end. At the screen door, her little sausage of a dog snaps and hisses.

And watching Mrs. Whitcomb, Paul sees something he's never seen before: a raisin-like mole protruding from her neck underneath one earlobe.

"What's that on my apple tree?" she asks.

As though thrown, he streaks down to carry out an inspection. In its well of stone, that tree is even older than its owner. Paul's the one who mows her lawn; the stone protects the tree. It's motionless with apples now, even in the wind, for the fruit restrains the limbs—except for one bizarre branch that, as he can see, has spontaneously generated on one of two forks an explosion of blossoms; the other holds apples. He breaks it off to bring it back. "Oh, my tree!" she exclaims, tromboning her voice from complaint to astonishment. He presents it to her, this mid-autumn wonder of regeneration. Later, when the reporter from the *Wire Valley Leader* comes to take a picture, having been summoned, it's Paul whom he snaps gripping the branch with its delirious mutation of alpha and omega—of apple blossoms and apples. And the next day, it's Grandma who clips the photo from the paper, with its caption declaring that on the branch of a tree holding full-grown apples in Mrs. Whitcomb's yard—two days short of October—miracle blossoms had appeared.

So the recluse thinks of how summers never stay, but this one did. He clings to it, this picture of his innocence. All his life, he saves it from the dark gulf. He holds the clipping in his fingers, then folds it in his notebook. Then leaves the notebook amid piles of waste in his house.

I'd like to rephrase the English journalist's either/or—the one who declared that life is either sacred or intrinsically of no account. Either all of us waste our lives—or none do. Either life itself is a waste, or there's a reason to live instead of not. In the Pascalian scale of the universe, "life itself" is a backwater, a barely audible squeal dwarfed by the eternal silence of those infinite spaces. It's such a thin veneer, a membrane ballooned to the airiest of skins around chasms of emptiness, that we wonder where it gets its fine tensile strength. Quantum physicists tell us that the universe is running down, due to entropy. It recedes from greater to lesser complexity, and someday all will be still and cold. Life on earth, however, apparently reverses this process, via evolution. It moves through random variation and natural selection toward greater complexity, not lesser. So what if life on earth, in quantitative terms, is just a brief moment in the drama of the universe? The same could be asked of life on distant planets. The planets themselves, in fact all the elements heavier than helium and hydrogen, make up less than 1 percent of the matter in the universe, and living matter is surely far less than 1 percent of that. *So what?* Life itself may very well require that enormous pyramid of stuff to occupy its little pinprick on top. And if the human brain is life's apical flower (Jean Paul's phrase), then, as Emily Dickinson said, "The brain is wider than the sky."

Watching that truck haul off Paul's waste, I felt like doing a jig. I was momentarily overwhelmed by a sense of renewal and new beginnings. As A. R. Ammons says in his long poem *Garbage:*

> here is the gateway to beginning, here the portal
> of renewing change, the birdshit, even, melding
>
> enrichingly in with debris, a loam for the roots
> of placenta.

3

ORIGINS

WASTE. LIFE. Competition for survival is produced by waste — by the excessive production of new members of a species. Waste and life are married, then. Out of two hundred million sperm, one penetrates the egg. A codfish lays as many as five million eggs in one spawning, an oyster eleven million, a sunfish three hundred million. Naturally, only a fraction survive. Excessive production is necessary to ensure that a few do make it—to ensure variation too—and both make natural selection possible.

Waste. Life. The ancients believed that life was born from waste. "Abiogenesis" is my *Britannica*'s term for the older phrase "spontaneous generation." The article under its heading describes Alexander Ross's comments on Thomas Browne's doubts as to whether mice may be born from putrefaction:

> So may he (Sir Thomas Browne) doubt whether in cheese and timber worms are generated; or if beetles and wasps in cows' dung; or if butterflies, locusts, grasshoppers, shell-fish, snails, eels, and such like, be procreated of putrefied matter, which is apt to receive the form of that creature to which it is by formative power disposed. To question this is to question reason, sense and experience. If he doubts of this let him go to Egypt, and there he will find the fields swarming with mice, begot of the mud of Nylus, to the great calamity of the inhabitants.

The *Britannica* says this was the common opinion until the seventeenth century—that life was born spontaneously out of waste—implying that it died with the Scientific Revolution.

It didn't. Our old friend Robert Fludd believed in abiogenesis, as a good Paracelsian. For Paracelsus, the "Mysterium Magnum" was mother to all things, and the generation of life was simply part of the great chemical putrefaction. Cheese being generated from the mysterium of milk, then, was no different from maggots and worms being generated from the mysterium of cheese. Even Fludd's colleague William Harvey, the first to assert that every animal comes from an egg, allowed an exception for some creatures, who "differ in respect of the primordium, which . . . bursts forth, as it were, spontaneously. . . . Whence some animals are spoken of as spontaneously produced." Let's not leave out Descartes in this reunion of cronies. He too believed that generation could be spontaneous, but largely because life is mechanical. For generation to take place, all one needs is heat—itself a form of motion—acting on putrefied matter, agitating both its light and heavy particles, and lo, an elephant springs forth.

Fludd was more subtle, if more mystical. He thought that wheat contained the essence of life, and he experimented with reducing it to a *prima materia,* in the manner of the alchemists. What he got was a black, putrescent goo in his flask. He dumped it in a stone vessel, and "after a few days were passed I espied the water to swarm with worms of a strange shape . . . very long, slender and passing white." One thinks of Stanley Miller who, in 1952, filled a flask with the gases presumed to have been in the earth's atmosphere at the dawn of life, then sent repeated charges of electricity through it. In a few days, brown gunk containing a variety of organic molecules, including amino acids, coated the sides and bottom of his flask.

Miller, of course, did not believe in spontaneous generation, in the notion that life still springs from inert matter. He knew that what Fludd observed, or what Paul held out to the camera as Miracle Blossoms, were due to life's reproductive tenacity, not to abiogenesis. Give it any opportunity, even the slightest crack, and biological life will leak through and burst forth, if only because of the default command in its genes: *Be.* But all biologists concede that at some point in the distant past, life did arise from dead matter, if not once, then more likely innumerable times, until the idea caught on and pulled itself up, as it were, by its bootstraps. Even today's textbook accounts of the origins of life can't avoid the suggestion of spontaneity. The usual explanation posits a carbon-rich pre-biotic soup some three and a half billion years ago, containing amino acids, nucleotide bases, and sugars. A critical diversity of molecules in a small space — in a gelatinous bubble, or smeared on clay, for example—resulted in the appearance of chemical systems that had the ability to catalyze their own reproduction. Biologists speculate that RNA came first, because DNA does not self-replicate—it needs a surrounding medium of protein enzymes. RNA, they think, may have been able to replicate without such assistance, but no one really knows; efforts to duplicate the process in a laboratory have failed.

A further question remains: where did the pre-biotic soup come from? From thick clouds of dust settling on the waters, some spewed by volcanoes, some scattered by asteroids and comets smashing into the earth. Its most essential ingredient, carbon, was born in the stars —as were all elements heavier than helium and hydrogen. Carbon is the sine qua non in any standard account of life's origins, because of its unique bonding properties, without which strands of RNA and DNA could not exist. It began in the stars and was scattered in space by supernovas.

Consequently, the origin of life is intimately connected to the origin of the universe.

MUSKRAT

Many stories of origin start with a seed, a drop of sperm, a grain of sand, a glob of spit. Einstein is not the only occupant of a nutshell to count himself a king of infinite space, or to create a picture of the universe that manages, Humpty Dumpty fashion, to keep on cracking open and spilling out. In Asian myths, an egg bursts open and becomes the cosmos. A Canadian Algonquian myth begins with a raft containing all the animals and their chief, the Great Hare. No world or universe exists yet, not quite—just a raft on water. The Great Hare orders various animals to dive down and bring up some mud so the world can get started, but those who try can't seem to reach bottom. At last their little runt, the muskrat, dives in, and is gone a full day.

He reappears belly-up. They drag him onto the raft. One by one they examine his feet, and between the claws of one paw find a tiny grain of sand. The Great Hare pinches it and drops it on the raft. It starts to swell. As it grows, he grabs a handful of the stuff and scatters it around, providing a sort of overdrive boost, not unlike what today's theorists of the Big Bang call inflation. At last he starts to run around the world, which makes it grow even more, and he hasn't stopped since—he's still running around it, perpetually unsatisfied with his expanding universe, always making it grow larger.

BIG BANG

Our own storytellers—our particle physicists, cosmologists, and astronomers—likewise describe a world that swelled up out of something even smaller than a grain of sand. Their myths, however, though sifted through the evidence, may scramble one's little egg of a brain. The expansion of the universe, the fact that regardless of where we look, objects in space are drifting away, was predicted by Albert Einstein, identified by Edwin Hubble, and confirmed by the discovery of microwave background radiation in 1964 and by the COBE satellite in 1992. Einstein's prediction, contained in the general theory of relativity, was so startling that he felt obliged to fudge it—to eliminate the expansion his mathematics indicated—a move he later called his "biggest blunder." Hubble demonstrated in 1929 that the universe really is expanding, and Einstein's restored equations, without the fudge factor, provided the explanation.

The rest should be familiar. The galaxies and clusters of galaxies we can see in the sky with instruments that have grown increasingly sophisticated since Einstein and Hubble are drifting apart, but not *through* space; rather, space itself is stretching. And if those objects are drifting apart, they must have been closer together in the past. Extrapolating backwards leads to a single event when everything started from a single point, space itself included. Our gargantuan universe, then, began at a point somewhere in nowhere, a location with no location, no size, weight, extension, or position—no dimensions of any sort. This is the ultimate spontaneous generation, the cosmological abiogenesis. Needless to add, it is also our myth of origin, our egg containing all in souped-up potential—including myths of origin.

WIRE VALLEY

Almost seventy years ago (a lightning blink in history), my mother climbed the stairs in Grandma's house, followed by my father, for their own Big Bang. She was sixteen, he twenty.

I won't describe this primal scene, which occurred sixteen years before my eyes were born. Wire Valley, a town west of Worcester originally called Whitney, had been saved from extinction by the Industrial Revolution in the mid-nineteenth century, then renamed for the wire factory that wound up employing my immigrant grandfather. Since my grandfather was dead by the time my parents eloped, the one they were defying must have been Grandma. Yet they returned to live with her, having no choice, because my father's job as apprentice to a printer paid only a pittance.

I've seen photos of my father and mother at this time, he in his Model T, she standing by the door. Impossible to conceive of what happened to that car, to their clothes, to those events, to that burning love. Their love still exists, I know, like the strong force that binds nuclei together. But hasn't some of it gone out into the world, like the weak force that governs radioactive decay? My mother, in particular, never has had any other life but life itself—contact with people, un-ceasing work both at home and in her jobs—meetings, sing-alongs, church, shopping, cooking—the life of being caught up in the melee. Seventy years ago she was like any sixteen-year-old, and lived on the edge of her green and raw radiance. She only knew what she was doing when she did it. Today her reservoirs overflow with a love that contin-ues to expand, and whenever I visit, her embrace dubs the universe: it seems to surround me from the inside.

BEFORE

To look into the past, as we do with the Big Bang—to extrapolate backwards—is a form of return. And a return is nothing more than the dream of immortality pulled inside out. The Big Bang may be the closest we come to a kind of immortality, inside out and upside down. But unlike immortality, it appears to have a limit. What came before it?

What indeed. Cosmologists acknowledge the question is meaning-less, then proceed to speculate regardless. One speculation goes some-thing like this: Our universe may be a local region in a larger meta-universe of high density and temperature. This region—our universe —underwent a transition from one state to another by means of the Big Bang. If this is true, and if the larger universe is infinite, ours could be one of many worlds—one of an infinite number. The notion that there are infinite worlds goes back in history through Giordano Bruno (who was burned at the stake for it) to various ancients, includ-ing the great Roman poet-philosopher Lucretius. If there *are* an infi-nite number of universes, incidentally, our eternal return would be guaranteed, and in the most Sisyphean manner. Mathematically speaking, if there are infinite worlds, it was not only inevitable that ours came into existence, but it must have existed before, and will exist again. In fact, it has existed and will exist an infinite number of times.

A variation of this idea says that our universe may both expand and contract—it passes through cycles that bounce at their limits—so that periods like our own, of expansion, are succeeded by periods of contraction (the Big Crunch), and periods of contraction by periods of expansion, and the cycles never end. However, this particular eternal return might not be so eternal. Some cosmologists suggest that under this scenario, the universe would change slightly with each new cycle; gravity might be stronger, or the strong force weaker. The cycles might even wear the universe down.

Those who offer this Big Bang/Big Crunch story also point out that time will run backwards when the universe contracts. This means that stars will soak up carbon instead of producing it, living things will grow younger instead of older, and causality will be reversed so that effects precede causes. These are not new ideas. In his dialogue *Statesman*, Plato talks about reports that the sun used to rise in the west and set in the east. The reason for this, he says, is that God himself once guided the world and held it in its course; but when a cycle was completed He let it go, and it turned around and began a new cycle in the opposite direction. When this happened, the lives of all living creatures came to a standstill. Then, slowly at first, they began to grow younger. The white hair on old men grew dark again, the bodies of youths grew soft and small, and the dead rose from their graves.

There is one hitch, though. Since time would run backwards in a Big Crunch, we'd be thinking backwards too, says John Gribbin, so we wouldn't notice that the universe is contracting. We'd probably think that it's expanding. So we could very well be in a Big Crunch now without even knowing it.

TADPOLE

Sperm are quite small—twenty-five hundred of them would fit inside the period at the end of this sentence—but we've all seen their portraits, blown up. They look like tadpoles, of course. Inside my father's body, since adolescence, the sperm had been hatching in his testes—roughly three hundred million every day—and stored in coiled tubes, called epididymides, behind each testis to await their summons. Each sperm has twenty-three chromosomes, and half of all sperm contain the X chromosome, half the Y. One of these would determine whether my mother's fertilized egg was male or female.

My mother had carried her eggs in her body—or the primitive germ cells that would become her eggs—since she herself was nothing but an egg in *her* mother's body. After fifty days in her mother's womb, her developing ovaries held about six hundred thousand of these cells, or primary oocytes, and after five months, seven million. That was the peak. For the rest of her life, they began to dwindle. The egg cells numbered five hundred thousand by the time she was seven, and four hundred thousand, give or take a few thousand, when she led my father up those steps in Wire Valley nearly seventy years ago.

Under orders from her pituitary gland (the size of a pea, at the base of her brain), one of the oocytes had matured in her ovaries (the size of almonds, hung on her uterus) into an ovum, or egg, also containing twenty-three chromosomes, including the X. She could not produce Y's.

At fertilization, an X plus a Y will result in a male, an X plus a X in a female. We can assume that the sperm that won the race—the one that became Paul—contained the Y chromosome. Y chromosomes are smaller, and their host sperms somewhat lighter, which may account for the marginally more males than females conceived worldwide.

The ovum, or egg, is the largest cell in any human body, because of its cargo of yolk, and perhaps that very morning in Wire Valley—or maybe afternoon—it softly fell into my mother's oviduct, ushered there by the hair-like cilia whose only job it is to sweep an egg along. Meanwhile, the sperm swarmed out of my father's testes, made a circuit up and around his bladder, and—blended with secretions from his seminal vesicle and his prostate gland (which gives him trouble now, at the age of ninety)—waited in the ejaculatory duct, poised at the urethra, for the gates to fly open. Already, those sperm snapped around like springs, also lashed their tails, did headflips and cartwheels, crowded one another, swam in circles, and generally postured like pent-up adolescents eager to be off.

At the moment of crisis, fanfared by whatever my mother exclaimed and my father echoed, by their shouted or whispered words of passion, this armada charged forward and entered my mother, then began their quarter-inch-every-three-minutes race. They were hopelessly ragtailed—not the fault of my father. As Carl Sagan reports, a surprising percentage of normal male sperm have two heads or tails, or no heads, or no tails, or misshapen heads, or bent or broken tails. Meanwhile, the healthy sperm, like a cloud of hairs, surged toward their distant goal, though it didn't take long for even some of them to fall by the wayside.

PLANCK ERA

Max Planck, one of the pioneers of quantum mechanics, pointed out in 1913 (when my mother was two) that the fundamental concepts of physics may be combined in such a way as to produce numbers representing the smallest possible length, the earliest possible time, and the lightest possible mass. Physicists have a horror of zero—it makes their best equations spiral out of control—so they welcomed the prospect of a Planck time, or length, or mass, as close to zero as possible without actually being zero.

That's why we say now that the universe began just *after* a singularity impossible to imagine, except to concede that it contained infinite density, a volume of zero, and an infinite curvature of space-time. Definition of singularity: a place where the laws of physics break down. After that, the fun begins.

Cosmologists therefore consider the Planck time, 10^{-43} second, as the closest we can come to the beginning of the Big Bang. The diameter of the universe at the Planck time was 2×10^{-33} centimeter, enormously smaller than the one ten-thousand-billionth of a centimeter (more or less) that is the diameter of an atom's nucleus. At the Planck time, gravity was equal to the other three forces of nature: the strong force (which holds particles in nuclei together), the weak force (which governs radioactive decay), and the electromagnetic force (which binds electrons to their orbits around nuclei and binds atoms into molecules and molecules into solids). In other words, the four forces were one. This didn't last long. As the Planck Era dawned, gravity split off, or was "frozen" out.

The density of the universe at the Planck time was 10^{90} kilograms per cubic centimeter. That's 1 followed by 90 zeros interlaced with 30 commas. By comparison, the density of a rock is a few grams per cubic centimeter. All of the universe—all of its mass-energy today, all the stars and dark matter, the earth and all its mountains, all philosophy and gallstones, galaxies and fox hunts, love, death, worm holes, thermometers, coronas, assassinations, cosmic dust, dog food, betrayals, T. Rex, cheese puffs, blood cells, the trash in my brother's house, *The Iliad*, and Duke Ellington—was squeezed into an "egg" infinitely smaller than a proton with this inconceivable density. This is madness, of course. But hey, so is Being itself. By all the rules of logic (discovered by us beings), Being should be utterly impossible.

The temperature at the Planck instant was possibly as high as 10^{31} degrees Kelvin (K).

There were no atoms or molecules yet, just elementary particles colliding with the energy of freight trains going a thousand miles an hour.

BINGO

They had a long way to go, my father's sperm. Their fifteen-inch voyage through my mother's reproductive system would be equivalent to a mob of full-sized human beings wriggling for nine miles with no arms and one leg through a system of drainage pipes. Sperm are comparatively simple creatures, with bubble heads—to protect the nucleus—spiral necks like the springs in click pens, long whip-tails wrapped with a thinner spiral filament, and (for some) tailpieces like the tassels on graduation caps. The space-helmet head comes equipped with odor receptors, and the egg ("egging them on," says Carl Sagan) sends out chemical signals for the sperm to follow—a sort of homing beacon. Really, all a sperm is, is a self-propelled package for the chromosomes in its nucleus. Blindly, the crowd of them swam upstream in my mother's body, and in a prodigious waste of life millions died along the way, drying to infinitesimal wafers, like snot or crusty spit waiting to be flushed in the next wave of mucus, when the cells peeled off in successive tidal waves and rippled away.

By now, Dad was sleeping but Mom lay awake and percolated. She must have sensed that her body was being altered—the pot being stirred down below, beyond her supervision. Or she could merely have been restless, thinking about the evening she and Dad had just spent at the Wire Valley Hotel, a white clapboard structure larger than a barn, with a wraparound porch behind thick white columns. Ten years later it burned down. There, Dad played alto sax in a little jazz trio while Mom sold tickets outside the room with the sawdust-covered floor that passed as a ballroom. They did this every Friday night; it was 1928. And Mom later complained, when she told me of those years, that she never ever got to dance with my father, since she was selling tickets and he making music—as though some sort of religious prohibition had separated them as effectively as the wall of a cloister.

They made up for it, however, later in the evening, upstairs in Grandma's house.

At last she drifted off while her enormous egg on its throne, surrounded on all sides by its ladies in waiting, or "corona" of nurse cells, presided over that ragged cotillion of sperm. Each bubble-headed courtier on the dance floor below her manufactured an enzyme to eat its way through those guardian cells, only to meet a final barrier, the beautifully named pellucid zone (*zona pellucida*), the egg's own protective bubble. One gutsy sperm out of the two hundred million or so that began the epic journey drilled its way through that membrane, encouraged by the egg. It lost its space helmet, lost its tail.

But it entered the egg. And as soon as it did, the egg shut its gates and rejected all remaining spermatozoa. The egg began to vibrate, discarding some nuclear material, while its pronucleus, with its twenty-three chromosomes, made its way to the center. There it met the sperm's pronucleus, and both swelled up like mating birds, peeled off their final membranes, and stood before each other naked. Then the chromosomes, in a long embrace lasting twelve hours, united in twenty-three pairs, one member of each pair from each parent. Bingo.

THE GUT ERA

At 10^{-35} second, the Grand Unified Theory Era comes and goes in a microblink. As the universe expands, it cools — relatively speaking — and as it cools, the grand unification of the three basic forces ends. Gravity had already separated out at the dawn of Planck time; now the strong nuclear force and the electroweak force (combining the weak nuclear force and the electromagnetic force) are about to decouple. Particles are still colliding with one another, and annihilating one another, at alarming rates. To think of them as matter, though, would be grossly misleading; we haven't yet reached matter as we know it. We haven't even reached protons and neutrons. Protons and neutrons, also called hadrons, are composed of more elementary entities called quarks and gluons. "Three quarks for Muster Mark," said James Joyce in *Finnegans Wake,* the passage cited by physicist Murray Gell-Mann when he applied the word "quark" to these elementary particles that he wasn't sure existed. Quarks, we are told, come in six "flavors," labeled u, d, s, c, b, and t, for up, down, strange, charmed, bottom (or beauty), and top (or truth). Gluons are the things—or the force—that hold quarks together inside protons and neutrons, hold them so well that no linear accelerator has ever succeeded in knocking them apart.

But in the GUT Era, all that existed, say the physicists and cosmologists, were quarks and gluons, along with leptons—considered by some to be identical to quarks—and X-particles, vector mesons, and photons. These unstable beings—go ahead, call them particles—spinning and colliding, annihilating one another, releasing radiation, spiced up a hot and boiling soup, or "quark-gluon plasma." Hot? In round figures—more or less, just an estimate—ten thousand million million million degrees.

ZYGOTE

With their circuitry of genes guiding the process—semaphoring to each other across endoplasmic lumens—Paul's chromosomes took their sweet time in doubling themselves, about thirty-six hours, but at last his zygote dimpled and pinched, cleaving in two to make a pair of cells. All the rest was downhill. The next cleavage took another twelve hours, and at the end of four days there were seventy-odd cells. They made a morula, from the Latin for mulberry, and in fact they did look like a cluster of berries hung on a tree. As the morula grew, it began to emigrate, from the oviduct down the fallopian tube and into the uterus.

The morula flattened out, curved around itself, and formed a hollow sphere—the blastula. Then a small group of cells began to specialize, forming another mass inside the sphere—the blastoderm, embryo of the embryo. Specialization, once under way, follows branching paths until the human body, at full development, contains 256 different types of cells. In Paul's blastoderm, this differentiation had already begun with three major divisions: ectoderm, endoderm, and mesoderm. Out of the first, the brain began to bud, also the spinal cord, nerves, sensory organs, and skin. Out of the second grew the innards, and out of the third the skeleton and muscles.

Meanwhile, the blastula implanted itself in my mother's womb, where its outer sphere of cells unfolded and expanded and rooted into the uterine lining to become a sort of flattened lung called the placenta, the place where Paul's and my mother's blood exchanged his oxygen and waste.

By now, my mother's estrogen and progesterone levels had risen enough to cause swings of mood from the giddy to the black. She was only sixteen, she'd dropped out of high school, and if her personality then was anything like what it is now, she probably shrugged and said to herself, No sense having a conniption fit about it. There's nothing *I* can do.

HADRON ERA

At the Hadron Era's dawn, something marvelous occurred, called by physicists "inflation," and still a matter of controversy. "Hadron" means particles that feel the strong force, such as protons—but we're not at protons yet. Protons are one of the results of inflation. The

Hadron Era gave birth to conditions that gave birth to protons, and it lasted from only 10^{-35} to 10^{-6} second. In that superthin slice of time, the universe increased by a factor of one million million million million. This means that it went from a region 10^{-36} times smaller than a proton to one about the size of a basketball. It expanded—blew up—exponentially, in other words. It doubled itself more than seventy times in a micro-microsecond—that is, it increased by a power of 10^{70}. This is the real Big Bang. Thinking about it should leave any rational person sucking his thumb. Also, inflation could outstrip the speed of light because the universe wasn't moving through space-time; in other words, space-time itself was inflating.

Explanations of inflation are highly technical, but have to do with something called a sudden phase transition. The decoupling of the strong force from the electroweak force, about to occur in the GUT Era, was delayed in the same way the freezing of water may be delayed when it is suddenly plunged below the freezing point. And just as water gives up a burst of heat when "supercooled" in this manner, so did the universe. Stephen Hawking says that this extra energy would have had an antigravitational effect, a repulsive impulse that outweighed the inward gravitational pull of the dense universe and caused it to expand at an ever-increasing rate.

Some cosmologists assert that without inflation the universe would have begun expanding then collapsed in its own gravitational pull, and both would have occurred in a fraction of a second. We may liken this to a trenchcoated man in a dark alley trying to light his Zippo lighter in a stiff wind. Repeatedly the spark goes out. Then at last one catches, and the universe is born. It may be that baby universes are born and die every second of our lives in this manner. The universe that survives amid such a profligate waste is the fittest, we Monday morning quarterbacks know—because the fact that we are in it, wondering how it began, means that it overcame its own annihilation.

PHYLOGENY

Later in the first week, Paul's embryo underwent its own puny version of inflation, doubling its size every day when the hemorrhaging tissue of my mother's uterus liberated glycogen, a starch, on which he fed. By the end of a month, the human seed who would be known as Paul had gone from one cell to a million cells, and grown to a quarter of an inch long. Unpacking the evolutionary history of its species — its phylogeny — it grew six pairs of gills, a tail, and a kidney-like structure that resembled the kidneys of primitive eels. Later, this kidney would be replaced by one more like those of frogs and fish, and still later by a recognizably human kidney.

Paul's eyes appeared on the sides of his head, as in serpents and fish.

His heart began beating by the fourth week. Distinct limbs and bones began to form by the eighth. A yolk sac about the same size as his body rose up like a yellow balloon from his belly, as though tied to a button on a child's coat. On the twenty-eighth day, his mouth fell open.

LEPTON ERA

Leptons are light particles, which take part in both the electromagnetic and the weak forces. Once the electromagnetic and the weak forces separated, the mass slaughter of quarks, antiquarks, and gluons began, at 10^{-6} second. When a quark and an antiquark meet, they annihilate each other, producing leptons (including electrons) in the process. This annihilation was so complete that only one out of a billion quarks failed to find a willing partner for mutual obliteration. Yet there were so many quarks to begin with that the ones left behind, as the universe cooled below 10^{13} degrees K, were enough to lock together into all the protons and neutrons we needed to make a universe. So this was the era of nucleosynthesis, when what we know as matter began, and now we are talking about comprehensible time—it actually lasted several minutes. But in those several minutes, all the matter now existing in the universe was born.

FETUS

Paul's embryo began to look human. Gradually his eyes migrated from the sides of his head to the front—in other words, his head grew rounder. This head by now was fully half of his existence, more or less equal in size to his torso. If that proportion stayed the same through birth into adulthood, we'd be a race of elephant men, unable to stand without flopping over.

His bones were forming everywhere—snapping into place—and beginning to brew up blood in their marrow.

Between the first and second month, my mother began to feel something was up. She'd missed her period, felt queasy in the mornings, threw up several times. She went to the doctor—no, the doctor came to her, this was 1928—and she heard the shocking news.

Was she happy? Scared? She'd grown up, it seemed, in just a few weeks, yet felt helpless as a child again. Why *hadn't* she and my father ever danced? Her youth was wasting away, she was going to have a baby, and her own mother wouldn't speak to her because of her elopement. Don't worry, said my grandma, whose home Mom was sharing. You have me, she said, I'll take good care of you.

And my mother, still a child, gratefully agreed.

PLASMA ERA

The universe now contained protons, neutrons, and electrons, wandering freely in a plasma, as in the sun and stars today. Its temperature when a minute had passed was about one billion degrees and falling.

We were on the slippery slope toward overcoats. After three minutes, the synthesis of protons and neutrons stopped. In the next thirty minutes, helium nuclei formed (two protons and two neutrons), also the nuclei of deuterium, or heavy hydrogen. After ten years, the universe had grown to ten light-years across. As it expanded it cooled, and as it cooled it expanded, and it continued doing this for several hundred thousand years.

Still, most cosmologists agree, it was nonetheless a fireball, not unlike our sun. After three hundred thousand years, a final significant decoupling occurred. When the temperature dropped below 6,000 degrees K—the same as the surface of our sun today—protons and helium nuclei began corralling electrons, and the first atoms formed. Atoms are electrically neutral, so photons had nothing to react with anymore. In other words, the radiation of the Big Bang's heat decoupled from matter. And matter could now form galaxies, stars, planets, and chickadees, while the radiation was free to fade away and cool on its own. Today the radiation is at a uniform temperature throughout the universe: somewhat less than 3 degrees K. This is the same microwave background radiation discovered in 1964, our relic of the Big Bang. It comprises, for example, about 1 percent of the scratches and hisses you hear between stations on the radio.

When radiation and matter decoupled, it was like a heavy mist lifting. A theoretical observer could actually see the universe now. For the first time, it became transparent. Yet it was just an embryo. An embryo five hundred million light-years across.

COMFORTABLE

Paul's face became Paul's face, with eyelids and eyelashes. He began to suck his thumb. His nipples appeared. In the fourth month, he nearly doubled in size and quadrupled in weight. His posture improved—it became more erect. He developed touch pads on his fingers and toes, and his body furred over with a fine down of hair. He never kicked much, my mother has told me, but often seemed to be just trying to get comfortable.

My mother, though a healthy seventeen (by now), was growing tired. She began to gain as much as a solid pound a week. She noticed a dark line running straight down beneath her navel, and wondered if maybe she was about to split open. She ate and she ate—couldn't stop eating. Occasionally she felt a contraction.

She still sold tickets at the Friday night dances. It didn't take much exertion.

As for Paul, he needed a haircut. A green paste of meconium—dead cells and bile—thickened in his intestines. He grew greedy, sucking up iron for his blood cells, calcium for his bones, protein for his growth. He drained them from my mother. His skin was so wrinkled it looked like an old man's. His brain filled with neurons.

My father placed his ink-stained hand on my mother's belly, as all fathers must, to feel his son's hiccups. Grandma did too, and her gentle hand lingered.

GALACTIC ERA

When radiation and matter decoupled, the matter was nearly all hydrogen and helium, in a ratio of about three parts hydrogen to one part helium. The remaining matter in the universe, about 1 percent of the total even today, was cooked in the stars, especially in the young hot stars that supernovaed all over the sky when the universe was new.

Matter is freeze-dried energy, after all. First helium and hydrogen were formed in the fireball of the Big Bang, then the heavier elements fused in the stars, including carbon, life's Lego, and were blasted into space when the stars blew up.

The Galactic Era—the one we live in—began with that hot gas of helium and hydrogen. During inflation, tiny fluctuations of density had occurred. About a billion years later, the fluctuations had resulted in regions of gas whose expansion was slowing due to gravity from their mass. Gradually these regions attracted more matter and began to collapse upon themselves and rotate about their own axes. "Gradually" means billions of years. "Matter" means enormous slow-moving storm-ships of gas clouds hundreds of thousands of light-years across. Inside those whirling clusters of matter, smaller whirls formed, in the manner described by L. F. Richardson:

> Big whirls have little whirls,
> That feed on their velocity;
> And little whirls have lesser whirls,
> And so on to viscosity.

Gravitation collapsed those "little" whirls more and more, heating them up, until their atomic nuclei began to fuse—the first thermonuclear reactions—and the stars were born.

The evolution of galaxy clusters, some of which contain tens of thousands of galaxies—the evolution of galaxies themselves, also stars, solar systems, planets, and moons—the evolution of the whole lumpy universe as we know it today—is still going on. And meanwhile, across wastes of space, the emptiness is inconceivable. So is the cold, punctuated here and there by heat engines of light, whose distance from us, and from each other, reduces them to stubble in the night sky. Keep in mind that some of the "stars" we see at night are galaxies. Some contain a hundred billion stars.

Goodness. If we didn't live in a busy local world, one that nicely bubble-packs that crush, we might be inclined to see ourselves as small.

PAUL

Grandma boiled the sheets. Paul was born at home, in the same bed in which he'd been conceived forty weeks earlier. "I'm going to have a baby," said my mother, as though to reassure—or convince—herself. Dad called the doctor. It was Paul himself who initiated these procedures, when his adrenal gland secreted cortisol, which ordered my mother's uterus to switch on its compactor.

Actually, my mother hadn't even told my father, but she'd been feeling contractions all day. By the time Grandma boiled the water and the doctor pulled on his gutta-percha gloves and probed Mom's little secret, her cervix had dilated five or six centimeters. *I'm going to have a baby,* she told herself repeatedly, refusing to believe it. Soon she said it out loud: "I'm going to have a *baaaaaby,* I'm going to have a *baaaaaby,*" slinging each declaration across the rise and fall of successive contractions.

Years ago, she told me that she'd done this: relieved her unmedicated pain with this outcry. Later on, I stole it for a novel.

With a washcloth, Grandma wiped the face of a woman I've never once seen sweat in my life. But this was August, and upstairs. Before the open windows lace curtains hung motionless. Darkness was falling, crickets sang. Dad was not present during these proceedings, as fathers then were considered squeamish and unreliable. He was downstairs in the parlor with Uncle John.

After each contraction, the longitudinal muscles of my mother's uterus remained a little shorter. Paul felt this, felt the shrinking space and growing pressure. His head, after all, was being forced through a bottleneck in raw flesh only seventeen years old. He did what he could to help: as he pushed against the cervical opening, the three plates of his skull slipped over one another, shaping his head like a small rocket. He'd already twisted to face my mother's back, but only his head—the shoulders hadn't caught up yet. The pressure of his face had pushed her coccyx backwards and squeezed her rectum shut.

Did he feel the lobster claw of the doctor's sudden grip, those terrible forceps? The oxygen in his blood had diminished because of all the pressure; perhaps he was fainting and didn't feel a thing. Grandma grasped my mother's shoulder so hard that Mom, confused, looked up at her in alarm. Then she sang out, "I'm going to have a *baaaaaby*," as her perineum stretched and bulged over Paul's face. Now her abdominal muscles were pushing, just when they weren't needed. Paul must have felt the change—felt his head rising up like a rubbery bubble with his torso in its wake, felt the air for the first time, the first grip of gravity, the doctor's meaty hands. Released, he fountained out toward some future origin, all covered with cheese.

A blue and red rope seemed to fill the room. After one last surge of blood from the placenta, the doctor cut the cord. The carbon dioxide in Paul's bloodstream then increased, stimulating his medulla oblongata, the respiratory center where his brain met his spinal cord. This sent a signal to the muscles of his chest, which contracted, billowing the rib cage and tugging on the diaphragm. He sucked air into his lungs. And for the first time, blood passed through his lungs and through his pulmonary vein back into his heart. Pressure rose in his left atrium and dropped in the right. This shift of pressure folded two flaps of tissue across the opening between the two sides of his heart, the opening through which his blood had flowed for the past nine months, bypassing his lungs—the same opening that Galen had claimed existed in adults and that Robert Fludd watched William Harvey prove did not exist, except in fetuses.

This opening closed and permanently fused for the rest of Paul's life.

With a wail he exhaled, driving fluids out of his nose and throat. Once the cord was cut, his last set of kidneys began functioning immediately, and now he pissed in midair, in a long yellow arc, striking Grandma's sleeve. She was already up, in motion toward the doctor, reaching for her grandson.

"I'll take him," she said.

CODA

3:08 A.M. I lay in bed beside Hannah, unable to sleep. I was thinking of Paul, of writing something about him, a poem or novel, to exorcise his ghost. Chiseled in darkness, the red numbers on the clock, made from elongated hexagons, froze the endless minute, then blinked and froze another, as if proving that time has no substance. The only things visible in a room erased by night were those red numbers. The clock sat on the dresser, I knew, but the time of day floated in empty black space. This was the night I'd driven home in darkness, after Jud and his crew had emptied out my brother's house and I'd bought a thermometer and built those front steps.

To exorcise his ghost. I'd arrived at 2 A.M. Our house was filled with things too, I noted, but they weren't trash yet. Furniture, silverware in drawers, linen in closets, photos in boxes. Each thing, in its place, possessed its own history. Together they produced a cadence of sorts. I could walk through them blindfolded, threading the pattern. I felt safe at home. Such feelings are brittle. Would my life too end up in a dumpster?

At least the world seemed to weigh less now. When I'd entered our room, Hannah had switched on the lamp beside our bed and thrown off the covers, and we embraced. "You're crazy for driving home this late," she said.

"I was wide awake. I can't believe it's over."

"I don't see how you could do it."

254 · A BOOK OF REASONS

"I was lucky I found those guys."

She watched me undress. "What happened to your thumb?"

"Banged it with a hammer."

"Doing what?"

"Building front steps for the house."

"You? Building steps?"

"It wasn't too bad."

"Which?"

" 'Which?' "

"The steps or the thumb?"

I told her. I sat beside her in pajamas. She had that unfolded quality of the newly awakened, still creased and soft. Hair flat on one side. Her breath smelled like bread. The room smelled of bed sheets, Tide, and dried sweat. "The place still stinks," I said. "You should have seen it."

"I'm glad I didn't."

"You wouldn't have believed it."

"I can imagine."

"No, you can't," I said. I felt lighter than helium, yet plugged up, congested. The heaviness returned out of nowhere—it condensed— and I stood up as though in spreading slow motion, chained there by ripples trailing my silhouette. "I'm thirsty," I said.

"I got some beer yesterday."

I walked out of the room. Down the hallway in darkness. I checked the boys' rooms, those explosions of books, clothes, rock collections, shells, pencils, candles, Walkmen, Bob Marley tapes, rulers and compasses, cups, plates and tissues, candy bar wrappers, folders and notebooks, day packs, shoes, Clearasil, paper clips. Somewhere in that confusion lay my sleeping sons.

In the kitchen, I found the beer and didn't drink it. The silverware drawer, with the church key I didn't use, held crumbs, trash stickers, bottle caps, twist ties, a peeler *sans* handle, lids of jars, corks. I pictured pots and pans breeding in the cupboards, the flow of charge back and forth inside objects, spores and mold exploding. Little pink mice the size of cashews born from piles of old clothes. Give me a bucket of mud, I thought—I'll make my own world. Could we relearn to count with five fingers on one hand, six on the other?

Piles of tires catching fire. Coal mines smoldering for decades under towns in central Pennsylvania.

I walked through the house. We were not the best housekeepers. Threads of dust tended to collect behind doors or catch in rug fringes. Newspapers lay on the floor for days, books and magazines were always scattered on the couch. I had the reputation in our family of possessing the greatest mania for cleanliness. I regularly wiped counters. Washed the dishes. Put bowls away so they nested in each other. I did not, however, alphabetize the dry goods in our pantry or throw out the rotten celery in the fridge, not unless it smelled. Sometimes I dusted. I don't do windows. From the time I was a child, I'd always loved to vacuum.

From closets and cupboards, from forgotten shelves and drawers, from boxes in the basement, in the space below the stairs, from old dressers, file cabinets, and utility shelves, from glove compartments in our cars, from trash cans and trunks, came the rattle of chains, flowed the cold grease of things, droned the machinery of ownership, the hoarse buzz of production—crawled the mortal rot of possessions.

To exorcise a ghost? One never exorcises ghosts. The world becomes a ghost when its familiar meanings die. When I made it back to bed, Hannah was asleep again, and I lay there in darkness, heart kicking in my neck.

My life had changed. When? When I saw my brother's house? I doubt it. Change does not occur when the catalyst appears. Even when the chemical reaction begins, when the atoms pop and the molecules fountain, one clings to old shapes as though holding on for dear life to a tent in a sandstorm. It wasn't when I saw Paul's house but when I phoned Hannah and doubled up in tears and told her what I'd seen that I became a different person. Changes don't occur until you tell the story.

Now she lay asleep beside me. Hannah could always sleep with nose whistle, but I never could. I could not simultaneously produce body sounds and achieve oblivion. Anyway, I wasn't sleepy. I'd passed beyond sleep, to that realm of humming consciousness and glow-in-the-dark voltage where all your vital circuits have absorbed a power surge. I did not have a body but an electric appliance. I was happy to be home, cozy and wide-eyed. But I felt sore all over and knew I'd never sleep again. I was a stranger, I thought—to my home, to my family.

And Paul was my brother. Was it fortune or accident that gave him the life I didn't lead, the one I'd escaped? The necessity of history, hardwiring in the brain, a chance whim of the gods? We'd shared the same parents, had a common flesh and blood. What made his life so different from mine?

Then I thought, *It wasn't different,* and started dropping through space. I'm part of his life, I thought, he's part of mine. The contents of life from nursery to nursing home may be wishes and dreams, sadness and waste, hopes and disappointments, all punctuated by shining beads, like spilled mercury—by luminous moments and gusts of generosity, each a sputtering universe—but they are never the exclusive property of any of us, from CEO to abject solitary. Life itself leaks. It leaks into one's possessions, one's neighbors and kin, the cars driven, the houses lived in. It leaks into the memories and souls of survivors, and leaks into history and the vastness of space. If each of us is connected to history, then each of us is plural, and we're connected to each other. This is not a consolation. It does not solve or even diminish the mystery of other people's lives. It simply means that even the least of human beings also leaves his mark upon others, and so upon the universe.

I *could* write something about him, I thought. I could link his life to the past, to the history of small and large things—of commonplace objects, planets and stars, and biological life as well, our blunt and sudden bubble. How could a timid and small life, I wondered, proceed from that extravagance, from that delirious profusion, from that upstart of the universe, life itself? They call it a miracle. Yet life is more or less the saturated state of something instead of nothing; its glow comes from engines fueled by history's litter. Maybe history instead is the miracle — the largesse of space and time. That and the connection between time on the one hand and our own little pinpricks of subjectivity on the other.

Or maybe the true miracle is consciousness, which *feels* somehow endlessly extended, though thick with inclusion. What happens to such a finely tuned instrument when its labyrinthine circuits fail? This is like asking where the potential energy goes when a tightly wound mainspring gets thrown into the sun. Did Paul's consciousness vaporize? Did it take another form? Pass into other bodies?

Had it passed into mine?

I lay there nearly tipsy with fatigue, beside my sleeping wife, and attempted to imagine what being Paul would feel like. If the greatest mystery is other people's lives, what it felt like to be Paul could have been what it feels like to be any of a million forgotten and diminished ones, the nameless in our midst. It could also have been its own forty-watt glory. Paul often seemed depressed. The usual culprits came to mind: unrelieved tedium, quiet desperation, loneliness, soothing wafers of denial, as well as, in the intervals, consumerist distractions, which are stuffing for the emptiness.

I saw him now through a darkened mirror, and almost understood. I remembered him lighting up in Hannah's warmth, touched by a voice of animated interest, and for an hour or two called into existence like a blossom in autumn, when everything goes moribund. Would *his* life have changed if he'd told it to someone? Now was too late, and instead I'd do the telling. As far as I knew, Paul had never had someone. Hannah may have come closest. I pictured her, from his perspective, as

the single representative of a new race of beings full of contradictions
—exotic and down to earth, strange and ordinary, beautiful and engrossed. Engrossed in *him*. Lying there, I saw him hunched in his chair
and, jowls aflutter, slowly shaking his head while waving one hand,
theatrically rejecting some advice she'd just proffered—to get exercise, maybe. "Me? Not me. I'm an old man." He must have been sixty,
sixty-one at the time. I could even hear his laugh, a deep mulish
chuckle, and the way it diminished to a low sputter before he withdrew
as though running out of fuel, or worse, as though suddenly remembering himself.

What self did he remember? What inner being? He was nothing like
you or me, be assured. Yet he was—he was the stranger in our souls.

WORKS CONSULTED

Note

Throughout this book, the chief source of information, both commonplace and recondite, is the eleventh edition of the *Encyclopaedia Britannica* (Cambridge, England: Cambridge University Press, 1910–11). In most cases, I've indicated this in the text itself.

Occasionally, allusions in *A Book of Reasons* come from memory. I've tried to trace these to their sources, but haven't always succeeded. Such potentially specious references are few and far between.

I. HEAT

Bishop, Morris. *Pascal: The Life of Genius.* Westport, Conn.: Greenwood Press, 1968.

Braudel, Fernand. *The Structures of Everyday Life: The Limits of the Possible,* vol. 1 of *Civilization and Capitalism: 15th–18th Century,* trans. Siân Reynolds. New York: Harper & Row, 1981.

Calvino, Italo. *The Cloven Viscount,* trans. Archibald Colquhoun, in *The Nonexistent Knight & The Cloven Viscount.* New York: Harcourt, Brace, 1977.

Cardwell, D. S. L. *Turning Points in Western Technology.* New York: Science History Publications, 1972.

Cole, John. *Pascal: The Man and His Two Loves*. New York: New York University Press, 1995.

Crosby, Alfred W. *The Measure of Reality*. Cambridge, England: Cambridge University Press, 1997.

Davis, Lennard. *Enforcing Normalcy: Disability, Deafness, and the Body*. London: Verso, 1995.

Dawkins, Richard. *The Selfish Gene*. Oxford: Oxford University Press, 1976.

Debus, Allen G., ed. *Robert Fludd and His Philosophicall Key*. New York: Science History Publications, 1979.

Drachmann, A. G. *The Mechanical Technology of Greek and Roman Antiquity*. Madison: University of Wisconsin Press, 1963.

Fahie, J. J. *Galileo: His Life and Work*. London: John Murray, 1903.

Fludd, Robert. *Mosaicall Philosophy*. London: Humphrey Moseley, 1659.

Godwin, Joscelyn. *Robert Fludd: Hermetic Philosopher and Surveyor of Two Worlds*. London: Thames and Hudson, 1979.

Hero of Alexandria. *The Pneumatics*, trans. and ed. Bennet Woodcroft. London: Charles Whittingham, 1851.

Keynes, Geoffrey. *The Life of William Harvey*. Oxford: Clarendon Press, 1966.

Knowlson, James. *Damned to Fame: The Life of Samuel Beckett*. New York: Simon & Schuster, 1996.

McGee, Thomas. *Principles and Methods of Temperature Measurement*. New York: John Wiley & Sons, 1988.

McMullin, Ernan, ed. *Galileo: Man of Science*. New York: Basic Books, 1967.

Middleton, W. E. Knowles. *The History of the Barometer*. Baltimore, Md.: Johns Hopkins University Press, 1964.

———. *A History of the Thermometer*. Baltimore, Md.: Johns Hopkins University Press, 1966.

Nabokov, Vladimir. *Bend Sinister*, in *Nabokov: Novels and Memoirs, 1941–1951*. New York: Library of America, 1996.

Pascal, Blaise. *Pensées*, trans. A. J. Krailsheimer. Harmondsworth, England: Penguin Books, 1984.

Plutarch. *Plutarch's Morals*, trans. C. W. King. London: George Bell and Sons, 1889.

Russell, Bertrand. *The Autobiography of Bertrand Russell.* 3 vols. Boston: Little, Brown, 1967–69.

Russell, D. A. *Plutarch.* New York: Charles Scribner's Sons, 1973.

Whitman, Walt. *Complete Poetry and Collected Prose*, ed. Justin Kaplan. New York: Library of America, 1982.

II. TOOLS

Augustine [Saint]. *The City of God*, trans. Marcus Dods. New York: Modern Library, 1950.

Balzac, Honoré de. *Old Goriot*, trans. Marion Ayton Crawford. London: Penguin Books, 1951.

Barb, A. A. "Cain's Murder-Weapon, and Samson's Jawbone of an Ass," *Journal of the Warburg and Courtauld Institutes* 35 (1972), 386–389.

Berthelet, A., and J. Chavaillon, eds. *The Use of Tools by Human and Non-Human Primates.* Oxford: Clarendon Press, 1993.

Bonnell, J. K. "Cain's Jaw Bone," *PMLA* 39 (1924), 140–146.

Cabeza de Vaca, Alvar Núñez. *Castaways*, trans. Frances M. López-Morillas. Berkeley: University of California Press, 1993.

Clark, Ella E. *Indian Legends from the Northern Rockies.* Norman: University of Oklahoma Press, 1966.

Cohen, H. Hirsch. *The Drunkenness of Noah.* University: University of Alabama Press, 1974.

Crosby, Alfred. *The Measure of Reality.* Cambridge, England: Cambridge University Press, 1997.

Dart, Raymond. "The Predatory Transition from Ape to Man," *International Linguistic Review,* April 1953, 201–208.

Davidson, Iain, and William Noble. "Tools and Language in Human Evolution," in *Tools, Language, and Cognition in Human Evolution,* ed. Kathleen R. Gibson and Tim Ingold. Cambridge, England: Cambridge University Press, 1993, 363–388.

Dawkins, Richard. *The Blind Watchmaker.* Harlow, Essex: Longman Scientific & Technical, 1986.

Freud, Sigmund. *Civilization and Its Discontents,* trans. James Strachey. New York: Norton, 1962.

———. "Our Attitude Towards Death," in *The Standard Edition of the Complete Psychological Works of Sigmund Freud,* vol. 14, trans. James Strachey. London: Hogarth Press, 1957.

Ginzberg, Louis. *The Legends of the Jews,* 7 vols. Philadelphia: Jewish Publication Society of America, 1909–1938.

Goodall, Jane. *The Chimpanzee: The Living Link between 'Man' and 'Beast.'* Edinburgh: Alexander Ritchie & Son, 1992.

———. *In the Shadow of Man.* Boston: Houghton Mifflin, 1971.

Goodman, W. L. *The History of Woodworking Tools.* London: G. Bell and Sons, 1964.

Heidegger, Martin. *Being and Time,* trans. John Macquarrie and Edward Robinson. New York: Harper & Row, 1962.

———. *The Question Concerning Technology,* trans. William Lovitt. New York: Harper & Row, 1977.

Josephus, Flavius. *Jewish Antiquities,* in *Josephus,* vol. 4, ed. H. St.-J. Thackery. Cambridge, Mass.: Loeb Classical Library, 1967.

Kidder, Tracy. *House.* Boston: Houghton Mifflin, 1985.

Leakey, L. S. B. *By the Evidence: Memoirs, 1932–1951.* New York: Harcourt Brace Jovanovich, 1974.

Leakey, Mary. *Disclosing the Past.* London: Weidenfeld and Nicolson, 1984.

Lewis, Meriwether, and William Clark. *Original Journals of the Lewis and Clark Expedition, 1804–1806,* ed. Reuben Gold Thwaites. New York: Arno Press, 1969.

Mellinkoff, Ruth. *The Mark of Cain.* Berkeley: University of California Press, 1981.

Mercer, Henry C. *Ancient Carpenters' Tools.* Doylestown, Pa.: Bucks County Historical Society, 1960.

Montaigne, Michel de. *The Essays of Michel de Montaigne,* trans M. A. Screech. London: Allen Lane/Penguin Press, 1991.

Morábito, Fabio. "The Yearning of the Screw," trans. Geoff Hargreaves, *Harper's Magazine,* February 1997, 28.

Pagels, Elaine. *Adam, Eve, and the Serpent.* New York: Random House, 1988.

Proust, Marcel. *Swann's Way,* trans. C. K. Scott-Moncrieff. New York: Random House, 1927.

Ronda, James. *Lewis and Clark among the Indians.* Lincoln: University of Nebraska Press, 1984.

Schick, Kathy, and Nicholas Toth. *Making Silent Stones Speak.* New York: Simon and Schuster, 1993.

Shapiro, Meyer. " 'Cain's Jaw-Bone That Did the First Murder,' " *Art Bulletin* 24 (1942), 205–212.

Stendhal. *The Red and the Black,* trans. C. K. Scott-Moncrieff. Norwalk, Conn.: Easton Press, 1980.

Thoreau, Henry David. *Walden.* New York: Holt, Rinehart and Winston, 1963.

Tudge, Colin. *The Time Before History.* New York: Scribner, 1996.

Whitman, Walt. "Song of Myself," in *Walt Whitman: Complete Poetry and Collected Prose,* ed. Justin Kaplan. New York: Library of America, 1982.

Williams, David. *Cain and Beowulf.* Toronto: University of Toronto Press, 1982.

Yeats, W. B. "The Man Who Dreamed of Faeryland," in *The Collected Poems of W. B. Yeats.* New York: Macmillan, 1956.

III. BODY

Aristotle. *The Basic Works of Aristotle,* ed. Richard McKeon. New York: Random House, 1966.

Augustine [Saint]. *Confessions,* trans. Henry Chadwick. Oxford: Oxford University Press, 1991.

Blake, William. *Complete Writings,* ed. Geoffrey Keynes. London: Oxford University Press, 1966.

Burgess, Anthony. *A Clockwork Orange.* New York: Norton, 1963.

Butler, Judith. *Gender Trouble.* New York and London: Routledge, 1990.

Campbell, Neil. *Biology.* Menlo Park, Calif.: Benjamin/Cummings Publishing, 1987.

Davis, Lennard. *Enforcing Normalcy: Disability, Deafness, and the Body.* London: Verso, 1995.

Debus, Allen G. "Harvey and Fludd: The Irrational Factor in the Rational Science of the Seventeenth Century," *Journal of the History of Biology* 3:1 (Spring 1970), 81–105.

———. "Robert Fludd and the Circulation of the Blood," *Journal of the History of Medicine and Allied Sciences* 16 (October 1961), 374–393.

———, ed. *Robert Fludd and His Philosophicall Key.* New York: Science History Publications, 1979.

Doby, Tibor. *Discoverers of Blood Circulation.* London: Abelard-Schuman, 1963.

Doyle, Sir A. Conan. *A Study in Scarlet.* London: Ward Lock & Co., 1887.

Fiedler, Leslie. *The Tyranny of the Normal*. Boston: David R. Godine, 1996.

Gaskell, Elizabeth. *Mary Barton*. New York: Norton, 1958.

Godwin, Joscelyn. *Robert Fludd: Hermetic Philosopher and Surveyor of Two Worlds*. London: Thames and Hudson, 1979.

Guild, Thelma S., and Harvey L. Carter. *Kit Carson: A Pattern for Heroes*. Lincoln: University of Nebraska Press, 1984.

Harrison, Robert, trans. *Gallic Salt: Eighteen Fabliaux Translated from the Old French*. Berkeley: University of California Press, 1974.

Harvey, William. "An Anatomical Disquisition on the Motion of the Heart and Blood in Animals," trans. Robert Willis, revised by Alex Bowie, in *Classics of Medicine and Surgery*, ed. C. N. B. Camac. New York: Dover, 1959.

————. *The Circulation of the Blood: Two Anatomical Essays*, trans. and ed. Kenneth J. Franklin. Oxford: Blackwell Scientific Publications, 1958.

Homer. *The Iliad*, trans. Richmond Lattimore. Chicago: University of Chicago Press, 1951.

Kafka, Franz. *Amerika*, trans. Willa and Edwin Muir. New York: Schocken Books, 1974.

Keynes, Geoffrey. *The Life of William Harvey*. Oxford: Oxford University Press, 1966.

————. *The Portraiture of William Harvey*. London: Royal College of Surgeons, 1949.

Morgan, Elaine. *The Scars of Evolution*. Oxford: Oxford University Press, 1994.

Nourse, Alan, and the editors of *Life*. *The Body*. New York: Time Inc./ Life Science Library, 1964.

Pagel, Walter. *New Light on William Harvey*. Basel, Switzerland: S. Karger, 1976.

Plato. "Symposium," in *The Dialogues of Plato*, vol. 1, trans. and ed. B. Jowett. Oxford: Oxford University Press, 1953.

Regan, Tom. *The Case for Animal Rights.* Berkeley: University of California Press, 1983.

Robinson, James, gen. ed. *The Nag Hammadi Library in English.* San Francisco: Harper & Row, 1988.

Schwartz, Delmore. "The Heavy Bear Who Goes with Me," in *The Norton Anthology of Modern Poetry,* ed. Richard Ellmann and Robert O'Clair. New York: Norton, 1988.

Shelley, Mary. *Frankenstein; or, The Modern Prometheus.* London: Penguin Books, 1992.

Vogel, Steven. *Vital Circuits.* New York and Oxford: Oxford University Press, 1992.

Whitteridge, Gweneth. *William Harvey and the Circulation of the Blood.* New York: American Elsevier, 1971.

Yeats, W. B. "Crazy Jane Talks with the Bishop," in *The Collected Poems of W. B. Yeats.* New York: Macmillan, 1965.

IV. CORPSE

Ariès, Philippe. *The Hour of Our Death,* trans. Helen Weaver. New York: Random House, 1982.

Bendann, E. *Death Customs: An Analytical Study of Burial Rites.* New York: Alfred A. Knopf, 1930.

Bergon, Frank. *Shoshone Mike.* New York: Viking, 1987.

Chekhov, Anton. *Eight Plays,* trans. Elisaveta Fen. Franklin Center, Pa.: Franklin Library, 1976.

Enright, D. J., ed. *The Oxford Book of Death.* Oxford: Oxford University Press, 1983.

Erdoes, Richard, and Alfonso Ortiz, eds. *American Indian Myths and Legends.* New York: Pantheon, 1984.

Farrell, James J. *Inventing the American Way of Death, 1830–1920.* Philadelphia: Temple University Press, 1980.

Ferry, David. *Gilgamesh: A New Rendering in English Verse*. New York: Farrar, Straus and Giroux, 1992.

Flaubert, Gustave. *Madame Bovary*, trans. Francis Steegmuller. New York: Random House, 1957.

Foucault, Michel. *Discipline and Punish: The Birth of the Prison*, trans. Alan Sheridan. New York: Vintage, 1979.

Habenstein, Robert W., and William M. Lamers. *The History of American Funeral Directing*. Milwaukee, Wis.: Bulfin Printers, 1955.

Herodotus. *The Histories*, trans. Aubrey de Sélincourt. Harmondsworth, England: Penguin Books, 1954.

Huntington, Richard, and Peter Metcalf. *Celebrations of Death: The Anthropology of Mortuary Ritual*. Cambridge, England: Cambridge University Press, 1979.

Jones, Barbara. *Design for Death*. New York: Bobbs-Merrill, 1967.

Mann, Thomas. *Buddenbrooks*, trans. John E. Woods. New York: Everyman's Library, 1994.

Mitford, Jessica. *The American Way of Death*. New York: Simon & Schuster, 1963.

Nuland, Sherwin B. *How We Die: Reflections on Life's Final Chapter*. New York: Alfred A. Knopf, 1994.

Quigley, Christine. *The Corpse: A History*. Jefferson, N.C., and London: McFarland & Co., 1996.

Ring, Kenneth. *Life at Death: A Scientific Investigation of the Near-Death Experience*. New York: Coward, McCann & Geoghegan, 1980.

Rosenberg, David, trans. *The Book of J*. New York: Grove Weidenfeld, 1990.

Ruby, Joy. *Secure the Shadow: Death and Photography in America*. Cambridge, Mass.: MIT Press, 1995.

Sandburg, Carl. *Abraham Lincoln*, vol. 4: *The War Years*. New York: Harcourt, Brace, 1934.

Sandrof, Ivan, and Trentwell M. White. "The First Embalmer," *The New Yorker*, November 7, 1942.

Spencer, A. J. *Death in Ancient Egypt.* Harmondsworth, England: Penguin Books, 1982.

Swift, Jonathan. *Gulliver's Travels.* Oxford: Oxford University Press, 1977.

Taylor, John H. *Unwrapping a Mummy.* Austin: University of Texas Press, 1995.

Whitman, Walt. *Complete Poetry and Collected Prose,* ed. Justin Kaplan. New York: Library of America, 1982.

Wilkens, Robert. *The Bedside Book of Death.* New York: Citadel Press, 1990.

V. HOUSE

Beecher, Catharine. *A Treatise on Domestic Economy.* Boston: Marsh, Capen, Lyon, and Webb, 1841.

Beecher, Catharine, and Harriet Beecher Stowe. *The American Woman's Home.* New York: J. B. Ford & Co., 1869.

Chartier, Roger, ed. *A History of Private Life,* vol. 3: *Passions of the Renaissance,* trans. Arthur Goldhammer. Cambridge, Mass.: Harvard University Press, 1989.

Chase, George Wingate. *The History of Haverhill, Massachusetts.* Haverhill: published by the author, 1861.

de Camp, L. Sprague. *The Ancient Engineers.* Garden City, N.Y.: Doubleday, 1963.

Doctorow, E. L. *Ragtime.* New York: Modern Library, 1994.

Driver, Tom F. "Beckett by the Madeleine," *Columbia University Forum* 4:3 (Summer 1961), 21–25.

Duby, Georges, ed. *A History of Private Life,* vol. 2: *Revelations of the Medieval World,* trans. Arthur Goldhammer. Cambridge, Mass.: Harvard University Press, 1988.

Frederick, Christine. *Household Engineering: Scientific Management in the Home.* Chicago: American School of Home Economics, 1921.

Gardiner, Stephen. *Evolution of the House.* Wallop, Hampshire: BAS Printers, 1975.

Gest, Alexander Purves. *Our Debt to Greece and Rome: Engineering.* New York: Cooper Square Publications, 1963.

Giedion, Siegfried. *Mechanization Takes Command: A Contribution to Anonymous History.* New York: Oxford University Press, 1948.

Hedrick, Joan. *Harriet Beecher Stowe: A Life.* New York: Oxford University Press, 1994.

Herodotus. *The Histories,* trans. Aubrey de Sélincourt. Harmondsworth, England: Penguin Books, 1954.

Jones, Barbara. *Design for Death.* Indianapolis: Bobbs-Merrill, 1967.

Kafka, Franz. *The Complete Stories,* ed. Nahum N. Glatzer. New York: Schocken Books, 1971.

Kirby, Richard Shelton, et al. *Engineering in History.* New York: McGraw-Hill, 1956.

Mack, Arien, ed. *Home: A Place in the World.* New York: New York University Press, 1993.

Perrot, Michelle, ed. *A History of Private Life,* vol. 4: *From the Fires of Revolution to the Great War,* trans. Arthur Goldhammer. Cambridge, Mass.: Harvard University Press, 1990.

Pliny the Elder. *Natural History: A Selection,* trans. John F. Healy. Harmondsworth, England: Penguin Books, 1991.

Rapport, Samuel, and Helen Wright, eds. *Physics.* New York: New York University Press, 1964.

Richardson, Samuel. *Pamela; or, Virtue Rewarded,* ed. Peter Sabor. Harmondsworth, England: Penguin Books, 1985.

Rudofky, Bernard. *Architecture Without Architects.* New York: Museum of Modern Art, 1964.

Rybczynski, Witold. *Home: A Short History of an Idea.* New York: Viking, 1986.

Rykwert, Joseph. *On Adam's House in Paradise.* Cambridge, Mass.: MIT Press, 1981.

Sklar, Kathryn Kish. *Catharine Beecher: A Study in American Domesticity*. New York: Norton, 1976.

Strathern, Paul. *Descartes in 90 Minutes*. Chicago: Ivan R. Dee, 1996.

Thoreau, Henry David. *Walden*. New York: Holt, Rinehart and Winston, 1961.

Wood, John George. *Homes Without Hands. Being a Description of the Habitations of Animals, Classed According to Their Principles of Construction*. London, 1875.

VI. ORIGINS

Abel, Ernest. *Ancient Views on the Origins of Life*. Rutherford, N.J.: Fairleigh Dickinson University Press, 1973.

Ammons, A. R. *Garbage*. New York: Norton, 1993.

Beckett, Samuel. *Worstward Ho*. New York: Grove Press, 1983.

Campbell, Neil. *Biology*. Menlo Park, Calif.: Benjamin/Cummings Publishing, 1987.

Chamberlain, A. F. "Nanibozhu Amongst the Otchipwe, Mississagas, and Other Algonkian Tribes," *Journal of American Folk-Lore* 4:14 (July–September 1891), 193–213.

Chekhov, Anton. *The Kiss and Other Stories*, trans. Ronald Wilks. Harmondsworth, England: Penguin Books, 1982.

Debus, Allen G., ed. *Robert Fludd and His Philosophicall Key*. New York: Science History Publications, 1979.

de Duve, Christian. *Vital Dust*. New York: Basic Books, 1995.

Descartes, René. *Treatise of Man*, trans. Thomas Steele Hall. Cambridge, Mass.: Harvard University Press, 1972.

Dickinson, Emily. *The Complete Poems of Emily Dickinson*, ed. Thomas H. Johnson. Boston: Little, Brown, 1955.

Dillard, Annie. "The Wreck of Time," *Harper's Magazine*, January 1997, 56.

Douglas, Mary. *Purity and Danger: An Analysis of Concepts of Pollution and Taboo*. New York: Praeger, 1966.

Durham, Frank, and Robert D. Purrington. *Frame of the Universe: A History of Physical Cosmology*. New York: Columbia University Press, 1983.

Eliade, Mircea. *Patterns in Comparative Religion,* trans. Rosemary Sheed. Cleveland: Meridian Books, 1966.

Farley, John. *The Spontaneous Generation Controversy from Descartes to Oparin*. Baltimore: Johns Hopkins University Press, 1977.

Forster, E. M. *Howards End*. New York: Alfred A. Knopf, 1921.

Freud, Sigmund. *From the History of an Infantile Neurosis,* in *The Standard Edition of the Complete Psychological Works of Sigmund Freud,* vol. 17, trans. James Strachey. London: Hogarth Press, 1955.

———. *Notes upon a Case of Obsessional Neurosis,* in *The Standard Edition,* vol. 10.

———. *Totem and Taboo,* trans. A. A. Brill, in *The Basic Writings of Sigmund Freud*. New York: Modern Library, 1938.

Fritzsch, Harald. *The Creation of Matter,* trans. Jean Steinberg. New York: Basic Books, 1984.

Gribbin, John. *In the Beginning: After COBE and Before the Big Bang*. Boston: Little, Brown, 1993.

Harvey, William. *On Animal Generation,* in *The Works of William Harvey,* trans. Robert Willis. New York and London: Johnson Reprint Corp., 1965.

Hawking, Stephen W. *A Brief History of Time*. New York: Bantam Books, 1988.

Jones, Ernest. "Anal Erotic Character Traits," *Journal of Abnormal Psychology* 13:1 (April 1918), 261–284.

Kristeva, Julia. *Powers of Horror: An Essay on Abjection,* trans. Leon S. Roudiez. New York: Columbia University Press, 1982.

Levine, Philip. *Not This Pig*. Wesleyan, Conn.: Wesleyan University Press, 1968.

Narlikar, Jayant. *The Primeval Universe*. Oxford and New York: Oxford University Press, 1988.

Plato. *Statesman*, in *The Dialogues of Plato*, vol. 3, trans. and ed. B. Jowett.

Rachman, Stanley, and Ray Hodgson. *Obsessions and Compulsions*. Englewood Cliffs, N.J.: Prentice-Hall, 1980.

Rapaport, Judith. *The Boy Who Couldn't Stop Washing His Hands*. New York: Dutton, 1989.

Robinson, Edwin Arlington. *The Children of the Night*. New York: Charles Scribner's Sons, 1919.

Rowan-Robinson, Michael. *Ripples in the Cosmos*. Oxford and New York: Freeman, 1993.

Rugh, Roberts. *From Conception to Birth*. New York: Harper & Row, 1971.

Sagan, Carl. *Cosmos*. New York: Random House, 1980.

————. *Shadows of Forgotten Ancestors*. New York: Random House, 1992.

Silk, Joseph. *The Big Bang*. San Francisco: Freeman, 1980.

Trefil, James. *The Moment of Creation*. New York: Charles Scribner's Sons, 1983.

Vogel, Steven. *Vital Circuits*. New York and Oxford: Oxford University Press, 1992.

Weinberg, Steven. *The First Three Minutes*. New York: Basic Books, 1988.

Wiggins, Jayne DeClue. *Childbearing: Physiology, Experiences, Needs*. St. Louis: C. V. Mosby Co., 1979.